Character Theology

"Character theology explores the missiological potential of interaction with biblical characters experienced in the telling and hearing of the stories rather than the ideas that emerge from the reading of printed biblical texts. It is a promising approach to biblical interpretation in a post-literate global culture that outlines both the theory and the practice of character theology. This work is a beacon of hope."

—**THOMAS E. BOOMERSHINE**, author of
First Century Gospel Storytellers and Audiences

"Groundbreaking, profound, and practical. Tom Steffen and Ray Neu's seminal text on character theology represents a powerful move that both returns to ways people related to God in the biblical narrative and proposes understandings that better relate with the contemporary globalized world. The embrace of holistic character theology provides possible pathways for emerging generations of young people confronted with the sterility of modernist 'certainty' and the ennui of postmodern deconstruction. A must-read for all engaged in Christian leadership training in the twenty-first century."

—**PERRY SHAW**, author of *Transforming Theological Education*

"Steffen and Neu wade into waters much deeper than our modernistic prescribed approach to understanding God through the textually abridged account of his word. They take us into theologies emerging from a story. Behind every epistle: characters. Every song: characters. Every law: characters. Only when we soak in the intertwining scenes and real people do we truly get a glimpse of our God. That is theology. 'Narratized' characters lead us to know him by means that he intended in a never-ending story."

—**CHARLES MADINGER**, founder/CEO,
Institutes for Orality Strategies (I-OS)

"The questions Steffen and Neu discuss are highly significant but have strangely gone undiscussed in the theological world. Their book integrates the best of multiple disciplines while connecting to a fundamental aspect of the human experience—story. Few works do what this one seeks to do—bridge biblical interpretation with mission-ministry strategy."

—**Brad Vaughn**, author of *Reading Romans with Eastern Eyes*

"Tom Steffen and Ray Neu offer a new lens for understanding theology, one that focuses on what matters most: character. I highly commend this book to anyone looking for a practical way of communicating theological truth to emerging generations who don't connect with abstractions."

—**Kevin Ford**, author of *Attentive Church Leadership*

"Steffen and Neu challenge us to think outside of our textually constrained and literate hermeneutics to consider the relationships between the characters of the stories in the Bible, the God who saw fit to relate those stories to us, and how these stories continue to be impactful today. *Character Theology* will no doubt find its way onto the bookshelves of all those who seek meaningful ways to connect as much with post-Christian as with pre-Christian cultures."

—**Michael T. Cooper**, author of *Ephesiology*

Character Theology

Engaging God through His Cast of Characters

Tom Steffen

AND

Ray Neu

FOREWORD BY
Samuel E. Chiang

☙PICKWICK *Publications* · Eugene, Oregon

CHARACTER THEOLOGY
Engaging God through His Cast of Characters

Copyright © 2024 Tom Steffen and Ray Neu. All rights reserved. Except for brief quotations in critical publications or reviews, no part of this book may be reproduced in any manner without prior written permission from the publisher. Write: Permissions, Wipf and Stock Publishers, 199 W. 8th Ave., Suite 3, Eugene, OR 97401.

Pickwick Publications
An Imprint of Wipf and Stock Publishers
199 W. 8th Ave., Suite 3
Eugene, OR 97401

www.wipfandstock.com

PAPERBACK ISBN: 978-1-6667-7857-1
HARDCOVER ISBN: 978-1-6667-7858-8
EBOOK ISBN: 978-1-6667-7859-5

Cataloguing-in-Publication data:

Names: Steffen, Tom A., 1947–, author. | Neu, Ray, author. | Chiang, Samuel E, foreword.

Title: Character theology : engaging God through his cast of characters / by Tom Steffen and Ray Neu ; foreword by Samuel E. Chiang.

Description: Eugene, OR : Pickwick Publications, 2024 | Includes bibliographical references.

Identifiers: ISBN 978-1-6667-7857-1 (paperback) | ISBN 978-1-6667-7858-8 (hardcover) | ISBN 978-1-6667-7859-5 (ebook)

Subjects: Character. | Theology. | Hermeneutics. | Education. | Communication. | Anthropology.

Classification: BJ1521 .S72 2024 (paperback) | BJ1521 .S72 (ebook)

VERSION NUMBER 02/16/24

Jonah images are copyright @ Sarah Drobnack. Used by permission.

Scripture quotations marked CEV are from the Contemporary English Version. Copyright © 1991,1992, 1995 by American Bible Society. Used by permission.

Scripture quotations marked CJB are taken from the Complete Jewish Bible by David H. Stern. Copyright © 1998. All rights reserved. Used by permission of Messianic Jewish Publishers, 6120 Day Long Lane, Clarksville, MD 21029. www.messianicjewish.net.

Scripture quotations marked ESV are from The ESV® Bible (The Holy Bible, English Standard Version®), © 2001 by Crossway, a publishing ministry of Good News Publishers. Used by permission. All rights reserved.

Scripture quotations marked GNT are from the Good News Translation in Today's English Version. 2nd ed. Copyright © 1992 by American Bible Society. Used by permission.

Scripture quotations marked JUB are from *The Jubilee Bible (from the Scriptures of the Reformation)* by Russell M. Stendal. Copyright © 2000, 2001, 2010 by ANEKO Press, LLC. All rights reserved.

Scripture quotations marked KJV are from the King James Version of the Bible (public domain).

Scripture quotations marked MSG are from *THE MESSAGE: The Bible in Contemporary Language*. Copyright © 1993, 2002, 2018 by Eugene H. Peterson. All rights reserved.

Scripture quotations marked NASB are taken from the New American Standard Bible®. Copyright © 1960, 1971, 1977, 1995, 2020 by The Lockman Foundation. Used by permission. All rights reserved. lockman.org.

Scripture quotations marked NIV are taken from the Holy Bible, New International Version®, NIV®. Copyright © 1973, 1978, 1984, 2011 by Biblica, Inc.™ Used by permission of Zondervan. All rights reserved worldwide. www.zondervan.com. The "NIV" and "New International Version" are trademarks registered in the United States Patent and Trademark Office by Biblica, Inc.

Scripture quotations marked VOICE are taken from The Voice™. Copyright © 2012 by Ecclesia Bible Society. Used by permission. All rights reserved.

Contents

List of Illustrations | ix
Foreword by Samuel E. Chiang | xi
Acknowledgments | xv
Abbreviations | xvii

Setting the Stage | 1

Part 1: Character Theology Defined
1 Clarifying Character Theology | 23
2 The Role of Characters | 64
3 The Role of Orality | 101
4 The Role of Oral Hermeneutics | 140
5 The Role of Character-Centric Questions | 177

Part 2: Character Theology Demonstrated
6 Participant Responses to the Jonah Story | 217
7 An Interview with the Jonah Storyteller | 236

Tightening the Threads | 257

Appendix: Four Value Frames of the Gospel | 275
Bibliography | 277

List of Illustrations

Figures

Figure 1 Road Map to the Book | 16

Figure 2.1 Types of Characters | 68

Figure 2.2 Concentrate on Discourse | 71

Figure 2.3 Concentrate on Characters | 72

Figure 2.4 Characterization Components | 72

Figure 2.5 "Reading" Characters and Contexts | 73

Figure 2.6 Character Roles | 74

Figure 2.7 Concentrate on Setting and Surroundings | 75

Figure 3.1 Oral Hermeneutic Accents | 136

Figure 3.2 Timeline of Orality's "Devalued Currency" | 137

Figure 4.1 Two Forms of Logic | 150

Figure 4.2 Engagements of a Heart Hermeneutic | 157

Figure 4.3 Guarding the Story's Meaning | 175

Figure 5.1 Storytelling Cultures of Teller and Told | 187

Figure 5.2 Appropriate Theology | 191

Figure 5.3 A Surplus of Meaning | 196

Figure 5.4 Character-Centric Categories for the Storying Process | 202

Figure 6.1 Map of Jonah's Journey | 219

Figure 6.2 Sailors Throw Jonah Overboard | 223

Figure 6.3 Jonah Prays | 227

Figure 6.4 Fish Vomits Out Jonah | 232

Figure 7.1 Ninevite King and People Call on God | 238

Figure 7.2 Jonah Awaits Nineveh's Destruction | 241

Figure 7.3 God Sends a Worm | 244

Figure 7.4 Jonah Wishes He Was Dead | 248

Figure 7.5 Discovering a Story's Significance | 254

Figure 8.1 Character Theology Accents | 264

Tables

Table 2.4 Pooling Faces and Topics | 92

Table 4.1 Focus Distinctives | 168

Table 4.2 Assumption Distinctives | 169

Table 4.3 Application Distinctives | 170

Table 4.4 Result Distinctives | 170

Table 5.1 Contrasting Two Models | 209

Table 8.1 Contrasting Two Eras | 260

Foreword

SOME FIFTEEN YEARS AGO, I read Phyllis Tickle's small book *The Great Emergence*. Tickle postulated that the church has a "rummage sale" about every five hundred years, at which time what was in the attic gets brought down, sorted, and reevaluated so as to accommodate the new. Then, over time, the old stuff and the new stuff get put back up into the attic. Tickle believed we are in one of those times now. Her prescient book provided a new lens for me to observe the renewed interest in orality.

When I entered the field of orality, I memorized, embodied, and internalized Bible stories, often gaining fresh insights through the vivid and imaginative work that orality entails. I also experienced an entire defamiliarization and relearning process as I became a practitioner of orality. But I always maintained an inner tension: Where was the theological foundation to support what we are rediscovering prior to adaptation into the Gutenberg textual galaxy? Over the last two decades, numerous books and videos have left a trail of breadcrumbs that point towards the reemergence of orality globally. But how does one get their arms around the subject of orality when it spans multiple generations, is distributed across all cultures, and inhabits multiple disciplines of study?

I first met Tom Steffen at a conference. He was quiet, listened deeply, and asked deep, probing questions, almost as if he was struggling and working through orality as a missiologist-theologian. Little did I know then what Tom would produce: beyond the doctoral students, thousands of correspondences, and many articles would come the birthing of books on the subject of orality. This book is the final one in the trilogy.

I first came to learn of Ray Neu several years ago through his reputation for "oralizing" written curriculum. After meeting Ray and learning more about what he does, I continued to hear about the fruits of his work from many ministry leaders, all of whom described the measurable impact of Ray's ability to "orallze" their textual curriculum and enhance their orality-based training.

I was delighted when I learned that Steffen and Neu had teamed up to explore what I believe will be one of the most significant questions in this upcoming church "rummage sale." Here is that question: Can an orality-oriented theology—one that impacts textual style and structure through sound and symbol, thereby helping to anchor meaning and memory—offer an additional type of theology that encourages and enhances further textual insights in this "age of art and heart"?

I believe this question is significant for a number of reasons. First, it invites us to consider broadly the location and conveyance of meaning and memory, and the way in which spoken dialogue has been subsumed into the structure and organization of written language—that is, how it has been "textualized." This is a profound consideration in the missional and global landscape that is increasingly characterized by its interactions with oral cultures.

Second, this question is being posed at a time when unprecedented innovations are being achieved in the arena of artificial intelligence (AI), particularly with large language model systems and generative AI. Just as happened in Gutenberg's time, our relationship with knowledge, language, meaning, and memory is shifting. No longer will we be as heavily reliant on systems of writing as we have been over the past few millennia. I believe Steffen and Neu's exploration of this question offers the church and theology not only the chance to be part of the conversation around this shift, but also the opportunity to help lead and steward it.

Lastly, Steffen and Neu's question sets the stage for an important and central contention. They argue not only that orality-oriented theology supplements a theological system that has often overlooked the relational-narrative portions of our sacred text, but also that it complements our existing theological disciplines.

In *Character Theology*, Steffen and Neu masterfully weave a multidisciplinary and scholarly case for an "oral hermeneutic" that focuses on the location of meaning in biblical characters. This deeply human-centric and imaginative approach brings what missiologists have been learning and experiencing over the past forty plus years into theological scholarship.

Steffen and Neu have authored a tour de force that bridges several adjacent disciplines, opens up the opportunity for believers to be a part of and lead very important conversations, and paves the way for vibrant future scholarship.

The rummage sale is on. Which lens might you put on to examine the old and the new?

Samuel E. Chiang
Deputy Secretary General, World Evangelical Alliance
Orality Catalyst, Lausanne Movement
Hippo Lake, South Africa

Acknowledgments

No one is an island. So many from around the globe have been instrumental in what is found on the pages of this book. From recipients of our sometimes-mediocre attempts at communicating Scripture, to practitioners, to professionals, all have provided insights, critique, encouragement. We are humbled and grateful. Thank you all!

We want to express our deep appreciation for the insights Dave Maddox provided throughout the book. Dave is a walking theological library who knows how to make Christianity walk in multiple contexts. His ministry training pastors abroad or those recovering from drug addiction here at home demands such. Thanks, Dave, for your discerning and distinguishing contribution. This book is better because of you!

I (Tom) want to thank the Antipolo-Amduntug Ifugao of the Philippines for starting me on a journey I have never been able to conclude. Having reintroduced me to the role of story, I began to see Scripture in a very different light than how I was formally taught and trained. Rational moved to relational, restoring the intimacy the Author originally had in mind. *Eteng salamat kung hi-gayu* (My thanks is enormous to you all).

Saving the best to last, I want to thank my gracious wife of fifty plus years for putting up with what she calls my "virtual wife"—my computer. Love you, and thanks for your patience.

I (Ray) also want to thank my wife who, as Tom expressed, puts up with a lot when it comes to these endless projects. She knows, understands, and heartily supports those we serve.

I also want to thank the Maya, Kekchi, and Creole people of Belize who served as my "learning laboratory" in the earliest days of experimenting with orality. I had only a vague idea of the potential we were beginning to explore together. You demonstrated we were tapping into something that was incredibly powerful. Those who have continued this journey with me on several other continents have also been my teachers, especially across Africa. The continual expressions flowing from your empowerment through orality remain my biggest motivation even now. *Tuko Pamoja!* (We are together).

We want to express our deep appreciation to Pastor Teresa Page of Cross Bridge Church, Rockledge, Florida, for gathering participants to demonstrate the process of character theology, film it, and post the results online.[1] Thanks, too, goes to the film and editing crew.

---

1. Cross Bridge Church, "Engaging Jonah."

Abbreviations

AI	Artificial intelligence
BTB	*Biblical Theology Bulletin*
CBQ	*Catholic Bible Quarterly*
CBS	Chronological biblical storying
CurBR	*Currents in Biblical Research*
EBC	Engaging Bible characters
EBCs	Engaging Bible characters discussion groups
EuroJTH	*European Journal of Theology*
GNT	Greek New Testament
HOR	High oral reliant
JAAR	*Journal of the American Academy of Religion*
JAM	*Journal of Asian Mission*
JPS	Jewish Publication Society
LOR	Low oral reliant
OT	Old Testament
OTSSA	Old Testament Studies in South Africa
MIA	Missing in action
NT	New Testament
Them	*Themelios*
TMSJ	*The Master's Seminary Journal*
VBS	Vacation Bible school
WCIU	Imprint of William Carey International University

Setting the Stage

Joseph, Daniel, Abigail, Isaac, Mary, Jacob, Ruth, Joshua, Esther, Josiah . . . the wisest people in history are waiting for you! When you hang out with them, their insights and perspective of life will rub off on you.

—WAYNE CORDEIRO

Books are not meant to be believed, but
to be subjected to inquiry.
When we consider a book, we must not ask
ourselves what it says but what it means.

—UMBERTO ECO

WHO DOESN'T LOVE A good story? Who among us, having faithfully scoured the Bible, isn't aware narrative is God's choice instrument for carrying forward the story of the knowledge and joy of our Father's unfolding drama of redemption? His never-ending story began before time directing characters to join a story arc enacted as every person in every generation sprang to life until their family story culminates with a great feast.

Then the *new story* begins. We sing a new song in a new garden in the fullness of his presence in a story of unending praise and service to the King. Through this unfolding story *we learn who God is and what he intends for us* to experience, be, and think. Story aids and outfits hearers/readers/viewers of truth to become doers of truth.

Story draws us into the sacred space of holy awe, discerned as a felt sense of God's presence, and felt as one standing near his wondrous works. In addition, story—as God's favorite communication tool—also guards against falsehoods by removing the sight-blurring scales from our eyes to see storied truths about God working through Christ in past and future promises.

Story supports awareness and actionized wisdom beyond the moment. Through story we come to know and experience both the riches and richness of his grace, something our hearts long for desperately.

Clearly, God loves telling stories. He longs for his children to take into their souls the demonstrated details of the stories he tells to "learn of me." Based on human experience, story is not only primal but also powerful. All stories in the Bible are God-breathed, and as so, essential to our Christian faith and walk. And he has trusted *us* with *his* stories!

Why are stories brimming in significance and impact? In a word—*characters*. Characters involve us in the appreciation of the depth, breath, and heights of God's story that reveals our story. Characters are essential to story—the glue and vortex to all elements of a story. In brief, characters tell the story through surprise and suspense. If no characters, no story (developed in ch. 2).

Observing life's ups and downs, tensions, and heartaches and joys of a biblical character can be an unbelievers first introduction to a relational God and a new believer's first mentor-mentee relationship. These characters compel the unbeliever to rethink life's priorities. They compel believers toward deeper understanding of what it means to be "in the world but not of the world." In other words, the life of a biblical character affects the heart, head, and hands of present and future Jesus followers.

Building on the Past

Character Theology: Engaging God through His Cast of Characters continues the conversation begun in *The Return of Oral Hermeneutics: As Good Today as It Was for the Hebrew Bible and First-Century Christianity*. The process of oral hermeneutics (developed in ch. 4),[1] a facilitated communal-experiential interpretation tool to understand more richly and impactfully Scripture's narrative genre (developed in ch. 3), leads to a product—character theology.

---

1. Hermeneutics is a broad term used as an interpretive system in many disciplines. This book focuses on its interpretive role of the Bible in relation to theology and ethics.

Simply stated, *character theology* is engaging God through "reading" biblical characters in the context of story (developed in ch. 1).

Leland Ryken and Tremper Longman remind us, "The Bible is pervaded by the consciousness of God it constantly interprets human experience from a religious perspective . . . solidly didactic revealing God to people, instructing them about how to order their lives, and asserting a religious system of values and morality."[2]

Summarizing, character theology relies on earthy, concrete biblical characters to frame, enliven, and demonstrate divine abstract truths and ethics; they provide abstractions a home in which we can enter and explore. Through various interactions with the Supreme One and others, Bible characters positively or negatively display the Creator's character, thereby revealing his divinity to the nations.

How did God choose to multiply worshipers from among the nations? By purposely and predominately revealing himself through his interaction with Bible characters along with their interaction with other Bible characters.

> What is character theology?

This book explores how Bible characters—predominately but not exclusively from the narrative sections of Scripture—are creative and relatable iterations of what God intends for us to appropriate or abandon. How? Through a sensate experience (hearing, seeing, smelling, touching, and feeling) challenged by reason that results in identification with various characters.

We also seek to determine how God's story not only challenged the lives of biblical characters, but ours as well. In short, God appointed characters as load-bearing, storytelling emissaries to aid in drawing us to himself through salvific history and then transforming our relationships and routines through salvific history's multiple tributaries.

Who comprises these God-selected characters? Among others, these could include humans, spirits, animals, insects, weather, elements, cities. God-selected characters demonstrate (not define) theology and ethics, providing multiple pathways for recipients to enjoy and glorify their Creator, respect themselves, and serve others.

---

2. Ryken and Longman, *Complete Literary Guide*, 34.

> How did God choose to multiply worshipers
> from among the nations?

Characters, however, are not cardboard stand-alones. Characters find themselves in different roles designed by the Author-authors, e.g., protagonist, antagonist, foil, primary, and peripheral (developed in ch. 2). They also find themselves moving through various scenes and events anchored in specific times and settings that establish the mood and moment for some entangled arduous journey in search of a satisfactory solution that can regain some semblance of stability. For the narrative genre, *Author-authorselected characters serve not just as a justifiable hermeneutic tool to interpret Scriptures to reveal the God of and to the nations, but also as a natural, normal, legitimate means that best represents and respects the narrative genre* (developed in chs. 1 and 2).

Seeking Fresh Insights

In this book the authors wish to advance some fresh insights. Rather than asking "What were the three points of the sermon?" we ask, "Who were the main characters in the story?"

Through appeals, arguments, and a few autopsies, we wish to respectfully and artfully persuade the reader that character theology can *add* insights other theologies miss or minimize, especially today; that character theology is *not* a replacement of other theologies, *nor* their rival. Rather, character theology, because it respects the narrative genre's way of communicating, *adds* not only intellect, but also identification, appeal (beauty), and impact. And it calls for participation in the divine truth assertions embedded in Bible characters. Character theology moves interpretation beyond the shallow end of the pool.

Character theology can do the above without an "overly literate mind" that attempts to dissect stories for "more than the obvious"[3] through an oft-single emphasis of the abstract "individual words, phrases, and sentences in a literary pierce."[4] Character theology is naturally designed to make theology *caught experientially rather than thought rationally.*[5]

---

3. Kelber, *Oral and Written Gospel*, 55.
4. Kaiser, "Meaning of Meaning," 38.
5. Note the different types of curricula (explicit, hidden, null) that influence educational outcomes (P. Shaw, *Transforming Theological Education*).

There are, however, strong headwinds that can be summarized in two bifurcated types of knowledge. Michael de Certeau's adage is instructive: "What the map cuts up, story cuts across." The first, "the map," is "official, objective, and abstract." In the opposing corner stands "the story," which is "practical, embodied and popular."[6] This all too often results in the bifurcation between theory (theology) and praxis (practice). Character theology assists Bible communicators in the navigation beyond this long-held erroneous bifurcation by wedding the two.

While many questions will be raised from a multidisciplinary perspective in relation to the narrative sections of Scripture, the driving question this book seeks to answer intellectually, practically, and with fidelity and faithfulness to Scripture is: *Why is it important to know and practice character theology when interpreting and communicating Author-author truths?*

Some Backstory

Tom and his family lived among the Antipolo-Amduntug Ifugao (one of five dialects) of the Philippines for almost eight years. These industrious people, known for carving the sculptured wet rice terraces up the mountainsides ("stairsteps to the sky") of the Cordillera region of Central Luzon in Ifugao Province, taught this foreign Anglo-American Bible teacher much. I learned to *re*appreciate the role of story in communication (my mother continuously read stories to us before formal education intruded) and worldview (re)formation, which dramatically changed our ministry models.

> Who comprises these God-selected characters?

The Ifugao taught me about patron-client relationships and how they differ from egalitarianism, how honor and shame contrasts with innocence and guilt, our preferred value system for interpreting and teaching Scripture. They questioned my use of grammar when interpreting Scripture with this critical comment from Gumangan: "English is so, so hard to speak. You have all that grammar. Keley-i [their dialect] is easy to speak. It doesn't have all that grammar like English; we just speak it." Ouch!

They added dreams and the spirit world to our systematic theology (why were these so faintly visible?) even as they found our theological categories and copious content boring and easily forgotten. "They wanted

---

6. Conquergood, "Performance Studies," 145.

stories; I gave them systematic theology. They wanted relationships; I gave them reasons.[7] They wanted a cast of characters; I gave them categories of convenience. They wanted explorations; I gave them explanations. They wanted descriptions; I gave them definitions."[8] Pedagogically, we were two ships passing in the night.[9]

Not enamored with my Dallas Bible College (heavily influenced by Dallas Theological Seminary) hermeneutical credentials or mission agency or church affiliations, the Ifugao also challenged my sterile science-informed historical-grammatical hermeneutic (we call this "textual hermeneutics" with its plethora of practices[10]) while questioning my individualistic perspective of theology, not to mention life in general. For these and other insights, including the frustrations and failures, we remain forever indebted to our Ifugao friends of Central Luzon. Cross-cultural ministry has been a healthy learning experience. From uncomprehending frustrated faces to "aha moments"—*we* learned so much *together*! Some of that learning weaves itself into the fabric of this book.

Having not been raised in a typical "go-to-church-every-week" setting, I (Ray) missed out on hearing the many Bible stories most people absorb through the early years of Sunday School. I made up for it once I slowed down long enough for God to capture my attention. As a voracious reader, the Bible fascinated me—its characters, its crazy adventures, its catalytic impact on me. I was hooked!

For eighteen years, I did my best to convert my Moody Bible Institute knowledge into useful manners of expression for teenagers. While failing often, one thing was certain—I felt it my job to get people *into* the Bible and that the Holy Spirit would take it from there.

When in Belize to train pastors, I failed again. My words were too big, concepts too lofty, and learning too focused on tests. There I learned to listen, to experiment with adult learning modalities and implement whatever worked. I became a collector of andragogical tools. Orality is loaded with these deceptively simple, incredibly powerful gems. I was hooked again!

Once I started traveling globally to continue the teaching/learning journey that orality afforded me, the new vistas of cultural context and worldview opened my eyes and my heart. The Bible was *even more fascinating* than I had previously thought! I began to form new questions: Are we to

---

7. "In contrast with the West, relationships in traditional societies are often ends in themselves, and not means to an end" (Hiebert, *Anthropological Reflections*, 141).

8. T. A. Steffen, *Reconnecting God's Story*, 2 (emphasis original).

9. See T. Steffen, "Pedagogical Conversions."

10. Textual hermeneutics, as in oral hermeneutics, is not monolithic. See T. Steffen and Bjoraker, *Return of Oral Hermeneutics*, 11–18.

think God did not account for oral learners? Are we to believe that only we few literates who have this highly exalted slice of information are the only ones who have the potential to be correct? Would not God have foreseen all of this, and created space for various perceptions and preferences of the brilliant multifaceted diamond of his word?[11]

In ministry with oral learners at all levels of the continuum, we stress the importance of *active listening* so that we can maintain a posture of being learners ourselves. As a dear friend, James Sai Ruma, told me after his first orality Bible training, *"Thank you for giving me a brand-new Bible."* This exciting revelation remains just as true today. We hope that by rotating the diamond of character theology the reader will see beautiful new insights that were *always* there.

Why This Book?

The authors begin with a confession. We are both card-carrying members of Facts Anonymous (FA).[12] We love to collect, codify, catalog, and communicate abstract facts. It's a hobby we learned long ago in our nonformal and particularly in our formal education that rewarded it with papers prominently displayed on walls with letters behind our names.

Recall Charles Hodge's perspective that the Bible is a "store-house of facts" and "the duty of the Christian theologian is to ascertain, collect, and combine all the facts which God has revealed concerning himself and our relation to Him."[13] We are in the process of jettisoning *some* of this baggage through participation in group therapy with other like-minded fact collectors. "Hello, my name is _____ and I'm a 'fact addict.'"

> *Why is it important to know and practice character theology when interpreting and communicating Author-author truths?*

A long history has shaped us—science, the Enlightenment, the printing press,[14] the Industrial Revolution (developed in ch. 3)—which requires significant time to remedy through FA. But we are recovering!

11. T. Steffen and Bjoraker, *Return of Oral Hermeneutics*, 244.
12. Adapted from Tiede, *Great Leaders Ask Questions*, 2.
13. Hodge, *Systematic Theology*, 10–11.
14. Alexis Abernethy writes, "In his book *Ritual in Early Modern Europe*, Edward Muir describes the shift that took place with the invention of the printing press and its effects on the Protestant churches that arose out of the Reformation. Muir describes

Because of our "fact focus," we overlooked and therefore missed much that was already and obviously embedded in a Scripture story. For example, in narratives, facts are much more than facts; they are events, signposts, billboards; they are divine activities (recall acts of Jesus through the apostles) connected to the God-orchestrated historical-redemptive-eschatological story that allows interpreters opportunities to locate themselves in God's ongoing story. Facts remain relational in nature on multiple levels. Somehow, we missed this.

We also missed character theology, which is related to orality (developed in ch. 3), requires an oral hermeneutic (developed in ch. 4), and takes Bible communicators beyond the facts in a story to the sensory, creating a marriage moment. This helps interpreters, as C. S. Lewis posits, to "steal past certain inhibitions . . . steal past those watchful dragons."[15]

Because our fact fascination with its ties to modernity still lingers (we remain prisoners of our perspectives), we have not been as great Bible interpreters and communicators of the narrative sections of Scripture as possible. Why? Because later generations are no longer fascinated with the unfeeling facts we continue to feed them. These lonely, searching generations who seek authentic relationships primarily through oral, digital, virtual means, and wish to contribute something to the world, have swapped, for the most part, a fact-seeking rationale promoted by a former generation for a more experiential one.

Peter charges the people of "the Way" to "always be ready to offer a defense, humbly and respectfully, when someone asks why you live in hope" (1 Pet 3:15 VOICE). Jude 3 commands us to contend for the faith once delivered to the saints.

What comes to mind when hearing these verses? Debates? Reasoned apologetics? Definitions? "Line-upon-line" evidence? Winners and losers? Why is it that when we think of "critical thinking" we think of individual skills to solve problems through science-based methods?[16]

---

a division between the lower body, with the passions and feelings it contains and the intellect and objectivity of the upper body, privileging the objectivity of the upper body, privileging the upper over the lower. For most Protestant churches this resulted in word-centered worship series, with most actions in worship involving speaking or singing—if not listening to—words" (Abernethy, "Exploring Role of Embodiment," 68).

15. Lewis, *On Stories*, 47.

16. Ben Paris defines "critical thinking" as "the ability to evaluate the connection between evidence and potential conclusions. It is the ability to make logically sound judgments, identify assumptions and alternatives, ask relevant questions, and to be fair and open-minded when evaluating the strength of arguments" (Paris, "Failing to Improve," para. 21).

But is this the only way to make a defense for Christianity? Think about it? Shortly before his homegoing, Bill Bright concluded, "*I have come to the conclusion that a good novel on biblical themes can reach many more people than most theological works.*"[17] What Bright learned late in life, Someone centuries prior had already modeled. Why did Jesus revert to parables (approximately one-third of his teaching) and stories as an apologetic?

The reader by now is no doubt wondering what new heretical hermeneutic theories these two provocateur "babblers" are proceeding to pitch. What kind of hermeneutic headwinds are they trying to stir up? Have not our theological categories been long established? In this book we offer a new hermeneutic (actually an updated, old one[18])—oral hermeneutics, which naturally spins off a new theology—character theology.

Character theology, like systematic theology accomplished in a former era, will speak strongly to today's generations. Character theology is much more than a better bad idea or a stroll down a yellow brick road; it will be *one* of the necessary additions for this present era in which we now sovereignly find ourselves.

Character theology provides abstract facts a concrete home in which to reside, thereby making them more assessable, memorable, and easily replicable. Character theology breathes life into comatose concepts and dead dogma, connecting them to living people, events, and objects; it centralizes relationships, just as modeled in the Trinity (developed in chs. 1 and 3).

Character theology is a relational theology that compellingly connects with *all* cultures and religions (e.g., Buddhism, Hinduism, Judaism, Islam, Confucianism, Christianity, Taoism, Shamanism, secularism). As with soulless secularism, which seeks an elusive safe sanctuary, the same holds true for a postmodern, post-Christian, post-print, post-fact, post-truth, social-media–driven generation who have moved beyond dated modernity's individualism, rationalism, and fragmented facts.

Facts for these audiences are submerged within a broader story that offers a more communal, emotional, comprehensive, impactful way of life. Character theology seeks to communicate not over the head but through the heart to the head. This is one of the main reasons we wrote this book—to help Bible communicators connect a relational Trinity with fearful (only five to twenty years before global warming incinerates us all ["eco-anxiety"]), relationally starved generations in search of safety, friends, and self-/collective justification. Why? So they can advance beyond cancelling themselves,

---

17. Bill Bright, as quoted in Zoba, "Bright Unto the End," para. 3 (emphasis original).
18. See T. Steffen and Bjoraker, *Return of Oral Hermeneutics*, 135–63.

others, and their Creator. How? Through character theology, which highlights the uncensored lives of biblical characters.

Purpose

An initial question often raised about character theology is: Does this even warrant something we should be discussing? The answer requires a simple yes or no response, which is not all that helpful. A better question might be: *What does character theology offer that existing theologies often miss or minimize?*

> Why did Jesus revert to parables (approximately one-third of his teaching) and stories to make a defense for a new kingdom way of thinking and acting?

Answering this question requires engaged, humble discussion. That is precisely what the authors desire—engaged, humble discussion between professionals and practitioners representing the assemblies, the agencies, and academies. As Lady Wisdom sagely asserted centuries ago: "Wise men and women are always learning, always listening for fresh insights" (Prov 8:15 VOICE). They stealthily steal past those "watchful dragons."

Remember the story of Simon the sorcerer in Acts 8? This story had me (Tom) baffled until our time living among the animistic Ifugao in the Philippines. Why did Simon react the way he did to Peter's terse response—"May your money perish with you"—for wanting to purchase the ability to give people the Holy Spirit by laying on hands (Acts 8:20 NIV)?

When we arrived in Central Luzon, the Ifugao were beginning to transition from a predominately oral society to a more print-oriented one. One of the things I (Tom) learned from the Ifugao related to orality was the power of words. But words are just words, right? "Sticks and stones may break my bones, but words will never hurt me." Right? Wrong on both accounts!

For highly orally reliant Ifugao, *words have power.* You can bless someone with *words alone* as Naomi did with her Moabite daughters-in-law ("May the Eternal show his loyal love to you" [Ruth 1:8 VOICE]) or just as easily curse someone as Peter's spoken words did to the sorcerer intoxicated with the power of magic! No wonder Scripture gives so much attention to not only God's words, but to our words as well (Ps 141:3; Jas 1:26).

Then it hit me. As an oralist sorcerer, Simon immediately knew that words had power and that he was as good as dead. Peter had just cursed him! Hence his response. Simon didn't "want these terrible things to be true" (v. 24 [VOICE]) of him. Orality gave this highly print-oriented expatriate an insight into this passage I had completely missed. The sorcerer's response now made total sense.

In the oral-dominant world, words have power, spiritual energy; spoken words (sounds released with a mission) announce and create an actionized event—in this case Simon's *immanent death*! Simon took Peter *at his word*. How did I miss this?

Our main purpose in writing this book is simple and straightforward—offer Bible interpreters and communicators particularly of the narrative sections of Scripture, a natural, universal, concrete, relational, robust, appealing, impactful way to recognize intended truths that carry the Eternal's signature. Additionally, this model also incorporates an easy way to remember, retrieve, and replicate the embedded principles in daily life globally.

Character theology requires highlighting *human experience*. The reflective interpretive process promoted in this book should never have been lost. We therefore *reoffer* Bible communicators a means to advance beyond insightful facts to godly wisdom that increasingly honors the Speaking One, oneself, and others (Matt 22:37–40; Gal 6:10).

Some readers may feel challenged by such charges, challenges, and changes. Please note the authors consider this proposal as an intermural critique. We are *all* on the same team, trying to better what we each have been spiritually gifted and assigned to do by our Creator. Advancement will require active engagement with many mature conversations, and not a few group sessions at FA. We seek the welfare of "the Way."

> Why is it that when we think of critical thinking we think of solving problem through scientific means?

To help accomplish this, the authors will introduce the reader to a colorful cast of characters. These characters come from a wide variety of backgrounds—secular and Christian scholars from multiple theological traditions; our friends; and, of course, Bible characters who demonstrate faith to faithlessness, sageness to silliness, strength to spinelessness, stableness to stumbles. The authors assume that *"good theologians are good missiologists, and good missiologists are good theologians."*[19]

Missiologists tend to look at an issue from multiple disciplines, as does this book (theology, education, communication, anthropology, orality,

---

19. T. Steffen, *Worldview-Based Storying*, 209 (emphasis original).

hermeneutics, homiletics). This helps reduce culturally introduced myopia and expand appropriate means of interpretation.

The authors ask readers to forge beyond the blizzard and frozen snow to the edge of the storm where the snow is melting. The authors recognize any such journey can seem perilous, especially when traversing unknown terrain during stormy times. But the journey may be life changing not only for the reader but also for those God sends his/her way. *A new Bible may await!*

> *What does character theology offer that existing theologies often miss or minimize?*

The authors also recognize any fresh innovative concept requires some creative abrasion. Most readers can expect to experience some, as have the authors. We also recognize a pause in automatism is required, i.e., robotically returning to one's go-to hermeneutic and theologies. In that most transformative learning requires praxis, we seek your total involvement.

How Does This Book Differ from Similar Books?

In the late eighties, numerous books emerged on Bible characters, e.g., Edith Deen's *All of the Women of the Bible* (1988) and Herbert Lockyer's *All the Men of the Bible* (1988) and *All the Women of the Bible* (1988). Two decades later Richard Losch published *All the People in the Bible* (2008). In 2001, Paul Gardner edited the *New International Encyclopedia of Bible Characters*. Ruth Tucker contributed *The Biographical Bible* in 2013. More recent contributions include Jaime Clark-Soles's *Women in the Bible* (2020) and Shannon Bream's *The Mothers and Daughters of the Bible Speak* (2022).

While there are multiple ways to consider characters in Scripture—snapshots to life stories, biographies, autobiographies, fiction, the world of nature,[20] and levels (children to adults)—this book proposes a different approach. Each of the above books offers insightful information (e.g., cultural, economic, political, pedagogical, religious) and/or helpful devotionals. But how were the theological and ethical conclusions reached?

Today's world emphasizes story and symbol much more strongly than some previous generations. People of different ethnicities find themselves interacting much more frequently. Orality and intercultural communication are *no longer* luxury disciplines for today's Bible communicators. *All*

---

20. Institute in Basic Youth Conflicts, *Character Sketches*.

serious Bible interpreters and communicators today should be up to speed on what orality and intercultural communication can contribute to a globalized digital world.

The distinct model the authors offer in character theology considers characters in specific (and related) Bible stories. It calls for a particular hermeneutic—an *oral* hermeneutic—one that explores the lives of Bible characters in a natural way through character-centric questions (developed in ch. 5). It calls for knowing how *culture* (serves as a palace or prison[21]) influences our hermeneutic, homiletics, and theology. Why? As Peter Drucker was reportedly fond of saying, "Culture eats strategy for breakfast!"

This introduction to character theology uniquely offers a facilitative-inductive-orality-based-participative approach to discovering theology in stories. It focuses on something natural and universal—*characters*. The conversations, conduct, choices, commitments, and consequences of those choices of a colorful cast of Bible characters in specific contexts and times draws out the Creator's theology and morals.

Who Benefits from Reading This Book?

Because story forms and reforms our worldview,[22] every inquisitive, serious saint and scholar should find character theology at least thought provoking if not transformative. More specifically, who might comprise these readers? *All Bible interpreters*—from moms and dads to Sunday School and VBS (Vacation Bible school) teachers, from youth workers to pastors (think homiletics) to apologists,[23] to evangelists to church planter catalysts to Bible professors to psychologists to coaches to business and health personnel, to . . . All should benefit from *a cast of Bible characters who serve as the mother of meaning, meditation, modeling, modification, and memory.*

One of those "among others" we would like to spotlight. Often ignored and marginalized, this group will find character theology fitting like a pair of comfortable old jeans. Who? The world's largest unreached people group—seventy million deaf.

Another burgeoning group includes some 60 percent of the world—Asians. One delegate from a recent General Assembly of the Asia Theological Association representing thousands of schools and seminaries expressed concern: "If we do not start promoting orality principles and methods, we'll

---

21. S. Lingenfelter, *Transforming Culture*, 9–10.
22. See T. Steffen, *Worldview-Based Storying*.
23. See Eisenhower, "Why Should the Devil."

continue becoming irrelevant to the next generation of students."[24] Character theology addresses this educator's concern and advances it beyond Asia to the world.

Character theology also encourages a new army of story recipients to become involved in a natural, universal interpretive and communication process. Jack Deere asks,

> Does God give illumination to the ones who know Hebrew and Greek the best? To the ones who read and memorize Scripture the most? What if the condition of one's heart is more important for understanding the Bible than the abilities of the mind? Is it possible that the illumination of the Holy Spirit to understand Scripture might be given on a basis other than education or mental abilities?[25]

Referencing the dominant role of metaphor in Scripture, Marcel Danesi concludes:

> Clearly, metaphor is hardly just a figure of speech, as is commonly believed. In actual fact, it reveals how we think, how we talk, and why certain things are the way they are. Incredibly, *no special intellectual powers or advanced linguistic training are required to produce or understand metaphors. Every child is born with the faculty to do so.*[26]

Character theology is *not* about eliminating the formally trained Bible teacher. Rather it seeks to put the learner behind the wheel of the car *without* throwing out the driver's ed trainer. We seek a symbiotic relationship between teacher and student.

We agree with Ryken when he claims, "It is time to give the parables back to the group to which Jesus originally told them—*ordinary people.*"[27] Why? "While the Bible is hard to interpret correctly or definitively, it is also nearly impossible to misread totally."[28] Meir Sternberg offers support,

> The reader cannot go far wrong even if he does little more than follow the statement made and the incidents enacted on the narrative surface . . . follow the biblical narrator ever so uncritically, and by no great exertion you will be making tolerable sense of

---

24. Madinger, "Orality," 32.
25. Deere, *Surprised by the Voice*, 257.
26. Danesi, *Poetic Logic*, 11 (emphasis added).
27. Ryken, *How to Read Bible*, 203 (emphasis added).
28. Ryken and Longman, *Complete Literary Guide*, 31.

the world you are in, the action that unfolds, the protagonists on stage, and the point of it all.[29]

The power of the Holy Spirit just may surprise us through the contributions of "ordinary" Christ followers.

The authors are not interested in just writing for our professional peers. We desire that the storyteller-interpreter-practitioner benefit too. Using a music metaphor, we offer readers two distinct tones. One tone is for the practitioner community. We do not wish to ignore or isolate you through crafted lingo, abstract theories (although a few may slip in), or mislaid common sense. Rather, we attempt to provide helpful practiced paths conducive to enhance Bible interpretation that results in daily worship and works (John 14:12).

The second tone is for the professional community where we provide extensive footnotes to validate subject significance and suggest sources. General practitioners can wade in or just keep trucking ahead.

We wish to reward both types of readers—practitioners and professionals—with tones that resonate. Should *both* tones resonate (no tone-deafness), hearing enjoyment should increase drastically. Whether the reader hears one or both tones (scholarship for the street) they can expect to hear something familiar and foreign (Matt 13:52).

How Do the Authors View Scripture?

Thomas McCall provides a succinct summary as to how the authors view Scripture:

> I believe that Scripture is finally and supremely authoritative in theology. If we know anything about God and God's works, it is only because God reveals to us something of himself and his ways. I take the Bible to be the inspired and authoritative witness to the self-revelation of God that culminates in Christ. . . . As such, it is the "norming norm" (*norma normans*) that is authoritative above any other sources of authority and thus able to guide and correct our theological endeavors.[30]

For the authors, authority is not centered in the individual or covenant community or creedal traditions or the novel; none are infallible. We agree with Alister McGrath that "the priority of Scripture over all other sources and

---

29. Sternberg, *Poetics of Biblical Narrative*, 51.
30. McCall, "Relational Trinity," 114.

norms, including interpreters, must be vigorously maintained."[31] We seek the norm of the sacred Scriptures that bear light and life rather than the novel.

What Is the Book's Road Map?

As Jesus required a forerunner, so does character theology. Actually, it requires at least five. The first is *stories*, followed by *characters*. The third is *orality*. *Oral hermeneutics* follows, with the fifth being *character-centric questions*—the engine that propels interpreters to theological and ethical narratized truths.

We divided the book into two parts (see fig. 1). Part 1 considers the five forerunners and foundational issues in relation to defining character theology.

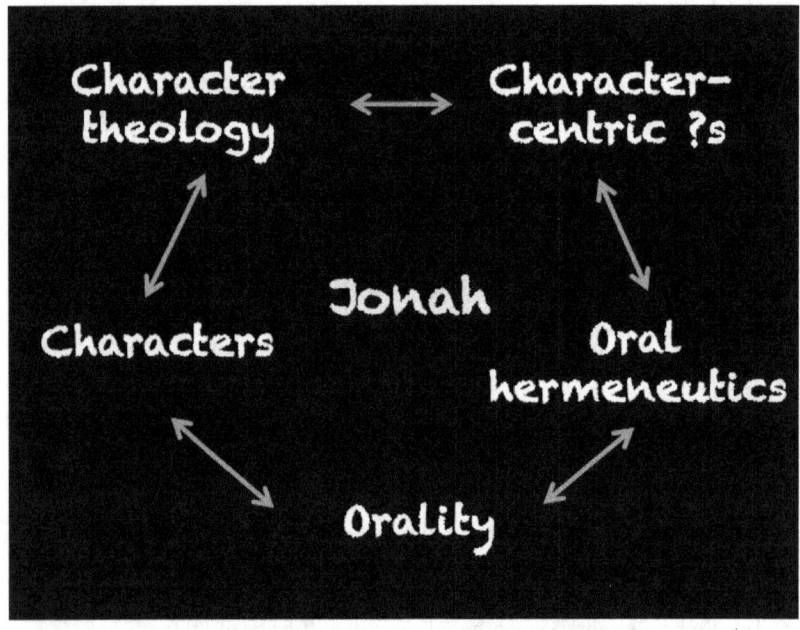

Figure 1. Road Map to the Book

---

31. McGrath, "Engaging the Great Tradition," 151.

SETTING THE STAGE 17

Part 1

Chapter 1 asks: Is a new theology required for a new era—the oral-digital-virtual-experiential world with strong emphasis on relationality? The chapter then considers the what and why of character theology. We begin this exploration with two questions: 1) What is character theology? 2) What are some of the benefits character theology offers? This is followed by the role of story (characters, plot, time, setting), the first forerunner in character theology. We conclude with foundational components that strengthen interpretation.

Chapter 2 asks: What is a "character"? It defines character, the second forerunner, and then digs deeper to ponder the purpose and key characteristics of Bible characters, and how they influence character theology. Curricula possibilities follow.

Chapter 3 argues one cannot understand character theology without a deep grasp of orality. Orality is the "big forgot," and the absence of voice is the "fatal flaw" in most hermeneutic models. This chapter takes a deep dive into orality, the third forerunner. Did God give his word first orally or textually? Were both authoritative? Did orality impact the written text? Downplaying orality results in a less robust understanding of the story which means a less defined portrait of the face of God.

Chapter 4 explores the role of oral hermeneutics, the fourth forerunner. While most modern-day Bible interpreters have been trained in the historical-grammatical method, the method fails to do justice to the narrative sections of Scripture. The first receptors and custodians of the Hebrew Bible provide us with a more natural, universal option that respects the narrative genre.

Chapter 5 concludes with the fifth forerunner—character-centric questions. It defines them and isolates the influential identifiers before laying out the character-centric question process. Illustrative questions are provided for each phase of the interpretive process.

Part 2

Part 2 documents the rich texture, significance, and impact of character theology. The voices of participants who engaged the entire, storied scroll of Jonah in one setting, as well as insights from the storyteller, are heard.

Chapter 6 documents not just what was interesting but what the participants experienced, felt, whom they identified with and why, how the characters in Jonah impacted them, and what they intend to habitually practice.

Chapter 7 has Tom interviewing Ray. The discussion covers insights and surprises noted while telling Jonah's story, leading the debrief, and offers possible implications for character theology at home and abroad.

We close the book with "Tightening the Threads," a succinct review that weaves together the foundational threads of character theology.

A Focus on Questions

Readers will note the extensive emphasis given to questions throughout the book. We seek to catalyze great questions. Why? Because great teaching is more than *telling or storying*; it also includes *asking*. Why? Because learners tend to move in the direction of the questions they entertain. Because their answers receive ongoing reflection. Because this book emphasizes *critical choices*.

Most of those *critical choices* have to do with the questions we ask ourselves. Great questions spark the imagination, evaporate the fog, generate new pathways, invite self-communal discourse, offer ownership for the answers given, increase long-term memory.

In *Change Your Questions, Change Your World*, Marilee Adams quotes Albert Einstein: "We cannot solve our problems with the same thinking we used when we created them." She then paraphrases, "Problem solving *begins by asking a different set of questions* because asking the same old questions will *not* advance one's thinking."[32]

The boxed questions set off throughout the chapters serve as a great chapter review. Rather than the authors choosing which questions the reader should review, we leave that choice to you. Choose a few communally and see what new insights the group discovers.

Looking Back and Ahead

In summary, as the media eras continue to change (oral to print to digital--virtual-AI [Artificial Ingelligence]). too many Bible scholars, and consequently pastors and Bible teachers in the West and beyond, lack capability to effectively communicate Scripture to millennials, Gen Z, and Gen Alpha who find themselves alone, confused, without purpose. These generations

---

32. M. Adams, *Change Your Questions*, 22 (emphasis original).

find little if any relevance in the Christianity offered by those stuck in modernity's sticky, abstract, fragmented systematic theology.

Biblical theology helped by providing a storied framework for the Bible, but we must go further. Character theology, without jettisoning former theologies, speaks to these generations by emphasizing the emotional, experiential, and relational, without negating the rational. Interacting with the human experiences of key concrete Bible characters paints the face of God in fuller definition.

Character theology relates, sticks, and transforms these generations. Why? Because people engage God most naturally and precisely through his interaction with biblical characters and their interaction with each other! Characters communicate the Creator's characteristics. *The road map to the recovery and expansion of Christianity in the twenty-first century will be through Bible characters.*

We pray your journey through this book will be transformative not only for you, but also for those God has and will bring to your ministry.

Part 1
Character Theology Defined

1

Clarifying Character Theology

> Theology is not a list of beliefs or rules, nor ought it to be. But it ought to be all truths. Where will we find these truths if all we receive from scripture is principles?
>
> —ROBERT WADHOLM

> Because you have stood with David at Ziklag, with Moses in the Sinai, with Paul in Athens, and with Esther in Persia, you know what to do.... No one could ever over-calculate the treasure of God's daily counsel spoken through the likes of Luke, Joshua and Samson.
>
> —WAYNE CORDEIRO

> The lives of the saints are the hermeneutical key to Scripture.
>
> —STANLEY HAUERWAS

A SEMINARY STUDENT WROTE this for one of my (Tom) classes: "Could this compartmentalization be the reason why I have struggled to maintain a vibrant relationship with God throughout my time in seminary? Could this be related to the fact that I have forgotten the stories of my powerful God and reduced him to a subject I study in seminary?" These discerning questions deserve reflective answers.

Why do so many Bible teachers at home and abroad immediately pursue a single proposition when interpreting a Bible story?[1] Why the fascination with "one-verse theology"? Why do many Bible teachers make Bible propositions so situationless? So eventless? So characterless? So emotionless? So aestheticless? So forgettable?

Are propositions the Bible's only interpretive outcome? Does not such a hermeneutic do a great disservice to the narrative genre, thereby minimizing meaning, appeal, impact, and memory?[2] Can we advance beyond two hundred plus years of history where proposition purveyors have made them the apex of Scripture interpretation over a dramatic framework centered on characters?[3]

Numerous types of theologies prevail—biblical, systematic, natural, missional, narrative, historical. During the Middle Ages the West's dissectors, dismantlers, categorizers, classifiers, and publishers of academic journals crowned science-Enlightenment–based systematic theology "queen," one to be served by all theologies. The "queen" tends to subjectively organize abstract doctrines under a limited number of classroom-categorized theological themes that answer the questions the West deems necessary to ask and answer.[4] Abstraction and argumentation tend to prevail.

---

1. Ryken and Longman note this common distinction: "Biblical scholars are often content with formulations that strike literary critics as reductionistic. Whereas literary critics are likely to see the many-sidedness of real life in a biblical text, biblical scholars often reduce biblical texts to a unifying idea" (Ryken and Longman, *Complete Literary Guide*, 22).

2. James Barr provides some history: "Failures to comprehend the literary genre led to a use of the biblical assertions with a wrong function. . . . Genre mistakes cause the wrong kind of truth values to be attached to biblical sentences. Literary embellishments then come to be regarded as scientifically true assertions" (Barr, *Bible in Modern World*, 125).

3. Vanhoozer, *Drama of Doctrine*, 16.

4. It is interesting how many key textbook *miss* mission(s). In Herman Ridderbos's *Paul: An Outline of His Theology* (587 pages), there is *no mention* of the mission of the church in eighty headings. In Wayne Grudem's *Systematic Theology* (290 pages), excluded header terms include: *missio Dei*, mission, justice, missions, kingdom of God. In William Shedd's *Dogmatic Theology* (922 pages), mission and missions are absent in all headers; *Missio Dei* and *missio Spiritus* are absent *in the entire text*. Can we assume theological categorization is a cultureless undertaking? To assume Eurocentric questions are sufficient for the world is ethnocentric (which Hiebert defines as "the human tendency to respond to other people's ways by using our own affective assumptions" [Hiebert, *Anthropological Insights for Missionaries*, 97]). To assume Eurocentric questions from a previous era are sufficient for the world is beyond ethnocentrism. Can one find any questions related to polygamy? Filial piety? Ancestor veneration? Female circumcision?

> Why do so many Bible teachers at home and
> abroad immediately pursue a single proposition
> when interpreting a Bible story?

Newly discovered theologies are conveniently placed under one of the static preexisting culturally influenced categories, thereby ensuring continued cozy control of tamed Truth (assumes Aslan can be tamed). Rote learning is all that remains (followed by testing in the academy). No need to generate new boxes through creative thinking as that task is now complete. Just digest what's been discovered. Is systematic theology the West's ethno-theology?

While systematic theology certainly offers strengths—I (Tom) built my library around it—it also includes weaknesses, not unlike *all* theologies. *No theology is cultureless, because no hermeneutic is cultureless.* Why? Because the "modern interpreter, no less than the text, stands in a given historical context and tradition."[5] "No one," claims Kevin Vanhoozer, "reads in a vacuum."[6]

Have We Entered a New Era?

Have we entered a new era that has shifted beyond systematics? Have we moved beyond the era of "reason" to the "experiential" where facts require faces and stats require stories? Are new tools in the toolbox required along with some resharpened old tools? Have incoming waves erased the footprints in the sand of a former era?

Richard Hays provides a helpful succinct historical overview relevant to these questions. Hays concludes that the Reformation's chief hermeneutical issue focused on relating Scripture to *tradition*. For the Enlightenment, it was how to relate Scripture to *reason*. For today, the "urgent question" becomes, how do we relate Scripture to *authority and experience*?[7]

---

5. Thiselton, *Two Horizons*, 11. I (Tom) grew up in the Apostolic Christian Church, an Anabaptist Swiss-German group with some five hundred churches in the US at that time, where we greeted one another with a holy kiss (literally). After all, that's what Scripture commanded, right? Or did it? As I learned more about customs in the Middle East, I had to begin to differentiate culture from commands in Scripture. I treasure that revelation.

6. Vanhoozer, *Is There a Meaning*, 382. Note the multiple views on the role of women in church (1 Tim 2:12).

7. Hays, *Moral Vision*, 211 (emphasis added).

In *A Whole New Mind: Why Right Brainers Will Rule the Future*, author Daniel Pink encapsulates the term "experience" as "right-brain rising."[8] For Pink, this minimally includes aesthetics, imagination, emotions, metaphor, holism, story, symbols, rituals. Is "right-brain rising" representative of our present era? To what degree have movies and music replaced reading?

> Have we entered a new era that has shifted beyond systematics?
>
> Have we entered a new era where voice must be reinstated?

Have we entered a new era where vision and voice must be respectfully reinstated? Due to social media, many, especially younger generations, no longer know how to express their feelings, hold a conversation, or even look up from their cell phones. Virtual relationships substitute for human relationships. Zoom replaces face-to-face classes and meetings. Loneliness, anxiety, depression, insecurity, addiction, suicide result.

Could an emphasis on the visual be more captivating for today's audiences? Could the heard voice of God help change all this? Could featured characters from the biblical world offer these cyber captives a competing means to return to genuine, face-to-face human relationships like twenty to thirty centuries prior?

Yes, we have entered a new era because a former era left behind too many exposed gaps. New eras require *new focuses* (without canceling all history). And a new era asks new questions, e.g., *"What is the equivalent of 'grammar' for oral hermeneutics when interpreting Bible stories?"* Rather than asking *"What is the point of the story?"* it asks, *"What are the characters telling us?"* It reviews old questions: *"How does God reveal his recorded character most naturally and precisely in Scripture?"* History demonstrates that new eras require new hermeneutics.

The answers to the above questions may correct some of the overreaches of a former era; they may maximize what was formally minimized, e.g., demonstrations over definitions, memory over manuscripts, the grand narrative over siloed fragments, more than one possible meaning per story. Is the strong focus on rational and abstract systematics reduced into controlled categories rather than appreciated for the possibility of new categories, for mystery, for unstifled imagination and emotions? For stories? For characters? Could such overreaches be one of the contributing factors to our seminary's continued decline in numbers?

---

8. Pink, *Whole New Mind*, 7.

New eras add fresh fuel to the conversation; they may even open a closed book for the masses. They may even overcompensate.

> *What is the equivalent of "grammar" for oral hermeneutics when interpreting stories?*

If the Bible is a product of its time, are not we? Have today's hermeneutic purists who simulate a former era become the petrified past for this current era? Have they forgotten the numerous emotional depictions of God in Scripture, such as joy, love, jealousy, anger, hatred, compassion, grief, mourning, sadness, laughter? Genesis 1: 21 reminds us we have been made in his image. Do emotional intelligence[9] and aesthetic intelligence rank equal with cognitive intelligence in God's eyes (Gen 8:21)?

In this chapter we will attempt to make a clear case for another theological emphasis by proposing a *new* "queen" for a *new* era. This new queen serves *all* subjects under her global reign. We then define and distinguish character theology, isolate its influential identifiers, and consider the role of stories (first forerunner) in character theology. We conclude by summarizing character theology distinctives.

A New Theology Required for a New Age?

Could an orality-oriented theology—one that impacts textual style and structure[10] through sound, symbol, and screen—help anchor meaning and memory in this "age of art and heart"?[11] Could it enhance further textual insights in what Jonah Sachs calls the "digitoral era"?[12] Could this type of theology help address some of the limitations of systematic theology by offering a more bottom-up approach to the complexities of life—more "come and see," more "taste and see," more "figure it out"?

---

9. See Goleman, *Emotional Intelligence*.

10. Structure markers in the Hebrew Bible were designed to tie to sound: "Texts were normally intended to be read aloud, whether one was reading alone or to an audience. Accordingly, an ancient writer was compelled to use structural signals that would be perceptible to the listening audience. Signals were geared for the ear, not the eye, since visual markers would be of little value to a listening audience" (Dorsey, *Literary Structure*, 16).

11. Pink, *Whole New Mind*, 247.

12. Sachs, *Winning the Story Wars*, 14.

> Is the strong focus on rational and abstract systematics reduced into controlled categories one of the main reasons seminaries continue to decline in numbers?

Other questions might include: Could helpful additions to existing theological categories include creative "character thinking"? Should other "strange theologies" be admitted to the theology club's categories that other cultures consider necessary, e.g., polygamy, ancestor veneration, reincarnation, graft and corruption, political repression?

Can we become humble, respected contributors as well as humble, respectful learners? Do we consider the whole as well as the isolated parts? The role of concrete characters in compartmentalized abstract theology? The journey along the way as well as the destination? How culturally sensitive is our theology? Curricula have a culture!

> Could an orality-oriented theology offer an additional type of theology that encourages and enhances further textual insights in this "age of art and heart"?

How could the answers to the above questions have changed the experience of this Gen Xer then enrolled in his first graduate theology course? He told our class that in all his undergraduate Bible classes he was "taught *what* to believe, not *how* to believe." He perceived all but one of the classes as "*indoctrination to conform* rather than *discovery to transform*." He felt he was "offered tasty delicacies before feeling hunger. Clarity came before confusion; answers before questions; meaning before mystery."[13]

Are we at a *kairos* moment that requires a new type of theology that a global audience can respect and reverence? *Has evidence that demands a verdict been replaced by demonstrations that require a cast of characters? Has a case for Christ been determined through the voices and actions of a cast of characters?* Does God reveal his "confusing, complex character"[14] in Scripture most naturally, precisely, and universally through his experiences with characters and their experiences with each other?

---

13. T. Steffen and Bjoraker, *Return of Oral Hermeneutics*, 103.
14. Keller, *Prodigal Prophet*, 133.

What Constructive Additions Could Be Added?

The theology category this book proposes aims to activate a holistic response. It is like how the whole body is captivated by a specific goal when one intentionally walks into a mall through the entrance where the Cinnabon store and its inviting aroma is located. Are you beginning to salivate? Who pauses to read the text of a promo flyer, making it the key persuasive medium and moment that allures one to step up to the counter and point at a certain cinnamon roll? When it comes to cinnamon rolls, the body reacts before the mind knows what is happening!

Not unlike all the compelling ingredients and aroma that comprise cinnamon rolls, the holistic theology this book proposes *adds the sensory* (how said) to often unfeeling documents (what said); it *adds aesthetics* to help offset illusionary abstractness; it *adds concreteness* to bring the conceptual down to earth; it *adds holism* to weave the flailing fragments of life together into a unified whole thus reducing reductionism; it *adds demonstration* that enlivens clinical dictionary definitions; it *adds chants* to charts; it *adds lived experience*, which gives cold confirmations incarnational credibility and celebrity; it *adds embodied relationships*, which provide reason a relational residence;[15] it adds *beauty* to blandness; it *adds communal analysis* to individual investigation; it *adds the experiential* to cognitive analysis; it *adds episodic presentation possibilities* to linear ones; it *adds becoming "like their teacher"* (Luke 6:40 GNT) to knowing about their teacher; it *adds nuanced perception* (imaginative, emotions) to mere cognitive recognition; it *adds spontaneous voice* (intonation, volume, rhythm) to written text; it *adds unleashed power* to the spoken word; it *adds a remedy* to a false and fatal dichotomy between the spoken and the written text. In brief, it *adds orality* to literacy, thereby adding familiar filters for the oral reliant; it *adds oral theories* to later print-literary theories; it *adds voice* to silence. We call this "character theology."

> *Has evidence that demands a verdict been replaced by demonstrations that require a cast of characters?*

Character theology, composed of a cast of characters who represent universal human experience, serve as the mother of meaning, meditation, modeling, modification, and memory. Character theology makes human

---

15. "The narrative paradigm does not deny reason and rationality; it reconstitutes them, making them amenable to all forms of human communication" (Fisher, "Narration," 2).

experience no longer MIA (missing in action) in theology. Character theology is a relational theology that shapes a sea of souls for sacrificial service. We will now consider the major components that comprise character theology.

What Is Character Theology?

Character theology is comprised of characters who reveal theology and ethics through embodied demonstration. We begin with the latter. "Theology" breaks down into two parts, *theos* and *ology* or *logos*. *Theos* is Greek for "God," while *ology* (words) or *logos* (events) give shape to words as events.[16] We define *theology*[17] simply as a human attempt to understand and construct God as revealed through characters and events demonstrated in the sacred book.

"Character" refers to those who participate in the story. This goes beyond humans to include spirits, places, objects, animals, insects, and so forth.

Character theology is *much more than impersonal, detached propositions*! "Narratives make story-shaped points," claims Vanhoozer, "that cannot always be paraphrased in propositional statements without losing something in translation."[18]

John Goldingay correctly contends "the Christian faith does not take the form of statements such as 'God is love' or 'God is three and God is one' but of statements such as 'God so loved the world that he gave.'" He continues, "*The Christian faith is a narrative statement*. One would therefore reckon that story would be a natural way to do theology, or to do spirituality."[19] How naturally would character theology come across to God's highest creation around the globe?

---

16. Kelber notes, "Gerhard Kittel has stressed the activist character of *logos* with a seriousness rarely encountered in Pauline scholarship: 'In all this the *logos* is always genuine *legein*, or spoken word in all concreteness. One of the most serious errors of which one could be guilty would be to make this *logos tou theou* a concept or abstraction.' As a rule, the Pauline reference to *logos* or *logos tou theou* is to the living, preached word of the gospel" (Kelber, *Oral and Written Gospel*, 144). For a tidy summary, see also Walton and Sandy, *Lost World of Scripture*, 121–27. "'Word' [*dabar* in Hebrew] is an event of effective power, an experience of intense interaction and personal engagement" (Bradt, *Story as a Way*, 176).

17. Kosuke Koyama points out the life-sustaining abilities of "theology," which he defines as "an exciting report on our having rice with Jesus" (Koyama, "We Had Rice," 19).

18. Vanhoozer, *Drama of Doctrine*, 93.

19. Goldingay, "Biblical Story," 5 (emphasis added).

What is character theology? Simply stated, *character theology is engaging God through "reading" biblical characters in the context of story.* We will now expand and unpack the definition.

Character theology is a memorable story-centric interpretive process that focuses predominately on the narrative sections of Scripture. Relying on the Grand Interpreter, a humble-hearted community comprised of committed Christocentric learners and storyteller-facilitators carefully employs an oral hermeneutic process to uncover the Author's/author's intended trustworthy truths and ethics in a natural, universal, earthy way—through characters. This enables appropriators of the narrative to "hear" God speaking from the social context, conversations, conflicts and contests, choices and consequences, commitments, and conduct of a cast of colorful characters explored through focused character-centric questions. The ultimate goal is to faithfully transfer the written text to the tablet of one's heart to influence the nations.[20]

Expanding the Components

Character theology is a memorable story-centric interpretive process. This hermeneutic tool calls for a learning, facilitator leader, a guide-by-the-side who can steward group discussion and reflection. This requires a "co-learner, guide, role model for critical reflection, and empathic provocateur."[21] He/she believes that iron sharpens iron when interpreting a Bible story, that the Holy Spirit can give spiritual insights to anyone (1 Cor 2:4–5), and that *all* can hear from the Author.

Character theology allows for bounded "flexibility in telling biblical stories *just as* the Gospel writers did when writing their accounts."[22] It recognizes that "writing is unable to reproduce nonlinear, overlapping speech because of textual restraints."[23] David Rhoads contends, "The medium is part of the message, if not the message itself. Studying these texts in an exclusively written medium has shaped, limited, and perhaps even distorted our understanding of them."[24] Valid interpretation requires *more* than printed text.

A major part of that "more" calls for participants to *enter* the story stage, *experience* with the characters, *emulate* the worthy.

---

20. Adapted from T. Steffen, *Worldview-Based Storying*, 211; T. Steffen, *Facilitator Era*, 149.
21. Payette, "Role of Holy Spirit," para. 15.
22. Wu, "Doctrine of Scripture," 321.
23. Bishop, "There's Nothing Natural," 61.
24. Rhoads, "Performance Criticism [pt. 1]," 126.

Performance-proclamation (oralized divine written discourse that creates an experiential, memorable event) promotes such holistic understanding. How? By adding *valid* extratextual dimensions through persuasive, participatory dialogue and actions that wed past to present.

Through voice and visual body enactment, performance-proclamation creates an immediacy with the audience, thereby shaping, amplifying, and expanding interpretation. These "gestures, facial expressions, eye movement, body position," Rhoads reminds us, "are not add-ons but integral parts of the dynamics that determine meaning and impact in a performance."[25]

> Does God reveal his "confusing, complex character" most naturally, precisely, and universally in Scripture through characters?

Character theology is an expanding process of understanding in that the metaphorical, analogical, imaginative, and nature of story and characters not only encourages but demands constant revisits and humble communal reevaluation. Whether written, aural, or visual, stories consist of concreteness, aesthetics, a blending of mystery and meaning, images, repetition, rhythm, among others, making them easy to internalize and lodge long-term in the hearts (thoughts and emotions) of teller and told. They perpetuate generationally God's trustworthy treasured truths. Character theology is a common interpretive assist that naturally and most fully engages the full spectrum of our God-imaged personality.

That focuses predominately on the narrative sections of Scripture. The Holy Spirit chose in his wisdom to communicate over half of the Bible in narrative, thereby giving it a strong focus on characters. Narratives—and the characters who drive them—also find themselves intertwined with other genres, e.g., proverbs, poetry, prophecy, letters.[26] Character theology recognizes *all* Bible genres are necessary to engage the fullness of Scripture and should be utilized as well.

---

25. Rhoads, "From Narrative in Print," 14.

26. John Harvey's *Listening to the Text* lays out what many commentaries on Paul miss—the oral nature of the epistles from beginning to end. From Paul's dictation of the letter to the rhetoric patterns within it to the communal reading of the entire letter (and most likely performance) by the deliverer, and the communal interjections throughout and/or following, a Hellenistic oral form dominated, all of which was necessary for a highly oral audience. See also Longenecker, *Narrative Dynamics in Paul*; Witherington, *Paul's Narrative Thought World*.

Biblical narratives exist to help learners and storyteller-facilitators more fully grasp the depth, richness, and feel the powerful impact of these much more than soap-opera worthy stories. These sovereignly selected stories involve a wide range of characters, both genders, and numerous personalities and ethnicities. Their human experiences speak life to us in ways that increase our awe and love for our Creator, calling us to greater allegiance and loyalty as we engage more fully the amazing and awesome God of love. Character theology makes faith magnetic.

Relying on the Grand Interpreter. Rather than relying on their own wisdom to ascertain what the story communicates, participants begin to, or already realize to some extent, that the Author is much better equipped to inform them of divine storied truths than they themselves. Bible interpretation is ultimately a spiritual matter.

A humble-hearted community comprised of committed Christocentric learners and storyteller-facilitators carefully employs an oral hermeneutic process. A biblical narrative's origin is apart from us, its preservation a mystery,[27] its full comprehension and color unattainable. Humbled by these realities, wisdom pushes interpreters away from isolation in search for others of similar humility, faith commitment, and ambition to honor our Lord. They rejoice in the work of his grace within a providentially assembled community. They acknowledge that *"knowers" don't learn.*

Such interpreters also seek to discover meaning from a Christocentric canon that unifies redemptive history from alpha to omega rather than "following a few simple rules of exegesis."[28] They agree with Vanhoozer: "Hermeneutics involves more than a wooden application of methodological principles; hermeneutics requires good judgment."[29] MBR (management by rules) alone cannot be trusted to get interpreters there. Good interpretive judgment requires a strong dose of humility (doubt is good), insights from past generations, the process of oral hermeneutics, and most importantly of all—the assistance of the Grand Interpreter.

In order to uncover the Author's/author's intended trustworthy truths and ethics in a natural, universal, earthy way they selectively chose certain characters within their stories. Authors of Bible stories wrote for a purpose, e.g., John explicitly states he wrote so that his readers might believe that

27. "A mystery . . . refers not to something that is irrational but to something that cannot be fully comprehended by reason, exceeding its capacity to discern and describe. The sheer vastness of God causes the images and words that humans craft to falter, if not break down completely, as they try to depict God fully and faithfully" (McGrath, *Narrative Apologetics*, 8).

28. Enns, *Inspiration and Incarnation*, 170.

29. Vanhoozer, *Is There a Meaning*, 140.

Jesus is the Christ. Matthew wrote to show Jesus was Israel's promised King. They also wrote for appeal and impact; they had things they desired interpreters to discover, ponder, implement; they desired interpreters become the interpreted so they could help others interpret themselves.

Through contrasted characters, emotionally based, storied concepts emerge that rely on trustworthiness (reflecting the oral world) rather than on truth (reflecting the scientific world) can be learned in a natural, universal, earthy way. Such Holy Spirit–driven storied concepts may even go beyond what the human authors understood at the time of writing. They may also require some simmering over generations for interpreters to begin to grasp their nuanced significance. It's difficult to downright drain drama.

Generally, personalities preceded propositions. Through conversations and embodied actions (genuine to fake) of biblical characters in specific contexts the Revealed One is discovered. Doctrines are found in the characters themselves rather than pried-out propositions that tend to dissect and dismember storied characters. Meaning is buried in its wholeness. Healthy propositions require holistic personification.

This enables appropriators of the narrative to "hear" God speaking from the social context, conversations, conflicts and contests, choices and consequences, commitments, and conduct of a colorful cast of characters. The colorful cast of characters includes humans (individuals and groups [e.g., elders, Pharisees], real and fictional), the supernatural (e.g., God, Satan, angels, demons, gods), animals (e.g., horses, donkeys, goats, roosters, ravens), insects (e.g., flies, locusts, ants), elements (e.g., whirlwinds, thunder, clouds, earthquakes), objects (e.g., trees, tents), cities (e.g., Babylon, Rome), and a host of others—fish, frogs, worms, vines.

Character decoding investigates the human authors' and the Holy Spirit's intent for recipients through a character's context and circumstance (setting, symbols, rituals), status (power relationships), role (major, minor, foil, real, fictional). Decoders also investigate personality traits given through the author or others (psychological [dress, appearance, judgments], physical [aggressive, passive, proximity]), and responses (conversations, questions, conduct [especially conflict between characters], choices, commitments, courage, compassion, collaboration, or the lack thereof). These are all driven by tangible and/or intangible aspirations and internal and/or external conflict and contests (active tensions). Character theology relies on earthy, concrete personages and places to frame and embed abstract concepts designed to tease observers into divine truth.

Writers are word shepherds. Storytellers are character shepherds. Interpreting words alone is inadequate to discern the full range of senses being unleashed through characters. The appropriate meaning behind the words also requires the character's character, context, and circumstance. Characters serve as the kindling of curiosity and the unravelment of the senses and meaning without bypassing text.

Conversation decoding plays a crucial role in character theology. Victor Matthews quotes Robin Wooffitt's definition of "conversation analysis" as "the systematic analysis of the talk produced in everyday situations of human interaction: *talk-in-action*."[30] Vanhoozer prefers "speech-acts," which he argues is "the main currency of personal relationships."[31]

Interpreting such conversations provide outsiders with insider societal insights such as power relationships—who can talk to whom, when, where, and how. Rhetorical responses reflect the risks and rewards of social reality and relationships.

Because "the dramatic impulse permeates the Bible . . . [to] read the Bible is to become an implied listener of the spoken voice."[32] Character theology creates in us a longing to hear God's authentic voice. Character theology sensitizes our heart and soul to hear God's voice in and through the narrative records of selected characters.

The Eternal One sovereignly chose to reveal himself to the nations primarily through Bible characters. Character theology, therefore, pursues a communal means to listen and faithfully respond to God's voice projected through a community of characters. Biblical truths portrayed through the lives of earthy biblical personages are best discovered and lived out as a covenant community.

Character theology recognizes the Bible is *not* a quiet printed text; rather, it is a speaking printed text. Scripture speaks strongly through Bible characters as it is *never* silent. Character decoding requires a strong oral sensitivity.

Explored through focused character-centric questions. Character-centric questions *begin* not by seeking content but by reading characters, not by seeking characteristics but by decoding conversations, not by seeking reasons but by identifying relationships, not by seeking propositions but by seeking personalities, not by seeking siloed fragments but by seeking wholeness.

The line of character-centric questioning that often follows the story will eventually secure the abstract content, but *after* the concrete characters have been decoded. Character-centric questions tend to sequence through

---

30. Robin Wooffitt, as quoted in V. Matthews, *More Than Meets Ear*, 68 (emphasis original).

31. Vanhoozer, *Drama of Doctrine*, 67.

32. Ryken and Longman, *Complete Literary Guide*, 32.

the concrete-abstract-hybrid circular interpretive model—from the concrete to the abstract and back to a hybrid as they follow characters working their way through plotline tensions.

The ultimate goal is to faithfully transfer the written text to the table of one's heart to influence the nations. The ultimate goal of character theology is *not* the interpretation of written text. Nor is it having the characters in the text interpret the interpreters. The ultimate goal of character theology *is* that the interpreters who have been interpreted learn to fear their Creator, stand in awe of him, find their fountain of joy in him, love him, love and serve others, and love themselves.[33]

Character theology is a spiritual exercise that can never be completely exhausted. Character theology is God's illustration or embodied (always a visible expressed event) explanation of the particulars of who he is, who we are to him and in him, and what he seeks from us.

Reflecting on the lives of biblical characters teaches recipients to fear and reverence their Creator (Prov 9:10). From the inspirational to devious conversations and conduct of Bible characters in specific contexts, godly, actionized wisdom emerges. This offers opportunity to habitually demonstrate it to others, thus bringing honor to the Source. Text on the page becomes text on the heart, which becomes text lived out in context.

As decoders continue to track granular and ever more extensive details resident in character theology, God's grace empowers them to turn away from sin, ignorance, lukewarmness, syncretism, a self-communal protective impulse. This then allows his followers to focus on blessing the nations by walking in loyal love as trophies of grace who exemplify God's glory.

Character theology shapes the whole person by appropriating the whole person Jesus is as reflected in, clarified through, and challenged by particular personages we meet throughout Scripture. Holy Spirit selected characters portrayed in natural life situations by human authors, and in their own language, acquaint us with a relational Creator who extends his hand to all. Character theology perceives the character of God primarily through biblical characters who challenge and help transform our lives, thereby influencing the nations for the Eternal One.

Characters convey their Creator. The goal of character theology is to center theology on characters so that their demonstrated treasured truths become *our* treasured truths, thereby making them memorable and modelable, all of which brings glory to the King.

---

33. This would include birth gender.

Isolating Influential Identifiers of Character Theology

Character theology's major influential identifiers will now be isolated. Character theology is:

- Centered on God's voice
- Story based
- Character centered
- Natural
- Universal
- Social, communal, relational
- Verbal and visual
- Holistic, fulsome (integrates imagination, emotion reason, spirit world)
- Based on narrative logic (developed in ch. 4)
- A dialogical peer process
- Ambiguous and mysterious
- Revealed through character-centered driven questions
- A repository for possible multiple divine truths (mega-message and mini-messages)
- Memorable
- Repeatable
- Designed for the nations
- Life transformative, resulting in honoring God, others, self

The above components and identifiers will receive further illustration and elaboration in the forthcoming chapters. We will now briefly introduce some key drivers of character theology.

Story Drives Character Theology

Story serves as the first forerunner of character theology. Mark Turner contends, "Narrative imagining—story—is the fundamental instrument of thought. Rational capacities depend upon it. It is our chief means of looking into the future, of predicting, of planning and of explaining. It is a literary capacity indispensable to human cognition generally."[34] That is because "humans are not mere intellects shaped by rationality, but rather embodied souls. Story reaches us as such, and locates us in a nexus of meaning."[35] Story, proposes Robert McKee, is a *"metaphor for life."*[36] For Kevin Bradt, it is "a way of knowing."[37] It is also a way of communicating, relating, and identifying.

Stories require characters. Characters drive stories through surprise and suspense as they seek a satisfactory solution. There are no good stories without characters. In the classic *Story Proof*, Kendall Haven quotes Mary Jo Puckett Cliatt and Jean Shaw: "All stories are based on character."[38] Note Haven's character-centric definition of story: "A detailed, character-based narration of a character's struggles to overcome obstacles and reach an important goal."[39]

Know any good stories absent characters? Good stories center on and illuminate characters. Stories serve as the scaffolding for characters to advance the author's plotline from simple to complex. Characters serve as the soul of stories as they live out their actions from selfish to selfless. Got characters?

Haven believes character-based stories spark our interest, giving stories inordinate power to draw us in as we seek to discover what hampers a character from reaching his/her goals and what they will do to solve the current dilemma in which they find themselves embroiled. In short, their lives reflect our lives, thereby transporting us effortlessly into *our* shared story world.

Minimally, a story requires the integration of a setting (urban, rural, terrain, season), characters (protagonist, antagonist, full, flat, foil), plot (intentionally introduced actionized tension by the author sequenced through scenes in search of resolution), and resolution (positive, negative, unresolved). Even so, life-changing stories are character-centric. Characters reign in a story because they engage the entire person. Like a local town fair, their different personalities draw in a wide range of onlookers.

> Know any good stories absent characters?

---

34. Turner, *Literary Mind*, 4–5.
35. Herring, "Re-Enchanting the World," 149–50.
36. McKee, *Story*, 25 (emphasis original).
37. See the title of Bradt's book: *Story as a Way of Knowing*.
38. Mary Jo Puckett Cliatt and Jean Shaw, as quoted in Haven, *Story Proof*, 77.
39. Haven, *Story Proof*, 79.

Daniel Taylor adds, "We remember characters from stories long after we've forgotten plot, language, and theme. The allure of character is the mesmerizing attraction of watching people struggle to make decisions."[40] So we watch, we listen, we imagine, we anticipate, we verbalize. As a story driven by characters, the Bible does *not* live in some abstract world of bygone days.

Just as honey draws ants, so stories pull us into the conversation and conduct of the featured characters. They do so because they "include the elements of surprise, hyperbole, paradox, and shock . . . the aesthetic mingling of the realistic and the surprise."[41] The words and works of certain characters are mesmerizing, magic, magnetic. Stories shout, "Picture this!" And we can't resist; we're hooked.

Stories refuse to remain a monologue. Stories demand ongoing dialogue between not only the story's characters, but also with the participants following the unfolding events. Justo Gonzàlez expands: "Communication is that mysterious bridge where intimacy and otherness meet. To read the Bible is to enter into dialogue with it."[42] When such happens, laughing, scolding, applauding, and disgust, among other responses, can be seen and heard as the story unfolds.

Often designed to meet the moment, effective stories influence and teach. Whether formal or informal, fictitious (e.g., *Veggie Tales*) or real, stories convey concepts related to contexts, moral values, humor, and so forth, and therefore have the potential to alter lives. Ineffective stories, on the other hand, do just the opposite. Stories "awaken sleeping wisdom."[43]

What comprises effective stories? They: "1) successfully engage and hold that engagement, and 2) also accomplish the communications purpose (your influence or teaching) for which they were created."[44]

Stories have their own modus operandi. Susan Shaw sagely summarizes: "The truths of stories are made, not by logical persuasion, but by experiential engagement. Stories do not convince by argument; they surprise by identification."[45] Andrew Le Paul posits, "Stories tell us who we were, who we are, and who we can be."[46] Stories do all this through suggestion rather than statement; they serve not "so much to convey a meaning as to

---

40. Taylor quoted in Haven, *Story Proof*, 77.
41. Kelber, *Oral and Written Gospel*, 60.
42. Gonzàlez, *Santa Biblia*, 14.
43. Simmons, *Story Factor*, 50.
44. Haven, *Story Smart*, 9.
45. S. Shaw, *Storytelling in Religious Education*, 61.
46. Le Paul, *Write Better*, 59.

wake a meaning."⁴⁷ The unspoken in stories can speak louder than a crack of thunder.

Authors of captivating stories wrapped in mystery, by design, often make it a difficult mental exercise for story listeners to decode divine truths. They may have a difficult time discerning the truths contained the first time heard, or even the fiftieth. Through time, reflection, dialogue and debate, fresh insights continue to bubble to the surface, dissipating the misty morning fog encompassing the pond.

> Has today's hermeneutic purists that simulate a former era become the petrified past in the current era?

Stories highlight propositions without bifurcating the two. Metaphorically, "story is the ring that provides a setting for the precious gems of propositions."⁴⁸ Bible propositions should not be stand-alone statements; rather, they should be narrativized. Attractive Bible propositions are compressed, dehydrated narratives.

Some will argue stories take way too much time away from the significant. Stories require a shortcut. Why waste time? Just get to the headline, the sound bite, the proposition.

Yes, stories do take time to tell, but we must never forget, they percolate and perpetuate in the recipient's mind long after the spoken words of the story have grown silent. Again, stories say, "Picture this!" because pictures speak visually and remain sketched in our minds. Stories shape the significant.

The imagined pictures suggest a story comprised of sensory images which ignite the imagination resulting in a long shelf life. As Richard Niebuhr notes, "We are far more image-making and image-using creatures than we usually think ourselves to be and . . . are guided and formed by images in our minds."⁴⁹ Vanhoozer adds: "Following the way ultimately requires using the imagination as well." Why? Because "the way of Jesus is more an embodied story than it is an embodied argument . . . it is largely thanks to the imagination that the disciples are able to relate the story of

---

47. MacDonald, *Dish of Orts*, 192 (emphasis added).

48. T. Steffen, *Worldview-Based Storying*, 138. Two self-published documents that were widely circulated among missionaries emphasized both integrated story and propositional doctrine (Team Ifugao, *Ifugao Evangelism*; Schultze and Schultze, *God and Man*). Does not metaphor do the same?

49. Richard Niebuhr, as quoted in Ryken and Longman, *Complete Literary Guide*, 17.

Jesus to the story of their own lives."[50] Knowing and remembering God requires more than the cognitive—it requires an assistant—the affective. Imagination leads to intimacy which leads to values.

The same held true for the Ifugao. They were not just hearing a Bible story being told. Like a movie, they were also viewing it in the theater of their minds; they were living the lives brought to their attention. They felt and experienced what the Bible characters felt and experienced—the sting of comments, the fear of dissent, the heat of pain, loneliness, the joy of a firstborn, the loss of a loved one. The invisible became visible, past events became present experiences. And these pictures painted on the canvas of their minds lingered, resulting in awe, amazement, anticipation.

On the flip side, imageless communication suffers memory loss.[51] Could one find not only long-term value but actual present enjoyment by becoming part of a story?

Story preceded Scripture, preexisting Gen 1:1. Michael Matthews perceptively proposes, "Story is inherently Trinitarian. Before everything other than the God of the Scriptures existed, there were characters (the Trinity), there was setting (the Trinity), and there was plot (the Trinity). Story consists of character, setting, and plot."[52] That is why people universally are called "storytelling animals."[53] As one aspect of orality, story has a strong theological basis.

Stories form our worldview. N. T. Wright adds: "Stories are actually peculiarly good at modifying or subverting other stories and their world views."[54] Steve Evans correctly claims, "It is not until the role of story in worldview and culture is firmly grasped that one can fully comprehend the necessity of story in worldview change and life and cultural transformation."[55] But could Evans go further with his proposal, beyond stories? Possibly.

Humans, made in God's image, are *homo narrans* because the Trinity is *Deus narrans*. Humans are also *homo symbolicus* because the Trinity is *Deus symbolicus*, and *homo ritualis* because the Trinity is *Deus ritualis*. The integration of symbols, stories, and rituals makes humans unique because the Trinity is unique. Symbols, stories, and rituals serve as the foundational roles in the (re)construction of one's reality and relationships.[56]

50. Vanhoozer, *Drama of Doctrine*, 15.
51. Haven, *Story Proof*, 69–70.
52. M. Matthews, *Novel Approach*, 85.
53. See Gottschall, *Storytelling Animal*.
54. N. T. Wright, *New Testament and People*, 40.
55. Evans, "Matters of the Heart," 192.
56. See T. Steffen, *Worldview-Based Storying*.

The integration of symbols, stories, and rituals continues to shape and reshape one's worldview. For example, as a rival story, the gospel restores communication and relationships lost in the garden and restored on a hilltop by the God-man. This requires followers of the covenant community to re-symbol, re-story, and re-ritual.

Stories increase and perpetuate memory. Roger Schank tells us why and how. Why? Because "human memory is story-based."[57] How? "Stories form the framework and structure through which humans sort, understand, relate, and file experience into memory."[58] Symbols and rituals also help preserve and protect memory.[59]

Part of that memory a story creates is an individual's and family's legacy. Stories keep family history alive for generations because they connect family members on a collective journey. Whether in grief or gladness, exchanged family stories have much to teach willing members even as they build a family member's legacy and family's legacy as well.

A story is a mysterious, unfolding struggle composed of characters (human or nonhuman, fictitious or real, prominent or periphery), who come with attitudes, attributes, activities. They experientially attempt to resolve the challenges, changes, and crises life throws at them internally and externally. Such challenges come in specific, often symbolic settings (e.g., legal, liturgical) and times (e.g., war, famine, peace). The whole story (which includes at least one counter-story) offers observers vicarious roles. Through suggestion and association, story triggers reevaluation of present realities and future possibilities. Tales tutor us.

Stories are powerful social constructs that feature multisensory (imaginative, emotive) characters who holistically (body, soul, spirit) connect and communicate with others, and engage in "spoken" actions (enactments that unleash learning); they make room for participants to reflect on their own lives in safe sanctuaries even as they serve as patterns for adaptive behavior.

Stories show rather than tell, enact rather than explain, illuminate rather than spell out, demonstrate rather than define, embody rather than conceptualize, encounter rather than detail, exhibit rather than exhort, suggest rather than state. Stories thereby intentionally leave much to the imagination and heighten emotions within the decoding community. Stories first and foremost speak from the heart to the heart. Stories exchange human

---

57. Schank, *Tell Me a Story*, 69.

58. Roger Schank, as quoted in Haven, *Story Proof*, 118.

59. Besides voice, note the numerous ways God instructed his highest creation before sacred print text arrived: a vast creation, animal skins, rainbows, doves, dry land, sacrifices. In the beginning were voice and symbols, rehearsed eventually through rituals.

experiences, offering a possible reimaged world. Stories create within us an insatiable hunger for more stories. Got stories?

The holistic participation of characters in the story is multisensory in nature, reflecting the creativeness and the engaging emotions of the Trinity. As the psalmist reminds us, "The *unfathomable* cosmos came into being at the word of the Eternal's *imagination*," which challenges us to "stand in awe" and "live in wonder of Him" (Ps 33:6, 8 VOICE [emphasis original]).[60]

Stories refuse to be limited to a fascination with facts or reason. Rather, they include the culturally colored sensory, aesthetic, emotional qualities. Characters kick-start our imagination and senses; we appropriate them by steadfast faith even as reason shows up to attempt to explain and rationalize.

Sensory stimulation in any venue is *not* a concession to humanity. Rather, it is at least as powerful as the meaning of the words themselves. Interestingly, this ancient wedding finds its roots buried deep in the holy Trinity.

How stories are told and interpreted differ from culture to culture. For example, how they begin ("Once upon a time . . ." or "It was a dark and stormy night . . .") and end (Mark and Acts end abruptly; Jonah leaves us hanging with an unanswered question).

Westerners tend to like happy endings—the hero wins (e.g., *Grease*, *Home Alone*, *Babe*); Easterners tend to like sad endings—the hero encounters tragedy or dies (e.g., *The Burmese Harp*; *The Last Emperor*; *Crouching Tiger, Hidden Dragon*). Who is considered a hero of the story? The Sawi made Judas the hero because he demonstrated their preferred value—deception. Gender,[61] different generations, and geographical locations—all of which influence choices and conduct—shape how stories are told and interpreted. While the use of stories is universal, expect how they are told and interpreted to always be culturally colored.

> Is systematic theology the West's ethno-theology?

---

60. Brueggemann calls this "abiding astonishment" (Brueggemann, *Abiding Astonishment*, 30).

61. The counterpart to Paxtun male revenge killings for females is sadness: "The main ingredient of a good story is gham (sadness) . . . beautiful stories that make you cry. . . . Almost every event a woman recalls in her life story is one that was marked by crying and visits, at which time no doubt she had to narrate the tragic circumstances to visitors over a dozen times. . . . They [women] are not considered to have begun living, and are even referred to as 'ignorant', until, beginning with their marriage, they experience the gham [sadness] of mature womanhood" (Grima, *Performance of Emotion*, 12–13).

Although originating from the past, stories refuse to remain history. History becomes the present as contemporaries identify with past characters. Stories easily become contemporary.

Stories were *not* meant to be studied—they are meant to be *experienced*. To begin to understand stories more fully and impactfully, we must engage them, live them. Living out the stories experientially suggests evidence of being captured by the characters within them.

The concepts that comprise story play a major role in the interpretation of Bible stories. While there is much more to orality than stories, stories remain "the life-blood of orality."[62] German philosopher Martin Heidegger adds, "Narrative is the primary scheme by means of which hermeneutical (interpretive) meaningfulness is manifested."[63] Stay tuned.

The Narrative-Centric Nature of Scripture

The Bible is replete with stories, comprised of some eight hundred major stories plus myriads of mini-stories found in the Psalms, songs, Proverbs, and elsewhere. These raw, concrete-relational stories name some three thousand human characters,[64] span around 1500 years over multiple ages (Bronze to the Roman), and are written in three languages.

The grand narrative summarizes hundreds of individual stories that comprise the biblical saga; it succinctly, yet unsystematically,[65] sketches the history of Scripture through all genres that captures God's storied actions from a mysterious origin, "in the beginning"[66] to a shadowy victorious conclusion. This choppily constructed canon remains a disjointed but unified story.

This unified sacred story centers on Jesus Christ, the Perfect Person and Chief Character. He is the storyline of Scripture—the centered core that ties all the individual parts into a cohesive whole (1 Cor 15:11).

---

62. Chiang and Coppedge, "Connecting Orality, Language," 8.

63. Martin Heidegger, as quoted in Haven, *Story Proof*, 107.

64. Herbert Lockyer estimates there are over 3000 named biblical characters (Lockyer, *All the Men*, 5).

65. This references 2 Tim 3:16, which eventually would include the New Testament.

66. In the beginning of what? Robert Munson offers four possibilities: 1) the beginning of God, 2) the beginning of the heavens and earth, 3) the beginning of space-time, or 4) the beginning of the story. He concludes, "I am not sure we always have to choose one interpretation. I certainly believe looking at the Bible as a story holds merit" (Munson, *Theo-Storying*, 5–6).

This "glorious mess"⁶⁷ with all its travesties and triumphs, still offers, yes, a complex, yet coherent story.⁶⁸ Even a child can comprehend its basics (Deut 6:4–9; Luke 10:21).

The "word of God" comprises the overall story found in Scripture. The "words of God" comprise the spoken⁶⁹ and written words that entail the overall story. The "Word of God" is a human-Divine person, the Chief Character—Jesus Christ—who is "alive and moving; sharper than a double-edged sword" (Heb 4:12 VOICE), and points to the triune God who speaks powerful words.

Bible authors periodically provided listeners helpful summary statements to make sure the whole was not lost over time due to fragmentation or memory loss (recall the numerous exhortations to "remember" [Deut 8:2; John 15:20] which includes actions⁷⁰). Some are quite brief, others more extensive. Each tends to build on each other, offering ever-expanding summaries of the sacred story. Characters who played vital roles are assumed in the story sweeps.

Part of those character sweeps include the extensive genealogies found in Matthew and Luke, thereby generating legitimacy for Israel's role in the unfolding grand narrative. The genealogical emphasis originates in Genesis where "each of the ten sections of Genesis begins with . . . 'These are generations . . . ,' and then gives a genealogy." Rather than "moral stories or philosophy," the Bible offers "a long epic of a family that God has chosen."⁷¹ Genealogies provide role legitimacy for Israel throughout the generations as they build the family of God, and they also make the honored firstborn Jesus a *real* person rather than a "fictional hero"!

Some Old Testament (OT) story sweeps include: Exod 3:15–17; 4:29–31; 6:6–9; 15; Deut 1:6—3:29, 6:10–25, 26:5–9, 32:7–43; Josh 24:2–15; 1 Sam 12:6–13; 1 Chron 16:14–22; Neh 9:5–37; Job 38; Ps 76; 78:1–4; 105; 106:6–12; 136; Jer 2:1–19. Story sweeps continue in the New Testament (NT), e.g.: Matt 1:1–17; Mark 12:1–23; Luke 3:23–38; 24; Acts 7; 13:16–41; 17:22–31; 28:23; Rom 9–11; Heb 11; Jude 1.⁷² As the narrative unfolds, so do

---

67. Sanders, *From Sacred Story*, 4.

68. If you have issues perceiving the Bible as a story, see N. T. Wright, *New Testament and People*.

69. Holly Hearon notes, "To understand a word as 'spoken' is to recognize that it references an immediate social context described by the location of a performer and audience in a specific place and time" (Hearon, "Implications of 'Orality,'" 100).

70. "Biblical remembering is a body activity, not merely a head activity" (Sarna, *Genesis*, 56). And in oral-dominated cultures, it is communal, not just individual.

71. Tverberg and Okkema, *Listening to the Language*, 71–72.

72. See Hood and Emerson, "Summaries of Israel's Story." Jackson Wu notes Richard

updated sweeps, aggregating into the grand narrative of Scripture, all aiding exegetical control.[73]

Characters mentioned most frequently (besides Jesus) in Scripture by name (not pronouns) include David (971x), Moses (803x), Jacob (363x), Saul (362x), Aaron (342x), and Abraham (295x [57 being Abram]). All are included in Acts 7 and Heb 11 except for Saul and Aaron. Their multiple inclusion, among other highly repetitive names, provide interpretive clues not only for a single story but also for the Story. "We have to study not only the spiders, or the Bible characters; it is equally important to study the web, or the meta-narrative . . . because God has chosen to weave this grand story with the smaller stories of particular people."[74]

Fullness of meaning is found in the aggregated fragments. For example, Chronicles revises and retells Israel's exodus and exile story from Genesis through 2 Kings for a later generation. Echoes of story sweeps and the characters who compose them provide a comprehensive and concrete means to understand the words of God. In the oral world, repetition of pivotal small stories is required for remembering the big picture.

How necessary is narrative in conveying biblical truths and ethics? While multiple genres comprise Scripture, more than half of the Bible is narrative.[75] As Eugene Peterson pithily proposes, "The Holy Spirit's literary genre of choice is story."[76] It may well be the telling of God's story is much more reliant on a multitudinous cast of characters than we've previously considered, and less dependent on doctrinal discourse than we've assumed and advocated.

What if narrative is embedded in theology rather than theology is embedded in narrative? Is the narrative mode a passive medium used to

---

Bauckham, "Reading Scripture as a Coherent Story" (2003); Paul House, "Examining the Narratives of the Old Testament" (2005); and other summaries not included in Hood and Emerson's list (Wu, "Biblical Theology," 275). Cf. Bruno et al., *Biblical Theology*. Note also in Acts 7, Stephen includes in his speech specific names for fourteen human individuals, eleven human groups, and eight good and evil individual spirits; while the author of Heb 11 mentions twenty-four human individuals, nine human groups, and two individual spirits.

73. "God knows where Scripture is going as a whole in a way that the Bible's human authors did not appreciate. All of this means that good exegesis pays attention not only to the meaning of a passage in its 'book' context but in its 'canonical' context as well, where the correlation of texts across authors becomes an important concern" (Bock, "Opening Questions," 25). Walter Kaiser notes that interpreting individual sections of Scripture is incomplete until it is run through the complete "promise-plan" (grand narrative) of God (Kaiser, "Must We Go beyond").

74. T. Steffen, *Facilitator Era*, 148.

75. T. Steffen and Bjoraker, *Return of Oral Hermeneutics*, 93–95.

76. E. Peterson, *Leap over a Wall*, 3.

convey God's message? Why were we reminded that "in the beginning was the *Word*" (not text) (John 1:1 NIV [emphasis added])?

How did most miss the dominant role narrative plays in Scripture? Alister McGrath believes the reason is that theologians and the biblical interpreters they trained "allowed themselves to be unduly influenced by the ideology of the Enlightenment," which "suppressed what is actually the dominant and most characteristic literary form of the Christian Bible: the narrative."[77] This significant oversight should compel *every* Bible communicator at home and abroad to ask: Which genre do I automatically default to when communicating the Bible to Christ followers? To potential future followers?

> How necessary is narrative in conveying biblical truths and ethics?

Interpreting the individual stories, however, is not as easy as it may seem. All too often Westerners (and some Easterners who graduated from Western-funded schools, often from the receiving countries of missions) have treated an Eastern book as if it were Western in our teaching and theological textbooks. Glenn Paauw warns the Minority World, "The Bible was written for us, but not directly to us."[78] Gary Burge believes, "We have forgotten that we read the Bible as foreigners, as visitors who have traveled not only to a new geography and pedagogy, but to a new century as well. We are *literary tourists* who are deeply in need of a guide."[79]

New guides, fortunately, are emerging. For example, Esa Autero writes, "Many students are surprised to discover that the Bible is an Asian book! Though the geopolitical definitions of the ancient world were not quite identical to ours, even the ancient Jewish historian Josephus viewed Israelites as *Asianos*. Hence, it is high time to return the Bible to its proper context."[80]

Actually, it is past "high time." Part of that "return" will require the incorporation of cultural backgrounds and orality. As "literary tourists" trying to interpret strongly Asian oral worlds and text, Westerners will need all the help possible. That would include theological insights from the too often

---

77. McGrath, *Narrative Apologetics*, 39–40.
78. Paauw, *Saving the Bible*, 69.
79. See https://preservingbibletimes.org/favorite-quotes/ (emphasis added).
80. Autero, "Seeing the New Testament," 180.

excluded voices of the Majority World,[81] the social sciences,[82] and especially the assistance of the Author—the Holy Spirit. Culturally bound pedagogies and their resultant theologies too often remain unassessed.

Characters Drive Theology

When you open the Bible, hear, read, or view a story, who comes to meet you? Content? Characters? We now take a brief look at how characters relate to character theology. We begin with the Chief Character.

Behind the Grand Narrative Is the Chief Character

While the Creator is behind all characters in a story, he does not always take an explicit role. Recall Esther. Even while not mentioned, however, the Liberating King is *always* there implicitly.

> Which genre do I automatically default to when communicating the Bible to Christ followers? To future followers?

Jackson Wu challenges the oft-repeated four-part summary of the grand narrative of Scripture—creation, fall, redemption, consummation—arguing this tells the story from a *human* perspective. He offers this alternative, "God created. God entered into a covenant. God incarnated in Christ. God commissions his Church to glorify him among the nations."[83]

Scott Duvall and Daniel Hays would agree: "If we miss God in the story, then we have missed the story."[84] Adding characters, in this case the Chief Character, helps personify, personalize, and mystify what follows.

---

81. For some diverse voices, see Gonzàlez, *Santa Biblia*; Adeyemo, *Africa Bible Commentary*; Simon Chan, *Grassroots Asian Theology*; Yong with Anderson, *Renewing Christian Theology*; Wintle, *South Asia Bible Commentary*; Jusu, *NLT Africa Study Bible*; Yeh and Tiénou, *Majority World Theologies*; Stephanous, *Arabic Christian Theology*; Gener and Pardue, *Asian Christian Theology*; Thomaskutty, *Asian Introduction*; Adewuya, *African Commentary on James*.

82. See Shaw et al., *Teaching across Cultures*; Flemming, *Contextualization in New Testament*. What if Christianity had been brought to the West from the East a century ago? How would Westerners have reacted to Eastern pedagogies?

83. Wu, *Saving God's Face*, 44.

84. Duvall and Hays, *Grasping God's Word*, 349.

Ernst Wendland provides these helpful aids to interpretation:

> In the Abraham-Isaac account, both Abraham and the narrator say that the Lord will provide, and he does (Gen. 22:8, 14). In the David-Goliath narrative, David says, "The battle is the Lord's and he will give you into our hand," and he does (1 Sam. 17:45–49). The main point in these narratives is not "Abraham obeyed a hard command and believers should, too" or "David was brave and Christians should be, too." The lessons are that "the Lord provides" and "the battle is the Lord's" (and then, also that he's certainly worthy of trust!). The stories' characters go on quests, face choices, and respond to God faithfully or unfaithfully—but the Lord is the main agent, and believers, unbelievers, and bystanders are always responding to him.[85]

Charles Koller concurs: "The Bible was not given to reveal the lives of Abraham, Isaac, and Jacob, but to reveal the hand of God in the lives of Abraham, Isaac, and Jacob; not as revelation of Mary and Martha and Lazarus, but as a revelation of the *Savior* of Mary and Martha and Lazarus."[86] Gordon Fee and Douglas Stuart tell us why: "Narratives are not just stories about people who lived in OT times. They are first and foremost stories about what God did to and through those people ... God is the hero of the story."[87] How strongly do our headers and titles focus on the hero of the story in our Bible stories? Story sets? Does the header create mystery or give away too much information?

When Bible characters do attempt to become the hero of the story, bad things tend to happen. Recall when Lucifer attempted to dethrone God (Ezek 28:11–19); or when Abraham did what was commonly done at that time, lied about his beautiful wife being his sister when entering Egypt (Gen 12:10–20); or when Jonah took a ship to Tarshish instead of Nineveh (1:2–3). But worst of all, the real Hero of the story is supplanted. Yes, we must prep the horse for battle but never forget who gives the victory (Prov 21:31).

> Is there any such thing as pure objectivity? Pure subjectivity?

Behind and before all Bible characters is the Hero of heroes—the one with outstretched arms on a cross, the one who continually knocks at the door, desires to tabernacle with us and call us friends—the *Chief Character*!

85. Wendland, "Interpreting the Bible," 6.
86. Koller, *How to Preach*, 32 (emphasis original).
87. Fee and Stuart, *How to Read Bible*, 75–76.

Character theology reveals the most famous person in the world as more than an historical figure or an idea; it introduces a *friend* to a cold and confused world.

Behind Interpretation Is the Grand Interpreter

C. S. Song challenges Bible communicators to read Bible stories *attentively* and *intentionally*. Be attentive, "because in the story you are entering a world alien to your own." Be intentional, "because you are making conscious efforts to interact with the world and the experience of the story with your own."[88]

While Song offers significant advice, storyteller-interpreters often fall short when interpreting. Fortunately, the authority of Scripture is not confined to our ability to interpret it as the original authors intended. Interesting, is it not, even within evangelical circles, how many different interpretations exist throughout the sixty-six books?

Ryken narrows the focus:

> Many biblical scholars have made unwarranted claims about how their methods establish objective controls on biblical interpretation. A survey of how biblical scholars interpret characterization in the stories of the Bible will reveal as much variability of interpretation as literary critics produce when they analyze characters in stories.[89]

Is there any such thing as pure objectivity? Pure subjectivity?

From amateurs to professionals, Bible interpretation has been and remains a mixed bag. Unlike us, the Holy Spirit has no problem identifying or respecting each genre used in Scripture,[90] knowing the various languages, cultures, geographical locations, historical context and times, or the audience's and author's preferred pedagogy and culture. He is well aware of the form of logic required in the different literary preferences. He is not overly enamored with soulless science nor willing to sacrifice his preferred genre—stories—for science or characters for concepts or "wise and persuasive words" (1 Cor 2:4; 4:20 NIV) for actionized demonstration.

The Holy Spirit loves beauty, teasing mystery, built-in ambiguity, creating emotive fascination, contradiction, wonder, discovery. He seems

---

88. Song, *In Beginning Were Stories*, 155.
89. Ryken, *Words of Delight*, 76.
90. We agree with O'Donnell and Ryken that not only is the content inspired, so is the form of delivery, in this case narrative. See O'Donnell and Ryken, *Beauty and Power*, 19.

to prefer to integrate the imagination, aesthetics, emotions, spiritual, and reason; he refuses to dichotomize these or minimize the spoken nature of his inspired written texts.[91] He seems unwilling to play only in the sandbox of siloed slivers and loves to communicate to those committed to the Author-author's sacred script. He also likes to reveal members of the Trinity through the convincing conversations, conduct, and commitments of a cast of chosen characters.

The Holy Spirit, the Grand Interpreter, is just what Bible storyteller-interpreters require, and he is *always* ready and willing to assist the "student on the stage" as well as the "sage on the stage." Have we overestimated our interpretive prowess? Underestimated the Grand Interpreter's? Got the Grand Interpreter?

> Which genre do I automatically default to when communicating the Bible to Christ followers and future followers?

Who better to assist Bible storyteller-interpreters than its Author, the "Spirit of truth" (John 14:17 VOICE)? And the Grand Interpreter offers promises as well! He will "teach you everything" and will "guide you in all truth" (John 14:26; 16:13 VOICE).

Because hermeneutics is *never* culture free, Bible interpretation is *never* cultureless. We must therefore remain totally dependent on the Author. Hermeneutics must be a strong Spirit experience.[92] May we as interpreters, tellers, and demonstrators become and remain humble dependents on the Grand Interpreter.[93]

Characters R Us

Brazilian poet Rubem Alves asserts, "Stories are not windows; they are mirrors."[94] The same could be said of characters—characters are not windows, they are mirrors. Bible characters reflect our lives, pulling us into their conversations, circumstances, clashes, compromises, cease-fires. Bible

---

91. Sadly, most textbooks on hermeneutics coming from the Minority World *give little or no attention* to the role orality played in biblical textual construction or implications for interpretation.

92. See Keener, *Spirit Hermeneutics*.

93. Corduan, "Humility and Commitment," 83.

94. Alves, *Poet, Warrior, Prophet*, 74.

characters are "alive, authentic, and utterly unpredictable.... Every emotion and enchantment found in the twenty-first century is somewhere lurking in the pages of Scripture."[95] Ancient characters remain forever young just as do their stories; the ancients continue living as our contemporaries.

Think how many different occupations and behaviors are mentioned in Scripture. All elicit positive or negative identification with the characters, no matter one's geography, gender, or generation. From prophets, kings, sages, fools, rogues, farmers, priests, military, politicians, murders, adulterers, the raped, the barren, the incestuous, scribes, Pharisees, crooks, apostles, doctors, teachers, tax collectors, farmers, artisans, businesspeople,[96] all our stories are present in someone within the sacred storybook. And each points us to the Chief Character.[97]

Our stories are found in the lives of those included in Scripture because of universal life similarities. This is all made possible because "all these things happened to them as examples for others, and they were written down as a warning for us" (1 Cor 10:11 GNT).

Recall Andrew Le Paul's quote: "Stories tell us who we were, who we are, and who we can be."[98] That is because, as Goldingay correctly purports, the "story-shapedness of Scripture corresponds to the story-shapedness of human experience."[99] The characters depicted in the stories found in Scripture represent us—past, present, and future.

Paul Bohannan digs deeper as to why stories grab us. "Stories are gripping not merely because we can identify with the characters, but perhaps even more because we understand the difficulties of the characters' choices, empathize with their need to make them, and learn more about the pattern."[100]

> Got stories?
>
> Got the grand narrative?
>
> Got characters?
>
> Got the Grand Interpreter?

---

95. Tucker, *Biographical Bible*, 2. See DeMuth, *Most Misunderstood Women*.

96. Jesus worked with his hands for around two decades (Luke 3:23) in a small business, which would influence his teaching—around thirty work-related parables.

97. T. A. Steffen, *Reconnecting God's Story*, 31.

98. Le Paul, *Write Better*, 59.

99. Goldingay, "Biblical Story," 6.

100. Bohannan, *How Culture Works*, 153.

To illustrate, Sarah's shameful barrenness caused her to ask Abraham to sleep with a servant girl to resolve her/their humiliation. Joseph had ample power and opportunity to take revenge on his brothers. Rahab and Esther were under tremendous pressure to compromise. Job could have easily turned his back on Yahweh. Joseph and family experienced extended family shame once Mary's pregnancy became public knowledge. The Samaritan woman at the well did not know what to think of the comments and conduct of this Jewish man who contradicted cultural stereotypes. The hair on the back of Adam's head no doubt stood up when he heard the Eternal calling, "Where are you?" (Gen 3:8 VOICE), as did the Israelite priests when asked, "Where is *My* respect from *you*? . . . Where is your fear of *Me*?" (Mal 1:6 VOICE [emphasis original]). The third crow of the rooster most likely stopped Peter in his tracks. The stories of Bible characters are raw, real, representative.

As observers watch Bible characters destroy themselves and others because of fear, greed, shame, or power, and/or restore themselves and broken relationships (e.g., David), we cannot help but empathize with them. Michael Goldberg states: "Narratives offer us a relatively safe way to explore our 'options' without first having to experiment with our own lives. They help us imagine what might follow from talking up and acting on one set of convictions rather than another."[101] The faces of fear and faith are right there for us to experience, internalize, emulate, or eliminate.

Whom is the Bible written to? Adults, of course. Wayne Rice thinks otherwise:

> As Paul wrote to young Timothy, "Don't let anyone look down on you because you are young" (1 Timothy 4:12). We have a treasure trove of biblical heroes to inspire teenagers who want to do something significant with their lives for God: Moses, Joseph, Samuel, Esther, David, even Jesus himself, who at age twelve declared, "I must be about my father's business." King Josiah began his successful thirty-one-year reign in Jerusalem when he was eight years old. Joan of Arc was only nineteen when she was martyred for her faith. There are many examples in history of teenagers who showed remarkable competence and courage as they assumed roles that today are reserved more or less exclusively for adults. And young people today are just as capable, if not more so.[102]

Bible characters on their life voyage, whether young or old, male or female, lure us into their lives; like a magnet they draw us up on the stage to participate with them as coactors. They don't just tell, they show; they don't

---

101. Goldberg, *Theology and Narrative*, 234.
102. Rice, *Reinventing Youth Ministry (Again)*, ch. 2, para. 34.

just explain, they enact; they don't just spell out, they illuminate; they don't just define, they demonstrate; they don't just conceptualize, they embody; they don't just assert, they present; they don't just state, they suggest.[103] Characters act upon us until we decide to brush them off or become coactors with them on the stage of life.

Nothing speaks like human experience. Bible characters R us.

> Have we overestimated our interpretive prowess?

Looking Back and Ahead

Character theology carries with it key distinctives that demonstrate its necessity for today's world. Whether "serendipitous" encounters like many of Jesus's or in the academy such as Tyrannus's lecture hall used by Paul, character theology has a major role to play. Bible storytellers who highlight the conversations, conduct, conflict, and contexts of the characters within a story, facilitate relevancy to life and therefore appeal through impact.

We now summarize the above conversation in which we sought to bring clarity to what we believe will be instrumental in changing people's perspective of Christianity in the twenty-first century at home and abroad—character theology.

A means to communicate. In that more than half of the Bible is narrative, character theology is a wise and loving God's most common, most natural, most universal way to discover theology, communicate it, and live it. Character theology focuses on concrete characters in the stories rather than conceptual philosophy, making them an obvious and preferred way to communicate and live theology globally.

A means to relate and identify. The Bible's "compelling immediacy"[104] and intimacy makes character theology universal, human, natural, earthy, visceral, mysterious, holistic, instantaneous. This is brought about in part through "participatory history," i.e., similar human experience the listener/reader/viewer encounters in a story. Harry Stout explains, "History stories are neither past nor present but both simultaneously."[105]

---

103. Was Matthew compiled and written to *prove* to the Jews that Jesus was their promised messiah? Or was it compiled and written to *demonstrate* Jesus was their promised messiah?

104. Alter, *World of Biblical Literature*, 210.

105. Stout, "Theological Commitment," 48.

Far from dead, past lives live on in the present. There are few things more powerful than experiencing the experiences of others whether in real time or ages past. Character theology offers choices between characters who offer the futility of foolishness, the well of wisdom, and everything between. Characters forge character.

The past is simultaneously the present, and vice versa; we participate on the living side of history, thereby making relational connection possible, often instantaneously with a character in the story. Bible characters have a natural, immediate way of leaving eternal impressions on our hearts; they tie the past to the present. Character theology renders warm relationships central over cold compartmentalization. Character theology offers pictorial perceptions through a parade of personalities, leaping beyond the rational to the relational. Likeness relates. Character theology meets the moment.

Spotlights the real heroes. Bible characters "are the real heroes who inspire us through their successes and disciple us through their scars. We will walk alongside their rough, unedited lives, without pretense and with no best-foot-forward performances."[106] We relate to reality; we relate to real heroes. Through their trials and troubles, we receive divine treasures and timeless, storied truths. Because we become whom we hang with, the Bible characters, who become not just friends but family members, spare us and others many wounds and scars.

Requires an oral hermeneutic. Character theology is an interpretive assist that naturally and most fully engages with the full spectrum of our God-created personality. Character theology recognizes and mines the oral nature of Scripture through an oral hermeneutic (with its plethora of practices); it recognizes the oral text as necessary as the written text;[107] it recognizes the Bible does not dichotomize the spoken and the written.[108] Rather, it assumes Scripture is the integrative *spoken-written* words of God requiring an oral hermeneutic.

Character theology creates in us a longing to hear God's authentic voice; it sensitizes our heart, soul, and mind to experientially and rationally

---

106. Cordeiro, *Divine Mentor*, 50.

107. Ruth Finnegan critiques the distinction made between the "superior" written and the "inferior" spoken, literate and oral societies, identifying it as the "great divide." She believes they interface on a continuum, constantly crisscrossing and cross-fertilizing each other, not unlike the spoken and written words of God. She also sees the relationship between oral literature and written literature as a "difference of degree and not of kind" (Finnegan, *Literacy and Orality*, 20; see also 39–105).

108. "The words *in this* book *are the words* of the Eternal One, which were told to Hosea" (Hos 1:1 VOICE [emphasis original]).

hear and heed God's voice in his numerous narrative records. Information and reason standing alone are insufficient for the Creator's highest creation.

Is revelatory. Character theology is God's illustration or embodied explanation of the particulars of who he is, who we are, who we are to him, and what he seeks from us.

Creates character-centric mystery. In character theology, ambiguous mystery, not precise propositions, reigns. This is because every prominent character personifies a mystery that our curiosity strives to unravel. Through a sequence of scenes, a cliffhanger emerges, intentionally leaving much to the imagination and emotions. We have far too often concluded that propositions reign, forgetting the powerful role of mystery.

Character theology has a unique way of arresting and retaining our attention—of making us wonder. Wise Bible interpreters follow the mystery being played out between characters through a sequence of events knowing they are on the path to life-changing meaning.[109] Personalities increase the potency of a message because they personify mystery.

It may well be the telling of God's story is *more* reliant on a multitudinous list of characters than we've previously considered, and *less* dependent on lists of doctrines than we've assumed, asserted, and advanced. What if the central hermeneutic question focused on the significance of characters rather than grasping for abstract one-liners through grammar?

Helpful Sources

Chiang and Lovejoy, *Beyond Literate Western Models*

Ryken, *Words of Delight*

T. A. Steffen, *Reconnecting God's Story to Ministry*

Communally oriented. Character theology calls for a communal pursuit to hear and faithfully respond to God's voice demonstrated through the lives of a cast of characters who surround us. Asian American Tom Lin eloquently concludes, "Individualism doesn't have much of a place in following Jesus. Bible study looks corporate; it doesn't seem like you can experience God fully until you have fully experienced and participate in the body of Christ incarnated in a community of believers."[110] Character theology calls for Christianity to be heard, discussed, and lived out *communally*, not just *privately* (2 Pet 1:20).

---

109. Bruner, *Culture of Education*, 121.
110. Lin, *Losing Face*, 76.

CLARIFYING CHARACTER THEOLOGY

> What if narrative is embedded in theology rather than theology is embedded in narrative?

Can we more fully understand and impactfully experience God when *corporately* participating in worship, prayer, Bible study, giving financially, serving? We believe so; this is one of the geniuses of character theology—corporately searching for biblical storied truth through a cast of Bible characters, and then corporately attempting to live out those demonstrated truths. The bottom line for character theology is transformed lives that habitually glorify the King.

As a community discovers granular and eventually more extensive specifics in the biblical narratives, God pours out his mercy and compassion, empowering and equipping his people to turn away from the sins of pride, laziness, ignorance, and self-aggrandizement, others. Character theology is based on God's narrated merciful and compassionate remedy to the suffocating power of sin and death in this world.

Character theology encourages *all* (leaders and led) to participate in unwrapping mystery's vagueness. It seeks deep dialogue and more together time around the "kitchen table," all of which require a listening-learning posture. Did Jesus listen more than he spoke?

> Can we more fully understand and impactfully experience God when *corporately* participating in worship, prayer, Bible study, giving financially, serving?

Good questions, which can connect existing isolated thoughts and help expand the participant's creativity and critique. Unravelers of the mystery offer ideas after which their merit is communally tested. Conclusions are summarized narratives to be revisited later. That is because "education is not an affair of 'telling' and being told, but an active and constructive process."[111] Jane Vella offers this warning and solution: "Teaching can get in the way of learning. The design of dialogue education . . . protects learners in their learning from teachers teaching that could steal the learning opportunity from learners by telling, or 'helping.'"[112] Have we allowed teaching to interfere with learning?

---

111. John Dewey, *Democracy and Education*, 38.
112. Vella, *Learning to Listen*, xxiii.

Character theology encourages an amateur army of foot soldiers, not just officers, opportunity to interpret Bible stories.[113] Why? N. T. Wright correctly contends that "to make the deep, life-changing, kingdom-advancing sense it is supposed to, it is vital that ordinary Christians read, encounter, and study scripture for themselves, in groups and individually."[114]

If Bible communicators believe in the Holy Spirit–engifted body of Christ, they purposely "provide space for intuition, feeling, sensing and imagination alongside the traditional skills of analysis, reason and sequential problem-solving."[115] Character theology is tailored and tooled for the average committed Christ follower to become a competent Bible story interpreter.

In summary, character theology is a public affair. The Bible story is proclaimed performed, heard publicly;[116] it is debated, interpreted, remembered, applied, and reviewed publicly. Such a living communal process also plays a major role in disseminating the message to the masses.

Interpretations eventually solidify, becoming part of the covenant community's local shared oral tradition. For example, "Theology in the African heritage was articulated not in treatises and manuals but in descriptive names and phrases, myths of origins, blessings and curses, greetings and expressions of gratitude, rituals, prayers, informal religious sayings, and in ordinary comments and explanations."[117] Character theology honors the role of community in Christianity.

Relies on character-centric questions. Character theology relies strongly on questions that focus on the characters in their roles and setting. Well-thought-through character-centric questions help keep the discussion focused, flowing, earthy, relational, relevant, reliable.

Offers vicarious life experiences. Like the Bible, character theology prefers *not* to offer defined lists of atomized, Aristotelian categories of theology. Rather, it prefers the observers experience the theology or ethics in a similar way as did the characters in the story. Such engagement often offers unheard, under-heard, or overlooked alternative ways to live life.

---

113. "The 'uneducated' still engage in biblical exegesis, but not that of a lone grammarian sitting before a text in the study. The value of 'exegesis' extends beyond the specialized work of a literary professional to the activity of one who intentionally participates in the prayer, worship, and reflection of the whole community and is challenged to live out one's life within that 'school'" (McCarthy, "We Are Your Books," 333).

114. N. T. Wright, *Scripture and the Authority*, 133.

115. P. Shaw, *Transforming Theological Education*, 282.

116. See Boomershine, *First-Century Gospel Storytellers*.

117. Mugambi, *African Heritage*, 59.

CLARIFYING CHARACTER THEOLOGY

Relies on the grand narrative. Character theology relies heavily on the grand narrative of Scripture that anchors all individual stories. While giving special attention to the individual stories, character theology recognizes that a grand narrative exists that not only unifies the book but also provides interpretive guide rails and guardrails for individual stories.[118] The grand narrative serves as a movie preview highlighting various scenes and pivotal players as it lays the foundation for what's to come.

None of this is new. As Birger Gerhardsson reminds us, "There was however a somewhat different way of learning an oral text collection. It was first learned as a whole; analysis and interpretation was undertaken later."[119] The grand narrative of Scripture is not a skeleton comprised of many bones; rather, it is a skeleton key that unlocks the meaning of all the bones.

The grand narrative does more than connect the dots, more than connect stories; it connects characters. In review, the grand narrative summarizes and unifies the total text, reveals the Chief Character, and interprets the individual stories. When should the grand narrative be storied in evangelism? Discipleship?

> When should the grand narrative, the big picture, be storied for evangelism? Discipleship?

Relies on the Grand Interpreter. No one knows a story better than the author. In relation to Scripture, this means the Holy Spirit. Not only did the Grand Interpreter tell select individuals what to say and write, and how to do so, he also helps us today interpret it.

Seeks a long-term ongoing discussion. Character theology begins a discussion as to what the Author-author wishes us to internalize from the mystery-laced story. It is not interested in ending the discussion as if there are no more marinated nuances to discover. Character theology prefers Bible story unravelers continue their attempt to crack the character code. While science is always a process, it nevertheless seeks to wrap up a discussion

---

118. "The 'grand narrative' of Scripture: 1) displays, defines, and deifies God through what he does (actions); 2) is Christocentric; 3) displays and defines God's creation through interaction; 4) encompasses the gospel; 5) frames trustworthy theology; 6) combats heresy; 7) places the spotlight on the significant; 8) interprets every part of Scripture; 9) unifies the multiple parts; 10) challenges all cultural biases in that meaning is influenced by our culture; 11) doesn't let us write the script; 12) summarizes to make the story economical to tell; and 13) shows connectedness to life" (T. Steffen, "Role of Grand Narrative").

119. Gerhardsson, *Memory and Manuscript*, 117.

through convincing evidence. Stories, on the other hand, seek to continue the conversation indefinitely through mystery. In character theology, "settled science" gives way to "unsettled discussion."

Is memorable. Character theology offers not only an engaging way to learn theology, but a memorable way to retain, retrieve, and replicate it. The context, conversations, and conduct of concrete characters enhance recall even as the "communal soul"[120] builds a shared oral-written tradition of faith. *Bible characters easily enter our lives through familiar pedagogical pathways and leave their footprints forever imprinted on our hearts, thereby challenging, and sometimes even transforming, present practices and postures.*

Is operational. Character theology suggests a natural teaching model most can emulate. In many passages of Scripture, the First and the Last revealed his character through characters as did the Father.[121] Following the Bible's model, personifying the lives of biblical characters to others is a natural, powerful means to reveal the Chief Character.

Is relevant. Character theology weds the relational to the rational. In so doing, it addresses the "quest for certainty" by moderns and the acceptance of "uncertainty" expected by postmoderns. Character theology weds experiential apologetics with evidential apologetics, thereby offering a more holistic approach to evangelism and discipleship. Character theology attempts to go beyond a legal value model (guilt-innocence) promoted in much Western ministry to include other key moral values conditioned by culture to serve as the social glue that holds communities together, such as relationships (shame-honor), control (fear-power), and hygiene (pollution-purity).

Character theology makes God's character clearer and more contagious because recipients recognize themselves in the conversations, conduct, and conflict of some of the cast of characters, thereby learning ways to become more Godlike personally and collectively. Corporately conversing about conversations and conduct can be life changing, not just for the individual, but for the community and nation as well. Many wounds and scars will be avoided.

Extends and enhances existing theologies. What makes character theology unique compared to other theologies? We answer the question with two questions: "Could character theology not exclude, but take us beyond biblical theology (diachronic), systematic theology (synchronic), and narrative

---

120. Ong, *Orality and Literacy*, 45.

121. "God is known and addressed primarily in the terms which relate him to society and to history.... Consequently, the only image of him possible is the mental image of a person, and the only language by which he may be addressed is drawn from the institutions of human society" (G. E. Wright, *God Who Acts*, 49).

theology (literary)? Could it help *integrate* all of these and others?"[122] Could it offer an interpretative beacon to billions? We believe so. Bringing Bible characters out of the shadows through character theology can help clear up the confusion that surrounds so much of Christianity around the globe, e.g., "Christianity is colonialism" or a "Western religion."

> What makes character theology unique compared to other theologies?

Character theology is not abstract theology; rather, it is a relational theology driven by chosen concrete characters. Relational theology puts abstract propositions in their place rather than dismiss them. Character theology adds to the theologies by personifying abstractness (recall the concrete-abstract-hybrid circular interpretive model).

Seeks a God-honoring, service-oriented goal. As interpretive skills sharpen, new insights create within us an extraordinary passion to bless others and to walk humbly as grace-and-truth–reflecting trophies of our Lord. Character theology returns us to the life-changing joy of God's presence in our lives and to wonder at the ways he works through us to serve Christ and others with renewed gladness.

Character theology acts as an interpretive lens, providing fuller, sharper vision of the glories of God. Characters seen, heard, touched, and smelled are the created, objectified illustrations of God's person and the sounds of his voice. Sounds awaken the senses, leading us into the space where we learn who the Eternal One is and our role in the Story. We can do no less than glorify our Creator.

As was common in antiquity, can we learn to process and organize biblical content around characters in a single story? A story set? The grand narrative? Can we become more comfortable with the virtue of vagueness? Could a little hermeneutic headwind bring more stabilization to Bible interpretation? Does this present oral-digital-virtual-AI era require a new queen of the theologies, one who serves all other theologies?

Characters have *never lost their centrality or creditability* in Bible interpretation and theology, just their *invitation* and *inclusion*; they have been all too often *cancelled* by the academy and replaced with the search for pithy propositions through grammatical analysis laid out systematically. Craig Blomberg provides a more balanced perspective: "The rhetorical power of the narratives is obviously lost by means of propositional paraphrase, as is

---

122. T. Steffen, "Pedagogical Conversions," 155.

a portion of their meaning. One must therefore not assume that dogmatic affirmations are adequate substitutes for narrative theology. Each has its place, and neither may be jettisoned."[123] There is no expiration date placed on character theology or other types of theologies.

Good drivers do not continually look through the rearview mirror. Nor do they only look forward. The former creates historians while the latter sets the driver up for potential accidents. A good driver continues to look both directions—building on the past while peering into an ever-fluctuating future. A good driver understands there are risks and rewards in looking in *either* direction.

> Can we become more comfortable with the virtue of vagueness?

If the church wishes to remain *irrelevant* in the twenty-first century to most of the world's population focused on the experiential, it is easy—just keep marching along the "straight black line of the Gutenberg galaxy"[124] while advertising and offering objective, abstract, rationally based propositions as the main entrée on the menu at Old Faithful Fact Church and Buffet Seminary. To become more contemporary, *change the menu*. Advertise Bible characters as the top entrée on the menu. This will do much inwardly for the health of the global church as well as her global advancement outwardly.

Is unique. For some, character theology will be like focusing binoculars from fuzzy to fully focused. It may take a few or possibly frequent adjustments to align one's view with that of the ancients but the crispness that awaits is well worth the time and effort.

Incapable of exhaustion. Like its Author, Scripture cannot be known in completeness. While character theology adds nuance, appeal, and impact beyond other interpretive models when applied to the narrative sections of Scripture, it, like *all* interpretive models, is incapable of complete understanding of a text or the Text. Even so, character theology provides a relevant and superior model for today's world and for the narrative sections of Scripture.

Recapping, character theology focuses on biblical characters because the Creator in his sovereignty chose to reveal his character most naturally and precisely through his interaction with characters and their interaction with each other.

---

123. Blomberg, *Interpreting the Parables*, 413.
124. Lou Silberman, as quoted in Kelber, *Oral and Written Gospel*, 1.

CLARIFYING CHARACTER THEOLOGY

Like Jesus required a forerunner, so does character theology. Actually, character theology requires at least five forerunners to make it operational. Stories comprise the first. We now turn to character theology's second forerunner—characters. What is the role of *characters* in character theology?

Reflection Questions

Time to review the questions highlighted throughout this chapter. Select two to three and dive in. If possible, do this communally. What new insights did you gain?

2

The Role of Characters

> In considering the total effect of any narrative, it is important to discover the focus of character, and to answer the question, "Whose story is it?"
>
> —CHARLOTTE LEE

> Character-affirming readings reflect (consciously or unconsciously) a "role model" hermeneutic. . . . The underlying assumption here is that the Bible is in the business of offering us characters to emulate.
>
> —DAVID GUNN AND DANNA FEWELL

> But there's only one Book in which you can meet with *all* the mentors specially selected by God to teach the saints. Only the Bible's men and women are His designated divine mentors. He has put His imprimatur on them alone.
>
> —WAYNE CORDEIRO

ARE CHARACTERS, REAL OR fictitious, the most influential force for good or evil for all age groups globally? Ask voters in Virginia in 2021 when given the opportunity to vote out the incumbent governor who advocated for the state and teachers to have sole control over the curricula taught to their kids in taxpayer-funded public schools. Droves of mama bears roared as they charged out of hibernation to voting centers. Having a much different perspective, many changed political parties. They clawed back by voting in a pro-parent governor who would challenge school boards advocating critical race theory, grooming for gender fluidity, and the 1619 Project, among others.

Ask the stockholders of the Walt Disney Company when it came to light that the most famous family-friendly entertainment corporation in the world was now promoting a gay-lesbian-transsexual-asexual-nonbinary agenda that targeted kids through long-loved and new Disney characters. Parents revolted, canceling theme park visits and cruises, and censored Disney movies for their kids. Stocks plummeted. As in the education world, parents did not want the beloved characters they grew up with in the entertainment world now being used to undermine family values.

Ask the Ifugao when presented with a very abstract sermon. The context was the celebration of the Golden Jubilee of the coming of Christianity to the Antipolo-Amduntug Ifugao of central Luzon, Philippines. The year was 2018. On the third day, Sunday, four sermons were presented, three by expatriates. The fourth sermon was based on verses from an epistle. The expatriate speaker divided the sermon into three parts. He immediately began using abstract terms, such as holiness, grace, free grace, salvation, justification, the righteousness of God, sanctification, predestination, and glorification, all with little or no accompanying concrete context.

The translator struggled, really struggled. The audience grew restless. When the translator could not translate a term, in desperation he added local prefixes to the English theological terms. On one occasion, he tried three times to explain "justification." In exasperation when he could not (and he knows English well), he said with a sheepish smile, "I think they understand." Neither the translator nor the audience had any clue what was being said by a very humble, charming, highly intentional Bible speaker.

Bringing it closer to home, LifeWay Research analyzed 450 sermons.[1] They discovered *50 percent* moved through a block text verse by verse. Certainly, a good thing, but where did the pastors focus the sermons?

Another *46 percent* focused on "a main theme, question or topic, using multiple Scriptures to support it." One wonders how character-centric the pastors made these thematic, topical organizational models?

---

1. See Stetzer, "How 450 Sermons Revealed."

> Are characters, real or fictitious, the most influential force for good or evil for all age groups globally?

The remaining *4 percent* organized the sermon around "one main character" with multiple supporting texts.[2] Much more concrete, personal, yet fragmented. If the Trinity is relational in nature, have Bible communicators flipped the script?

What drives Bible communicators to such all-too-common abstract presentations? Vanhoozer offers this possibility, "Modern theology is overdependent on a single form: dedramatized propositions, statements about God taken out of their context in divine communicative action."[3]

What if the speaker at the Ifugao service would have used concrete aspects of the life of Abraham (think Rom 4) to demonstrate the abstract concept of justification by faith?[4] Would the Ifugao have remained fidgety and expressed frustration through facial feedback along with a few interjected comments in a strongly shame-oriented society?

How did audiences at home respond to those 450 sermons? Whether in the educational, political, business, or religious worlds, *can we learn to tell better tales that highlight central characters at home and abroad*? Which best creates down-home choices—characters or concepts? How did the Transcendent become transparent?

In the last chapter, we considered who drives character theology behind the scenes—the Chief Character, Jesus, the One who assists in discovering the meaning of Scripture—the Grand Interpreter, and how Bible characters R us.

In this chapter we want to dig deeper into the specific role of those who drive individual Bible stories—characters. We begin by defining "character" followed by isolating its influential identifiers. The overall purpose of Bible characters is then pondered before closing with some key characteristics of characters that influence character theology and curricula.

---

2. Stetzer, "How 450 Sermons Revealed," para. 13.

3. Vanhoozer, *Drama of Doctrine*, 269. We would define "communicative action" as narrative.

4. Note how Paul relied on the Spirit's demonstration (in contrast to "persuasive elegance") to reveal the meaning of his sermons. Paul's sermons were "effective because I relied on God's Spirit to demonstrate God's power" (1 Cor 2:4 VOICE).

What Is a Character?

It takes more than setting, situation, and struggle to make a story. It takes *characters*. Story is the arena in which characters drive the plot to some conclusion. But what is a character? Simply stated, *a character is a person, spirit, or personified entity that advances or surrounds a conflict*. We will now expand and unpack the definition.

A literary "character" refers to humans and anything personified—spirits, animals, insects, plants, the elements, objects—that helps drive the story. Characters can be an individual or group, real or fictional, visible or invisible. Driven by imagination, motivations, and emotions, key characters acquire a descriptive personality profile through conversations, conduct, and change. Whether the protagonist, antagonist, foil, full, or flat, they find themselves entangled on some perilous journey (plotline) in search of an attainable resolution. The character traits projected by sovereignly selected characters are never neutral. Characters propose choices as they change or resist change, especially to observers who identify strongly with them. Possible flashbacks and flash-forwards make their arduous journey seldom a straight line. Focused character-centric questions will go a long way in revealing the thoughts and actions of others, and their implications for life's journey.

Expanding the Components

A literary "character" refers to humans and anything personified—spirits, animals, insects, plants, elements, objects—that helps drive the story. Characters in a story, when given human qualities or characteristics that advance the plotline, e.g., voice, actions, looks, include more than humans. These may include spirits, e.g., angels, demons, gods; animals, e.g., horses, donkeys, goats, roosters; insects, e.g., flies, locusts; elements, e.g., whirlwinds, thunder, clouds, earthquakes; and a host of others—fish, frogs, worms.[5]

Characters can be an individual or group, real or fictional, visible or invisible. Characters come in many types (see fig. 2.1). These could include individuals and groups, e.g., elders/Pharisees; real or fictional, e.g., the good Samaritan; or invisible spirits, e.g., angels and demons.

---

5. "A character is a person, animal, being, creature, or thing in a story" (https://literaryterms.net/character/).

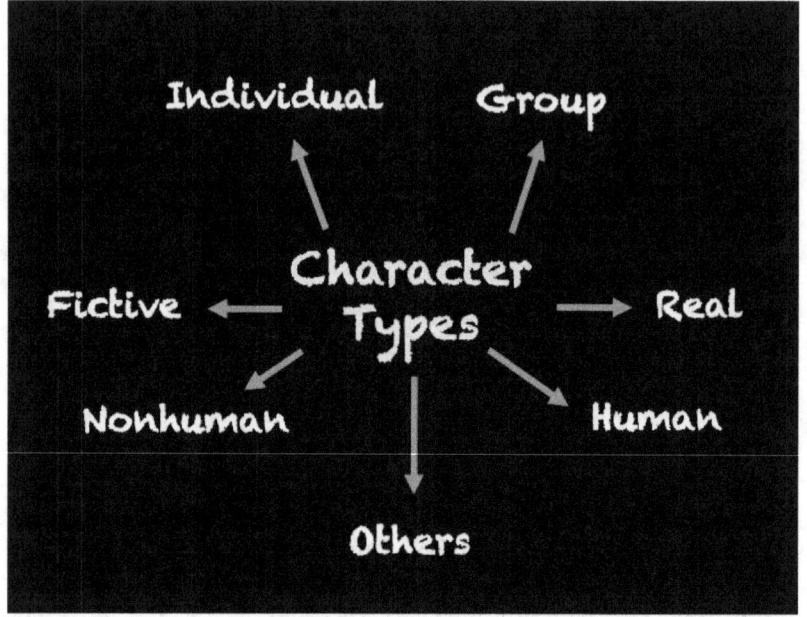

Figure 2.1. Types of Characters

They can be driven by imagination, motivations, and emotions. Characters respond to more than reason. Rather, imagination, motivation, and emotions (implicitly or explicitly expressed, which "are data, not directives"[6]) play a strong role in the decision-making process, even as they interact with reason. Through culturally colored imagination, characters tend to express feelings critiqued by reason.

Key characters acquire a descriptive personality profile through face-to-face conversations, conduct, and change. Different stories spark different conversations, thereby requiring different characters. John, e.g., following essentially the same Jesus story outline of other Gospel authors, offers a "quite a different way than his canonical companions . . . John primarily tells stories. But as Jesus speaks, his words flourish into conversations and discourse with all sorts and conditions of people, conversations brief and

---

6. David, "Gift and Power," 12:35. Matthew Elliot adds: "Emotions are not primitive impulses to be controlled or ignored, but cognitive judgments or construals that tell us about ourselves and our world. In this understanding, destructive emotions can be changed, beneficial emotions can be cultivated, and emotions are a crucial part of morality. Emotions also help us to work efficiently, assist our learning correct faulty logic, and help us build relationships with others" (Elliot, *Faithful Feelings*, 14).

lengthy, conversations pithy and elaborate, but always *conversations*."⁷ Stories create ongoing conversations through author-highlighted pivotal people who exhibit a kaleidoscope of faults, failures, feats.

Bible authors of the Gospels often use "surprising characters (e.g., widows, sinners, tax collectors) or an authority figure (Jesus)"⁸ to juxtapose the assumed with the unassumed. Referencing the "sinful" woman arriving with a flask of perfume, washing Jesus's feet with her tears, and wiping them with her hair completely contrasts host Simon's total lack of culturally expected hospitality (Luke 7:37–50), drawing this conclusion from James Resseguie. Resseguie deduces, "The widow's gift and Jesus's commendation remove the ordinary way of judging the value of gifts from its habitual context, which in turn makes the 'normal' method of evaluation seem arbitrary and strange."⁹

Using Victor Shklovsky's term *defamiliarization* ("making strange"), Resseguie argues this oft-used concept "strips away the 'film of familiarity' . . . that blurs our ordinary, routinized perception . . . in order to break the chain of automatized perceptions."¹⁰ In this case, the lower-class female "sinner" (noted twice for emphasis) outclassed the upper-class male Pharisee, thereby catching everyone by surprise. Premature conclusions involuntarily required unanticipated reflection because of Jesus's comments, thereby highlighting the need for some reverse thinking.

Resseguie summarizes these "special characters" and "authority figures" this way: "Defamiliarization relies upon shifting the reader's attention from an automatized habitual recognition of familiar phenomena, to a deformed, convention-violating expression which awakens the reader to a new perception of the world."¹¹ Because of unexamined habitual frequency (a "sinful" women brings and applies perfume to a male), more than a gentle nudge is often required for transformational learning to transpire—it requires "defamiliarization."

Conversations offer opportunity for discourse insights. Listeners and readers should look for, among other hallmarks of orality, repetition of words and phrases, concreteness, holism, nonverbal communication, artistry, formulaic expressions (see fig. 2.2).

Beyond author-provided conversations that highlight discourse features, they observe emotions and actions driven by internal thoughts (see

---

7. E. Peterson, *As Kingfishers Catch Fire*, 321 (emphasis original).
8. Resseguie, "Defamiliarization in the Gospels," 30.
9. Resseguie, "Defamiliarization in the Gospels," 31.
10. Resseguie, "Defamiliarization in the Gospels," 25.
11. Resseguie, "Defamiliarization in the Gospels," 25.

fig. 2.2). Dialogue within the text also offers the "potential to glean insights into the social world that it reflects rhetorically."[12]

Through author projection,[13] characterization (a personality profile) begins to emerge for key individuals[14] and background characters.[15] Sometimes this happens abruptly but more often incrementally. Through physical features, attire, name or new name (Abram to Abraham; Saul to Paul; Daniel to Belteshazzar), setting, implemented values, internal thoughts, emotions, internal and/or external conversations, a personality profile emerges, along with representative roles comprising assets and vulnerabilities.

Other key features introduced throughout the story could include a character's conduct (reactions to actions), experienced conflict (destabilizing actions that create tension) and controversies, choices, consequences, small to big changes (see figs. 2.3, 2.4, 2.5, 2.7). Such personality profiles serve as billboards that promote certain choices and consequences.

Any fluidity within the positioning of characters also has the potential to create tension. Such potential flash points should receive strong interpretive attention.

---

12. V. Matthews, *More Than Meets Ear*, 99.

13. "Noah was *a good man*, a right-living man, the best man of his generation; and he walked closely with God" (Gen 6:9 VOICE [emphasis original]).

14. David to Nathan: "I have sinned against the Eternal One" (2 Sam 12:12 VOICE).

15. Queen Esther about Haman: "He is vile, and an enemy to my people" (Esth 7:6 VOICE).

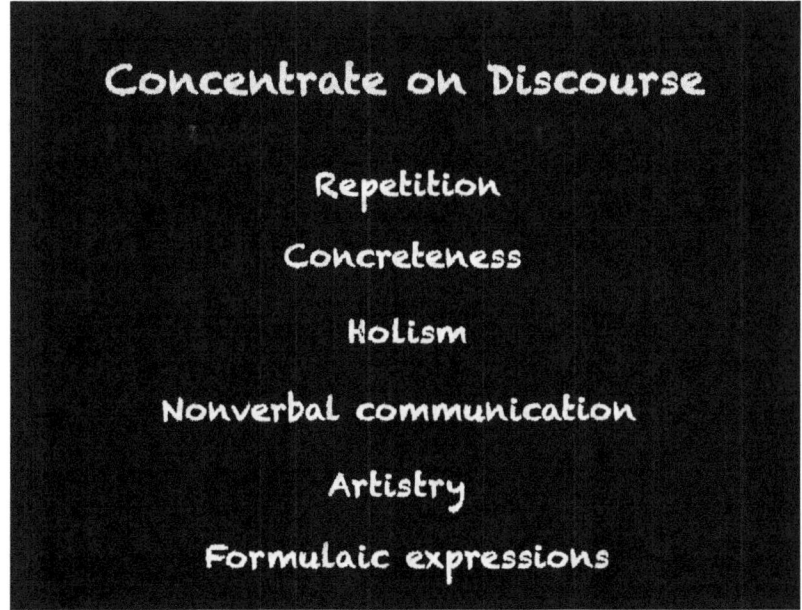

Figure 2.2. Concentrate on Discourse

Comparing and contrasting characters can also garner further insights. It can be assumed that the author's embedded dialogue in a story is "attempting to communicate not only meaning, but also relevance and context."[16] Such insight drives Matthews to conclude, "It becomes the task of the audience or reader to recognize strategic positioning by the storyteller, since characters in a drama only play the parts assigned to them by the actor."[17] Characterization reveals personalities through demonstrating face-to-face public roles and responsibilities in specific communal contexts.

Whether protagonist, antagonist, foil, full, or flat, a story requires a cast of characters. Two prominent characters often include the hero and villain who compete for supremacy. These can be individuals or groups. Sometimes a foil (e.g., Martha in the Mary-and-Martha story) is included, someone who contrasts with another to highlight differences and distinctives to frame the main character. Full characters receive a more three-dimensional definition than flat characters who tend to remain as background scenery (see fig. 2.6). Who sides with whom as the plotline unfolds through various events becomes a noteworthy meaning-marker.

16. V. Matthews, *More Than Meets Ear*, 33.
17. V. Matthews, *More Than Meets Ear*, 107.

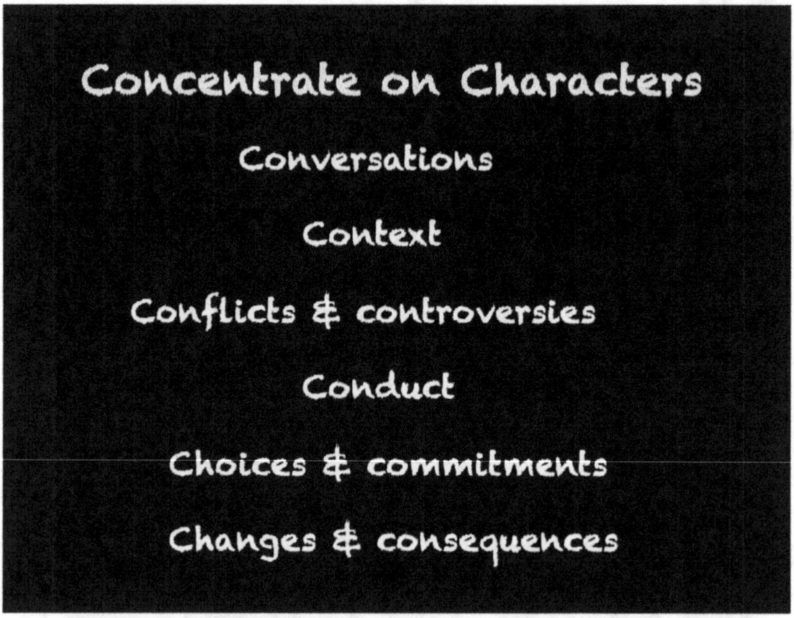

Concentrate on Characters
Conversations
Context
Conflicts & controversies
Conduct
Choices & commitments
Changes & consequences

Figure 2.3. Concentrate on Characters

External conversations
Internal thoughts
Characterization Components
Emotions
Actions

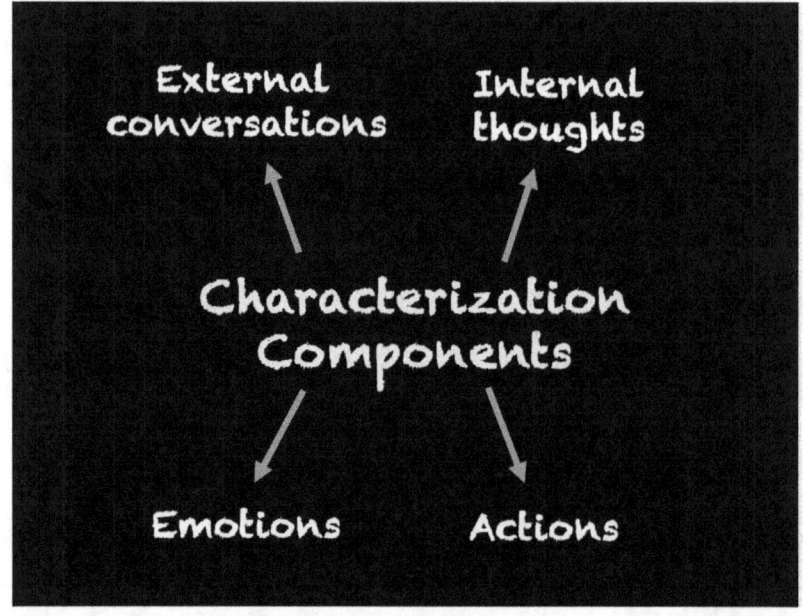

Figure 2.4. Characterization Components

They find themselves entangled on some perilous journey (plotline) in search of an attainable resolution. The more perilous the journey, the more interesting the story as it advances from scene to scene. Mystery, unpredictability, silence, tension, conflict, confusion, starts and stops, crises, catharses, conundrums developed in the plotline all create curiosity. Curiosity creates concern. The question that takes center stage in everyone's mind is: "How will this end for _____"? Got mystery?

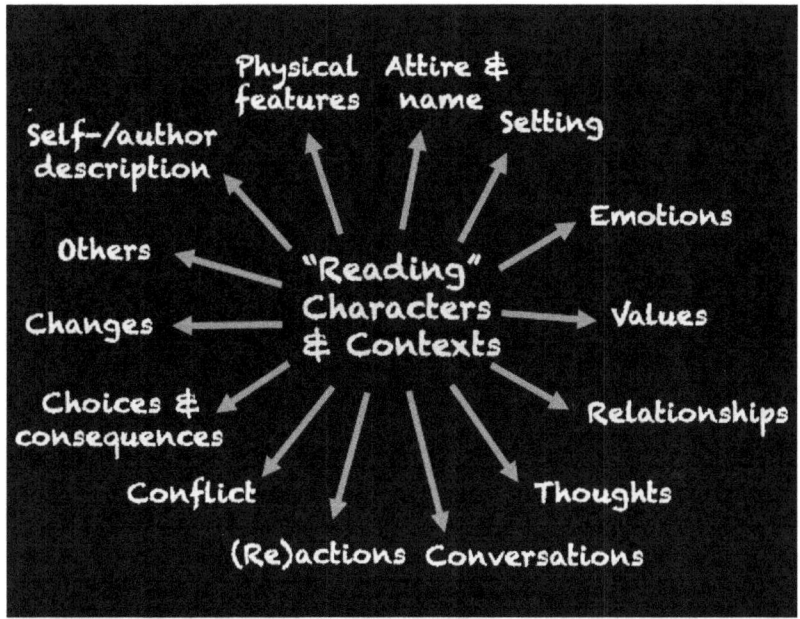

Figure 2.5. "Reading" Characters and Contexts

For Bible storytellers, two plotlines happen simultaneously. The first belongs to the Author, the second to the authors. The author's plotline is embedded in the Author's plotline, thereby providing participants opportunity to observe the complexity of life from a dual perspective. Characters introduced by the author and advanced through selected scenes in chosen settings (urban, rural; terrain) and times (season, attire, symbols, rituals) simulate the multidimensionality of life (see fig. 2.7). Onlookers become wrapped up in the characters, all of which point to the Author's larger story and where they fit in post-fall and post-Jesus.

The character traits projected by sovereignly selected characters are never neutral. Characters propose choices as they change or resist change, especially to observers who identify strongly with them. A cast of characters in a story serve as moral barometers and boundaries as they resist or make small to significant changes, thereby parading moral choices to observers. "The Bible does not merely invite response—it requires it," claims Ryken and Longman.[18] All actions and encounters made by Bible characters create opportunities to explore the character of the Chief Character and make decisive choices—"choose God or repudiate Him."[19] This is possible even through flawed characters. Characters convey convictions.

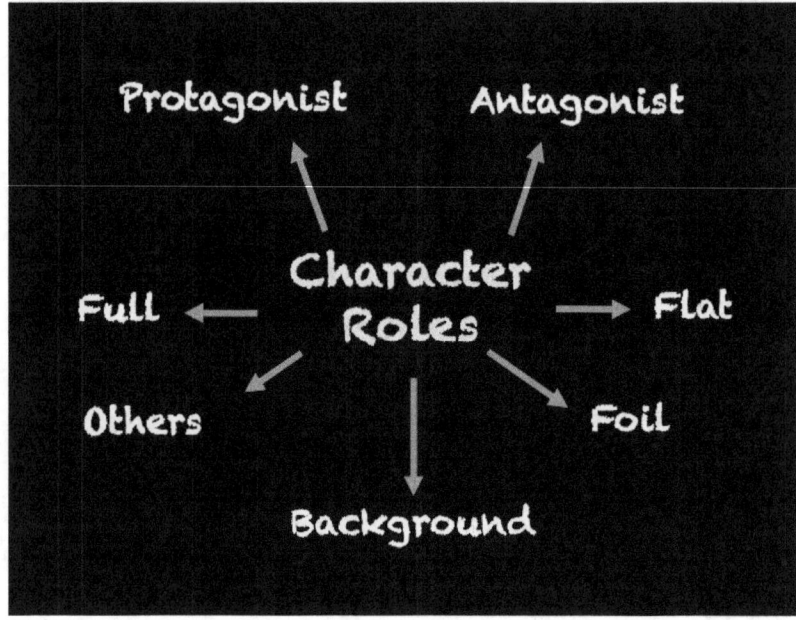

Figure 2.6. Character Roles

Bible characters (the good, the bad, the in-between) serve as catalysts to ongoing theological conversations; they are not there as ancient notables to help one pass the time of day or forget reality for a brief time. Their case studies become possible change agents.

Bible stories were never meant to be neutral because the characters within them are never morally free. Why? Because every character had a divine purpose assigned before God formed them in the womb (Jer 1:5; Ps 139:13–16; Gal 1:15). Nevertheless, even biblical humanity requires some humiliation along life's journey. Erich Auerbach summarizes, "There is hardly one of them who does not, like Adam, undergo the deepest

---

18. Ryken and Longman, *Complete Literary Guide*, 34.
19. Ryken and Longman, *Complete Literary Guide*, 34.

humiliation—and hardly one who is not deemed worthy of God's personal intervention and personal inspiration. . . . But their greatness, rising out of humiliation, is almost superhuman and an image of God's greatness."[20]

Alert to moral hazards, heroes of the faith like Adam, Noah, Joseph, Jacob, Abraham, David and Bathsheba, Ananias and Sapphira, and Peter lived out God's purposes even though they experienced tremendous personal and public humiliation. Personal failure resulted in humiliation, which led to life-changing transformation. When God is involved, however, failure need never be final.

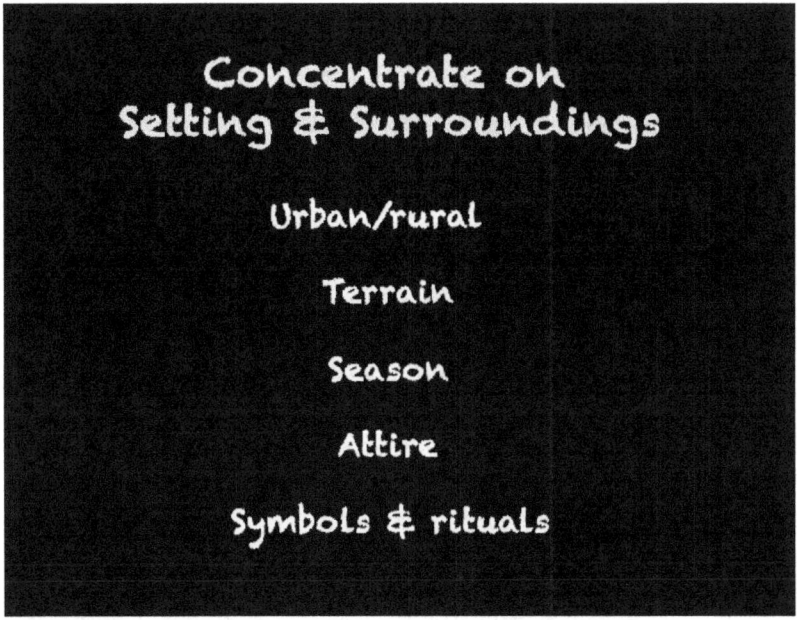

Figure 2.7. Concentrate on Setting and Surroundings

Characters who display authenticity also identify with observers in ways that confirm or conflict with their comfort zones. Central to changes for the observers is identification with the characters involved. This identification seems to come with little risk even as it makes one vulnerable. Characters serve as persuasive commercials or warning signs for their Creator; they offer restoration (re-*story*-zation) through "redeemed power."[21]

As noted previously, characters "read" other characters and contexts to discern possible courses of action (particularly in relation to conflict

20. Auerbach, *Mimesis*, 8.
21. Koeshall, "Navigating Power," 76.

[plotline]), motives, foundational secular and religious beliefs, and so forth. To discern probable immediate and/or future actions, character-centered thinkers listen, watch, contrast, feel, focus, think; they read others, they read contexts, something done naturally, universally, and daily; they are "street smart"; they have "situational awareness." Some, however, like many of our African and Asian friends, are far better at this than we the authors.

The Chinese character for listening (*ting*) captures the holistic nature of listening and hence its strong significance in the communication process. It calls for two ears to hear, ten eyes to see, undivided attention for focus, respect for the king in one's thinking, and an undivided heart to fully feel.[22] Listening holistically should be the great initiator for all Bible communicators (Isa 28:23; Jas 1:19), and it begins with our ears. Is listening holistically the currency to connection?

When interpreters decode characters, among others, they "have a keen eye for the obvious."[23] Why? Because *the body tells stories*. Decoders watch for actions, facial features, gestures, posture, proximity, dress, symbols and rituals, location; they listen for names and titles,[24] roles and relationships; they note life cycle (birth, youth, death); they interpret "direct speech, inward speech, a summarized or quoted monologue, or statements by the narrator about the attitudes and intentions of the personages,"[25] voice intonation and speed, repetition of words, phrases, actions; they contrast the interactions of characters, especially when conflict is displayed (review fig. 2.3).

Rather than using critical thinking—a rational, autonomous, individualistic, direct (often disrespectful in collectivist societies, especially when utilized by youth), Enlightenment-based model—oralists prefer another option. Uninterested in evaluating the strengths and weaknesses of evidence collected to prove a hypothesis, oralists tend to prefer "character thinking." Driven by relationally based narrative logic, character thinking provides a natural way to discern the characteristics of characters. When it comes to character analysis, what may seem surprising to the highly print-oriented is often intuitive for high to low oralists. But we get ahead of ourselves.

Robert Kaplan raises two simple questions central to critical thinking few have considered. While focused on reading and writing, both have implications and application for the oral reliant: "What is evidence?"

---

22. Bates, "5 Listening Insights," para. 2.

23. Ryken, *How Bible Stories Work*, 67.

24. Hebrew names often reflect former heroes and character attributes; they serve as identifiers answering the question "Who are you?" Who named someone, relatives (genealogies), and name changes, among others, also provide interpretive insights. Is the name respected? Shunned? Feared? Profaned? Desired?

25. Alter, *Art of Biblical Narrative*, 117.

and "What arrangement of evidence is likely to appeal (be convincing) to readers?"[26]

Referencing the first question pertaining to evidence, for some, if it is in print, it is gospel. For others, it's what's spoken or some combination of the two. Referencing the second question about evidence arrangement, some assume linear is logical. Others prefer a more circular, spiral presentation.

How do individualism and collectivism influence the collection and investigation of evidence? How one perceives, arranges, and investigates evidence is culturally colored. How well does the Bible communicator know the cultural context in relation to collecting and arranging evidence? Back to relationally based character thinking.

Relationally based character thinking goes beyond rationally based critical thinking by including emotions, life experience, and spirituality. Character thinking is relational in nature, considering the whole person—emotions, spirituality (moral direction), rationality.[27] Character thinking reveals the inner thoughts and outward actions through a character's words and works, both positive and negative. Such provides character thinkers leverage with which to respond. Character thinking is at least as complex as critical thinking, just different. Can we expand beyond the more cerebral "think the thought" to the more relational "think the character"?

If one wants to put his or her finger on the truths taught in a story, watch for changes in the protagonist. James Resseguie concludes, "Changes in the characters elaborate and develop a narrative's meaning . . . the way a protagonist responds to a crucial situation in his or her life will 'likely be the surest clue of the story's meaning.'"[28] Wise interpreters discover meaning through watching for changes in characters, particularly among protagonists.

Possible flashbacks and flash-forwards make the characters' arduous journey seldom a straight line. Authors introduce characters, exit them, and sometimes reintroduce them, e.g., Barnabas (Acts 9:27). Add to this flashbacks and flash-forwards, and a character's journey may look more like a toddler's piece of art than Aristotle's beginning, middle, and end. Nevertheless, whether circular ("a never-ending repetition of summer and winter; day and night, and birth, death and rebirth"[29]) or linear,[30] there is direction

---

26. Kaplan, "Foreword," ix.

27. See D. Erickson, "Developmental Re-Forming." Perry Shaw prefers to call it "constructive thinking" (P. Shaw, "Moving from Critical Thinking").

28. Resseguie, *Narrative Criticism*, 126.

29. Hiebert, "Conversion and Worldview Transformation," 85.

30. T. Steffen, "Clothesline Theology for World," 38.

and purpose. Fokkelman reminds us, "There is not only linear progress, but also circular coherence."[31]

Circular history, in contrast to linear history, tends to highlight tensions that reveal strong conflictive human choices. Think Israel entering or being removed from the promised land. These tensions also reveal that interpreting characters without such knowledge can be extremely complex and delicate. Characters, therefore, must be carefully read, especially between historical cycles when conflict tends to intensify, thereby requiring choices and changes between strongly competing and contested ideas.

Robert Alter assumes characters abandon themselves to "unfathomable freedom" thus evidence a "bundle of paradoxes." David, the most complex character in Scripture, fits this description.[32] To be able to read such complex characters with proficiency requires inquiry into their total life.

Focused character-centric questions will go a long way in revealing the thoughts and actions of others, and their implications for life's journey. It should first be noted that when storying Scripture there are multiple characters in the mix that influence meaning. Such include the Author, authors, storytellers, characters in the specific story, echoes of related characters in other stories, and the hearers/readers/viewers. All bring a point of view and therefore add meaning to the mix, some of which will be detrimental to the author's perspective. Questions raised behind and within the stories, therefore, will play a significant role in discerning the emotional-rational truths and ethics buried within a story. Such questions steer us into the hearts of characters who then get inside our hearts, thereby initiating an internal/external debate about choices. The lived experiences of characters lead us to their Creator as we join in their journey.

Isolating Influential Identifiers of Characters

The major influential identifiers of a character will now be isolated. A character may be:

- Anyone or anything personified or who drives the plotline
- Individuals or groups
- Real or fictional
- Visible or invisible
- Driven by motivations, emotions, reason

---

31. Fokkelman, *Reading Biblical Narrative*, 80.
32. Alter, *Art of Biblical Narrative*, 115.

- Competing and conflictive
- Descriptively profiled
- Entangled in some risky journey
- Searching for an attainable resolution
- Seeks confirmation or change
- Seldom on a journey that progresses in a straight line

The above components and identifiers will receive further illustration and elaboration in the forthcoming chapters.

What Purpose Do Bible Characters Serve?

The primary purpose of the OT (2 Tim 3:15 [including the NT to follow]) is to offer and promote God's wisdom to all his highest creation so they can display it in every area of daily life, thereby glorifying the Creator globally. How is this accomplished? Jack Miles offers a rarely recognized possibility: "God is like a novelist who . . . can only tell his own story through his characters."[33] God often uses biblical characters to portray himself, thereby challenging and modeling for us how to live wise, God-honoring lives.

Through the wise and unwise words and works of people we learn about our Creator. We learn about the Protector when we see a prostitute hide out Israelite spies. We learn about the Holy One when we see what happened to Moses when he hit the rock rather than speak to it. We learn about the Jealous One when we see Moses descend from the mountaintop with two stone tablets "inscribed by the *very* finger of God" (Exod 31:18 VOICE [emphasis original]) only to discover the Israelites worshipping false gods. We learn about Emmanuel though the lives of Joseph and Daniel when taken as prisoners to foreign lands. We learn about the Most High when we see what happened to Haman after Esther courageously visited the king. We learn about the Mighty One when a young shepherd boy defeats a giant veteran warrior. We learn about the All-Seeing when we observe what happened to Peter after three denials. We learn about the Restorer when we see what happened to John Mark after Paul and Barnabas's "sharp disagreement." We learn about the Merciful through Jonah's inconsistent actions. And the list goes on and on.

The purpose of the lives of Bible characters is to teach us to fear and reverence our Creator. Gaining godly wisdom begins by grasping the fear

---

33. Jack Miles, as quoted in Yancey, *Bible Jesus Read*, 37.

(unsettling awe that inspires living with integrity) of God (Prov 9:10). How is this accomplished? Through the healthy and/or devious conversations and conduct of Bible characters. These begin to paint in our minds a more detailed and defined portrait of the King of kings.

But it doesn't stop there. It also begins to perfect our messy attempts to paint our own portrait, making it a masterpiece; it begins to perfect our family portrait, our community portrait, our national portrait. God's desire is to see godly wisdom become communal and global.

Lesslie Newbigin challenges the Christian congregation to live wise lives in his chapter titled "The Congregation as the Hermeneutic of the Gospel."[34] Christ followers (committed to compliance), Newbigin cogently argues, are the interpretation of the gospel to their brothers and sisters in faith and those yet to follow Christ. Through their conversations and conduct in specific contexts, which can cause internal and/or external "disorienting dilemmas,"[35] we learn about the Creator and the godly, actionized wisdom he desires we habitually demonstrate.

Characteristics of Characters

Colorful characters come with characteristics that influence character theology. Some prominent follow.

Characters vary. Most stories have more than one character. When this occurs, a protagonist and antagonist emerge. When multiple characters appear, controlling characters (pivotal people) and background characters (supporting to flat) begin to distinguish themselves, providing the receptor suggestive clues as to the story's intention.

From the famous to the infamous, faithful to faithless, saints to scoundrels, pacifiers to provokers, ruled to rulers, princes to prodigals, victimizers to victims, selfish to the self-discrediting, characters come to life when we hear them dialog, note their appearance, view their actions and interactions, watch how they attempt to resolve disputes, make decisions, react to decisions. Some generalizations of inner and outer characterization that are evidenced in space and time could include:

- Personality: sweet, stately, standoffish, sincere, sleazy, silent, stiff necked
- Gender: male, female, eunuch
- Age: baby, youth, adult, senior

---

34. Newbigin, *Gospel in Pluralist Society*, 224–33.
35. Mezirow and Associates, *Learning as Transformation*, 22.

THE ROLE OF CHARACTERS

- Status: slave, priest, laborer, king, apostle, deacon, fisherman, daughter
- Ethnicity: Philistine, Egyptian, Roman, Hebrew (Jew), non-Hebrew (gentile)
- Appearance: clothing, hairy, tall, frail, beautiful
- Vocalization: stutter, slang, talkative
- Vocation: shepherds, tax collectors, kings, carpenters, businesspeople
- Action: thinking, worried, laughing, sick, aggressive, passive

Identifying character traits (personality pieces that create a profile) of the controlling characters will take interpreters to the core of a story.

Sometimes overlooked by Bible communicators is the universal representativeness of Bible characters. J. P. Fokkelman reminds us that "characters are in principle just as ignorant and insecure, arrogant or sad, just as smart or vicious or ironical or excited as we are in our own lives."[36] Edward Schillebeeckx contends, "People are the words with which God tells his story."[37] Bible characters carry great currency because they think, feel, talk, and act like us. Characters mirror our reality. Again, characters R us.

The characterization of Bible characters reminds Bible communicators of individual stories *and* helps them remember what they teach. These characters are *not* two-dimensional cardboard cutouts; they are three-dimensional. And the characters we embrace (or more accurately who embrace us) become the characters we seek to exemplify.

The Bible is not a compilation of unrelated texts. Nor is it a collection of theological statements. Nor is it a scrapbook of stories. Nor is it a grab bag of characters. Rather, it is a collection of characters sovereignly selected and sequenced in a purposely designed process within the Story comprised of many stories. Of the thousands of named human characters who grace the pages of sacred Scripture, some are sovereignly selected to take us on human journeys that reflect universal spiritual and ethical truths to be recognized, internalized, and habitually demonstrated.

Note also that human characters are often presented in binary pairs: Adam and Eve, Cain and Abel, Ruth and Naomi, Peter and John, Paul and Silas.[38] Some serve as archetypes (reoccurring patterns), e.g., Melchizedek and Moses. Characterization evidenced through the actions of binary pairs offers vital visual and textual images that aid in layered oral interpretation.

---

36. Fokkelman, *Reading Biblical Narrative*, 68.
37. Schillebeeckx, *Church*, xiii.
38. Do binary pairs lead to binary theologies—e.g., faith (Abel) and works (Cain)?

Nor are all Bible characters monocultural. Some of the most significant characters in Scripture were minimally bicultural, i.e., those who were able to view the world through multiple worldviews. These "bridge people" could include Joseph, Moses, Daniel, Esther, Ezra, Nehemiah, Israelites going into or returning from exile, Jesus, Paul.

Characters centralize and consolidate a story. Characters stand at the center of a story. "Characters carry theme."[39] While abstract plot is often said to drive a story, who drives the plot? Concrete characters.[40] We appreciate Haven's character-centric definition of story: "A detailed, character-based narration of a character's struggles to overcome obstacles and reach an important goal."[41] Know any good stories absent characters?

Reflecting on the narrative development of Acts, Beverly Gaventa, concludes, "We need to add questions about its characters. Luke appears to follow Aristotle's dictum that characters are included for the sake of action and not the other way around, but we need to keep the issue of character in mind." She goes on to ask, "What kinds of characters occupy this story? To what extent are Luke's characters distinct from one another? Do the communities (e.g., Christians in Jerusalem, Jewish leaders) function as characters?"[42]

Gaventa believes that "an adequate treatment of the theology of Acts needs to attend to the elements the narrative repeats, the information omitted, the appearance and disappearance of individuals and groups of people, the rich interweaving of story lines, asking what each of those suggests about the theology of the author." Such inquiry does "not easily lend itself to the conventional headings of 'doctrine of God,' 'theology of the Spirit,' 'eschatology,' 'ecclesiology.'" She therefore concludes, "The narrative of Acts is not to be reduced to propositional statements or systematic affirmations."[43]

Bible characters serve as a conduit to textual meaning; they vicariously convey one heart to another heart; they vicariously compare someone's experience to the experiences of others, thereby deeding and decoding the way to emulate observed positive attributes (1 Cor 10:11) or abandoning

---

39. James Scott Bell, as quoted in Myers, "Writers on Characters."

40. We weigh in on the longtime debate of which came first, plot or character?

41. Haven, *Story Proof*, 79.

42. Gaventa, "Toward Theology of Acts," 152. When I (Tom) taught Acts at Biola, I identified and titled each story, followed by categorizing every major/minor human character, group, and spiritual characters. Moving my hermeneutic to focus on God-Luke's selective use of characters opened my eye to new insights; e.g., Satan is mentioned only twice while the Holy Spirit is mentioned numerous times.

43. Gaventa, "Toward Theology of Acts," 157.

negative ones. Bible authors present such characters realistically, thereby challenging us to evaluate our own lives.

Grant Osborne observes, "Biblical narrative is replete with realistic figures seen in all their human frailty. . . . As a result they are all the more appealing and applicable to the reader."[44] He adds, "In every sense biblical narrative is theology seen in living relationships and enacted in story form."[45] It is those risky and rewarding "living relationships" that capture and consolidate the story, luring us into joining them on the journey.

Ideas are present in any story through a host of venues. Holly Ordway offers this insight, "The idea is embodied in particular details: this character, this location, this sequence of events, these colors and shapes. By the very limitation inherent in these specific choices of story, characters, and images, the truth becomes tangible, and thus more accessible and more engaging."[46] Ideas emerge from settings (desert, sea, mountains), from symbols (tassels, towel, whip), among others, but they all have interconnectivity and therefore influence in some way the people in the story. How good a job do we do in discovering meaning through the central characters who drive the story?

> Can we learn to tell better tales that highlight central characters at home and abroad?

Characters are embedded in other characters. Just as all stories are embedded in other stories, so all controlling characters are embedded in other controlling characters.[47] The Second Adam is embedded in the first Adam. Jesus carrying his own wooden cross is embedded in Isaac carrying the wood for the burnt offering sacrifice (Gen 22). Jeremiah's fear of speaking (Jer 1:6) is embedded in Moses's fear of speaking. David's steadfast faith in YAHWEH when facing the giant Goliath is embedded in the Israelites as they face giants when nearing the promised land (Num 13:30–33). Lying to save the Israelite spies, Rahab is embedded in the Hebrew midwives who lied to save Hebrew babies. Joseph fleeing with Mary to a foreign country is embedded in Moses fleeing Egypt. Ananias and Sapphira are embedded in Achan. The twelve NT apostles are embedded in the twelve tribes. Jesus

---

44. Osborne, *Hermeneutical Spiral*, 159.
45. Osborne, *Hermeneutical Spiral*, 171.
46. Ordway, *Apologetics and Christian Imagination*, 106.
47. The same could be said of symbols, e.g., the ark is embedded in Moses's basket placed in the Nile River. It is also true of rituals, e.g., the Passover is embedded in communion.

preparing a meal for shell-shocked disciples (John 21:1–14) is embedded in the stories of Hagar and Ishmael (Gen 21:8–21) and Elijah (1 Kgs 19:1–8). Controlling characters are social entities embedded in previous players who echo, silhouette, and help sculpt an ever-expanding pattern of divine truth over time and social-geographical locations.

Jesus was a genius at tying familiar characters to present stories, making it easy for his Jewish listeners to wed the two, thereby enhancing learning. In Luke 15, e.g., Jesus tells three stories (patterned repetition as a sticky memory technique and interpretive hint) on the same topic—searching for something someone lost. The third story of the lost sons has OT character connections that a Jewish audience would quickly recognize: a father had two sons. The Jewish mind is racing to connect characters—could that be Isaac whose sons were Jacob and Esau? They listen intently for more clues.

The younger son asks for his father's inheritance, infuriating the older son (Luke 15:12, 28). The parallel story of Jacob (younger son) stealing Esau's (older son) inheritance who had stayed home waiting for his father to die (Gen 27:41), which made him very angry, comes racing back to mind.

Jesus then adds a contrastive action (another memory enhancer). The younger son goes off with everything and returns with nothing while Jacob goes off with nothing and returns with everything.

Jesus's story then returns to parallels (another memory technique). A loving father rushes out to embrace and kiss his returning wayward son (Luke 15:20), just as what happened in Gen 33:4. But the older brother was totally upset with his younger brother just as Esau was ready to kill Jacob (Gen 27:41).[48] When "reading" the characters in a story, wise interpreters do some "backward mapping" to see who may serve as forerunners and what possible interpretive clues they may provide; they listen for echoes as they glance backwards in time.

Characters drop breadcrumbs. Just as crew members think, talk, and act on their voyage, thereby leaving behind a trail of breadcrumbs as to what happened, so Bible characters leave behind a trail of breadcrumbs that lead to theology and ethics the Author-author wishes recipients to appropriate. In relation to human characters, Bible authors present them as human, documenting their flaws, failings, fluff, and forces, thereby providing turn-key case studies. Cain killed Abel. Noah became drunk. Moses murdered an Egyptian. Boaz discreetly cared for Ruth. Phillip provided needed insight to a receptive foreign inquirer. Phoebe, whose name means "bright and radiant," served others with distinction. A jailed Paul purposely shames

---

48. We are indebted to Peter Williams for these parallels and contrasts. See Williams, *Can We Trust Gospels*.

THE ROLE OF CHARACTERS 85

Philemon into freeing Onesimus. Charlotte Lee believes this all happens because "a character moves and speaks as he does largely because of what he thinks and feels."[49]

> Know any good stories absent characters?

Everyone drops breadcrumbs along the journey, providing personal and spiritual clues for insightful interpreters. When collected and read, breadcrumbs become theological and ethic signposts, and possible central themes to a story.

What one thinks and feels is often expressed in conversations accompanied with body language. Jolyon Mitchell and Sophia Marriage believe "conversation lies at the heart of our human existence, at the heart of our cultural understanding and at the heart of our religious experience. It is fundamental to our being and allows us to express our thoughts, reach new depths of understanding and promote human growth."[50] How these conversations are expressed, however, tie to culturally colored relationships.

Susan Scott sagely states, "The conversation is not about the relationship; the conversation *is* the relationship. One conversation at a time, you are building, destroying, or flatlining your relationships. . . . Our lives succeed or fail one conversation at a time."[51] Conversations reveal the heights and depths of webs of relationships. Matthews claims a conversation goes further. It "creates and re-creates a people's social world. . . . personal identity, status, and power are continually being defined and redefined in every dialogue."[52]

When conflict and/or changes result from a conversation, especially when contentious, more breadcrumbs hit the ground. Watch for them.[53] Gather them. Whether many or few, like a good hunter, read the signs to discern the animal's intent.

Authors consciously create their characters and conversations, thereby providing interpretive clues *along* the journey. Collect all the breadcrumbs, noting especially the patterned, repetitive ones of the same size or shape or

---

49. C. Lee, *Oral Interpretation*, 393.
50. Mitchell and Marriage, *Mediating Religion*, 1.
51. Scott, *Fierce Conversations*, xvi (emphasis added).
52. V. Matthews, *More Than Meets Ear*, 101.
53. Ernst Wendland claims that the crucial clue to what the author wants us to learn is often found "in the climax-resolution nexus" part of a story (Wendland, "Interpreting the Bible," 61).

color.[54] Stir well, set the timer for longer than expected, and in communal dialogue with others and the Great Interpreter—who promises to guide us into all truth (John 14:26; 16:13)—surmise what the Author-author wishes recipients to replicate.

> How well do we see people and their relationships behind the ideas?

While conclusions most likely result in an imperfect interpretation (we can comprehend the Creator without knowing him fully), which is not unusual unless already stated by the author,[55] storyteller-interpreters are well on their way to grasping the Author more fully. "Understanding does not necessarily mean successful or harmonious understanding; nor is it realized in a single act of comprehension, subject to dialogue, conflict, and contest, it is a process carried out through revisions and reinterpretations that are, in principle, endless."[56]

All interpretation is a risk, as *all* hermeneutic models and methods are culturally bound theories. But it is a risk that cannot avoid. Only Jesus interpreted the Hebrew Bible flawlessly.

Human characters leave behind a trail of breadcrumbs not only through conversations, but also through their actions and commitments as previously noted. Actions generate more actions, all of which are tied to the unfolding plot. This reflects the role of the Trinity who has acted in history, leaving behind breadcrumbs over the centuries. The same is true of those representing the spirit world (e.g., Gen 3:23; 28:12; Matt 1:20) or animal world (Num 22:28–30).

Craig Blomberg believes, "*The key to interpreting most allegories lies in recognizing what a small handful of characters, actions or symbols stand for and fitting the rest of the story in with them.*"[57] Wise listeners-observers

---

54. "Everyone did what was right in his own eyes" (Judg 17:6; 21:25 KJV).

55. For example, in Matt 24:32, Jesus says: "Now think of the fig tree. As soon as its twigs get tender *and greenish*, as soon as it begins to sprout leaves, you know to expect summer" (VOICE [emphasis original]); or Mark 6:4, "A prophet can find honor anywhere except in his hometown, among his own people, and in his own household" (VOICE).

56. Brockmeier and Meretoja, "Understanding Narrative Hermeneutics," 6.

57. Blomberg, *Interpreting the Parables*, 64 (emphasis original). Blomberg believes each of the two to three characters in a parable "suggests that one point is associated with each. . . . *Each parable makes one main point per main character*" (88, 189 [emphasis original]).

attempt to anticipate the direction of a character's conversation, conduct, and commitment as they leave behind a growing informative trail of breadcrumbs.

To *bypass characters* in the interpretive process is to *shortchange theology* of its fullness. As C. S. Song states, "Theology worthy of its name has to be part and parcel of the dramas of life and faith."[58] Character theology begins when one assumes the theological nature of a sovereignly selected cast of characters highlighted in Scripture.

Characters carry concepts. Shipped goods do not reach their destination without some human involvement. Goods must be moved, marked, stacked, secured. This requires imagination, emotion, reason, not to mention some trial and error. An interesting question arises in relation to biblical propositions: Who carries the water in relation to biblical concepts and ideas?

Biblical ideas, propositions, or concepts, whether doctrines or ethics, were never intended to be isolated or naked. To do so is to devalue the spoken-written words of God. As Vanhoozer notes, "The church's script is not an inert object for critical analysis but an invitation to dialogue and participation. . . . Von Balthasar only slightly exaggerates when he says that the lives of the saints are themselves interpretations of the gospel, more true and more convincing than all exegesis."[59] Only through follower participation can a fuller, richer understanding of the script prevail. The difference is like adding milk rather than water to your favorite bowl of cereal.

The Bible was not given to us as a list of theologies systematically organized, including the attributes of God. Authors presented these through "inferences from events"[60] (embodied truths lived out relationally in space and time). Middle Eastern expert Kenneth Bailey fleshes this out:

> A biblical story is not simply a "delivery system" for an idea. Rather, the story first creates a world and then invites the listener to live in that world, to take on as part of who he or she is. Biblical stories invite the reader to accept them as *his or her* story. . . . [In] studying the Bible, ancient tales are not examined merely in order to extract a theological principle or ethical model. Instead, the Bible is read to rediscover who we are and what we must yet become, because the biblical story of sin and salvation, law and grace, is *our* story.[61]

---

58. Song, *In Beginning Were Stories*, 116.
59. Vanhoozer, "Drama-of-Redemption Model," 160.
60. G. E. Wright, *God Who Acts*, 57.
61. Bailey, *Jacob and the Prodigal*, 51–52 (emphasis original).

Bible stories are *not* simply delivery systems for abstractness. Rather, Bible stories convey clothed (narratized) ideas, clothed propositions, clothed concepts.

Uncovered concepts would be way too simplistic and one-sided for the Creator who prefers relationships wrapped in wholeness.[62] For example, "Jesus is Lord" makes little sense until we see him healing the sick, raising the dead, or rising from the dead. "God forgives" carries little impact until tied to the stories surrounding the humiliation and transformation of Adam, Joseph, Jacob, Abraham, David, and Peter.

Concepts require characters so they can dance together as they live out the rhythms of life in a holistic concrete manner. "The Christian faith," Goldingay reminds us, "*is a narrative statement.*"[63] Vanhoozer prefers "theo-dramatizing" so that the body and soul of the text, the point and parable, all remain intact.[64] How bifurcated have we made characters and concepts in our Bible teaching?

> How good a job do we do in discovering meaning through the central characters who drive the story?

Characters, who encapsulate and emulate the complexities of life, flesh out concepts, making them more heartfelt, nuanced, appealing, impactful, and memorable. Characters provide propositions a holistic pathway to display and demonstrate their earthiness; they wed affect to meaning.

Truth requires characters, and characters require truth. Fuller, richer, more appealing meaning is derived from character-enlivened, actor-based propositions. Cognitive content without affective stimulus risks an incomplete and inadequate understanding of God's universal, timeless truths.

While metaphor-based stories of characters tend to link the concrete with concepts, propositions tend to divide and isolate the two. The holism required of stories, however, relies, requires, and flourishes on the totalism of concrete experiences related to relationships (human, spiritual, material); it makes perceptions and projections possible even as it recognizes constant change driven by conflict, contradiction, and chaos within those relationships. It therefore seeks harmonization through compromise rather than control and fragmentation through rule-based categorization. Characters unleash multiple paradoxical perceptions through a holistic, integrative package.

---

62. See Buchanan, "Oral-Preference Communities." Brueggemann calls such dichotomies "phony polarizations" (Brueggemann, *Land*, 193).

63. Goldingay, "Biblical Story," 5 (emphasis added).

64. Vanhoozer, "Drama-of-Redemption Model," 159, 162.

Sharon Short perceptively observes Paul's different starting point in 1 Cor 10:

> There is a crucial difference between extracting a precept *from* a story and illustrating a precept *with* a story. In every allusion in this passage, Paul states a scriptural instruction first, and then clarifies it by referencing a specific event from the past. He begins by exhorting his readers "Do not be idolaters" (11:7) and *then* adduces the negative example of the Israelites and the golden calf (Exod 32:6). He commands his readers not to grumble, and *then* reminds them of how God punished the Israelites for grumbling by sending venomous snakes among them (Num 21).[65]

Paul, when serving in the Greco-Roman world, often started with propositions and then tied them to characters because he knew that characters draw or repel through demonstrated actions. A circular pattern of principle and people become evident.

Paul also notes that all Old Testament happenings "occurred as examples" to us (1 Cor 10:6 NIV). Paul may not be as abstract a communicator as some would have us believe.[66] Note Thomas Winger's perspective of Paul and others:

> The epistolary authors use language which suggests a conversation is going on between them and the receivers of the letter. Rather than a prosaic, philosophical "What shall we think/reason/suggest/propose about this?" Paul poses the dialectical question: "What then shall we say?" Such oral engagement continues as the "writers" use verbs of speaking rather than verbs or writing.[67]

Ben Witherington concludes, "*All* Paul's ideas, all his arguments, all his practical advice, all his social arrangements are ultimately grounded in a story, a great deal of which is told in the Hebrew scriptures, but some of which is oral tradition reflecting developments that happened after Old Testament times."[68] We would label Paul a well-balanced concrete-abstractionist.

In much of Western theology, intellect prevails over intuition, propositions over personalities, rules over relationships. Systematic theology has taught us to "*cut to the chase.*"

---

65. Short, "Formed by Story," 112 (emphasis original).

66. Here's an insightful question: "Do narrative elements 'exist' in front of the text, in the text, or behind the text?" (E. Adams, "Paul's Story of God," 41).

67. Winger, "Orality as the Key," 226.

68. Witherington, *Paul's Narrative Thought World*, 2 (emphasis original).

Ironically, the Bible puts systematics and propositions in their place. How? It tutors Bible storyteller-interpreters to "*cut to the character.*" Characters personify propositions; they humanize doctrines, ethics, symbols, and rituals (rarely systematically); they relationalize abstract ideas; they blend drama into the doctrine. Characters conceive concepts, keeping them earthy. Characters carry the water for concepts.

Character evaluation is required to discern concepts. How? By decoding a character, which requires evaluating:

- Context and circumstances (setting, symbols, rituals)
- The level of conflict with others or oneself
- Status (power relationships)
- Role (major, minor, foil, real, fictional)
- Personality traits (psychological and physical)
- Responses/actions (conversations, conduct, choices, commitments)
- Internal and/or external conflict to discern meaning and morality intent

Character decoding maintains the mystery in teaching even as it casts clues to reconstruct lost ways to become more Godlike personally and collectively (review fig. 2.3).

Characters in Bible Curricula

As noted in "Setting the Stage," characters can be observed in numerous ways—individual stories, a series of stories, biographies,[69] life histories, and so forth. What comprises comprehensive transformative character theology curricula when long-term ministry opportunities prevail? When short stints avail? What role should the grand narrative have in character theology curricula? How would all these differ for different age groups? Subcultures? Ethnic groups?

Just as the Holy Spirit brought order out of chaos and it was "*beautiful and* good" (Gen 1:4, 10, 12, 21, 25 VOICE [emphasis original]), so his curricula developers strive to do the same. The results, however, may not always immediately end up "*beautiful and* good."

To have some semblance of order, story curricula developers will pool (a form of systematization) characters in various ways for different purposes. For example, multiple evangelism models of differing lengths (e.g., from creation

---

69. Miriam Adeney held a workshop to produce biographical ballads from Adam to John on Patmos. See Adeney, "Feeding Giraffes, Counting Cows," 107.

to Christ; from creation to consummation [Revelation]), highlighting preferred Bible characters, already exist and the number continues to grow.

> Who carries the water in relation to biblical concepts and ideas?

The number of discipleship models also continues to grow. One could expect to see the same for followership, leadership, devotionals, whole book studies, theological studies, catechisms, VBS curricula, and so forth.

Grand narratives continue to emerge, offering different highlighted characters, scenes, events, actions, and lengths.[70] Beyond Bible history, often receiving little attention, grand narratives provide further possibilities of the characters behind the creeds and confessions, along with the early church fathers. Back to the Scripture story.

How will the Bible characters be pooled? Theologically? Thematically? Topically? Sequentially traced throughout a book? The possibilities for Bible character curricula are endless, making fragmentation a perpetual liability.

Wise character-centric curriculum developers begin with their "Character Collection" and "Who's Who List"[71] created from each book and letter of the Bible.[72] Bible personages project places, scenes, events, themes, topics, theologies, ethics, outcomes; they become the faces who paint pictures in the theater of our minds about *all* of life; they offer God-directed, actionized wisdom whether through constructive or destructive voices and actions.

For your family, Sunday School, VBS, camp, church, *who* comprises your "Who's Who" compendium of central Bible characters? How could these be built upon year by year? Which memory tools accompany each character? Does the number of stories or story sets match the host culture's favorite numbers (recall the three-point sermon presented to the Ifugao)?

In our theological institutions, what if Malcolm Knowles's whole-part-whole learning model[73] was adopted, where the whole encourages the need to grasp the parts even as it advances clues to the key pieces, all of which later must be put back together to complete the puzzle? Such holism offers oralists coherency and validity while enhancing long-term memory, all through pedagogically preferred tutoring.

---

70. See Panoramaofthebible.org.
71. T. A. Steffen, *Reconnecting God's Story*, 101.
72. See Jagerson, "Quintessential Characters, Stories."
73. See Knowles et al., *Adult Learner*.

What if Systematics 1–4 was replaced with Characters 1–4? Or better yet, Characters 1–4 embedded in the grand narrative (first *and* last course taken)?

Will new titles emerge, such as Systematic Character Theology? What are the strengths and weaknesses of such? How well do these categories match how the host audience sequence and categorize things? Will the focus on parts again minimize attention to the message of a complete book (e.g., Jonah) or letter? The complete Book?

How could Bible characters be communicated beyond a single story or story set? Table 2.4 offers some possibilities for pooling faces and topics.

Faces of Pride • Babel • Naaman	*Faces of Barrenness* • Sarah and Abraham • Rachel and Jacob • Hannah and Elkanah
Faces of the Marginalized • Ruth and Boaz • Israel in Egypt	*Faces of Trauma and Tragedy* • Tamar • Lot's daughters
Faces of Power • Esther and Haman • Pilot and Jesus	*Faces of Christmas* • Joseph and Mary • Angel Gabriel • Zechariah • Elizabeth • God • Emmanuel
Faces of Faith • Abraham • David and Goliath	
Faces of Genocide • Pharaoh • Haman • King Herod	*Faces of Government* • Deborah • Esther • Daniel
Faces at the Well • Rebekah • Zipporah • Samaritan women	*Faces of Contention* • Cain and Abel • Joseph and brothers • Older brother and prodigal
Faces of Fear • Spies of Israel • Moses requests Aaron	*Faces of Theology* • Abraham and justification • Adoption and Eli, Joseph

Table 2.4. Pooling Faces and Topics

J. O. Terry has developed numerous ministry-themed story sets. Some of these include: *Hope Stories from the Bible* (thirty-two stories); *Food Stories from the Bible* (forty-four stories); *Death Stories from the Bible* (forty-two stories); *Water Stories from the Bible* (twenty-two stories); *Grief Stories from the Bible* (thirty-nine stories); *The Holy Rosary Gospel Stories of Jesus* (twenty meditations); *Heaven Is for Women*; *God's Gift of Forgiveness Stories*; *Peace for Hindu Women Stories*; *Ebenezer Stories*; *HIV Hope Stories*; *Shepherd Stories*; *Healing Stories*; *Just Jesus Stories*.

In the twenty-first century, storytellers who are multi-communicators, i.e., those who can teach through the "middle way"—a hybrid of oral, print, and digital—will reign.[74] Which type of hybrid will you offer? But there is something that often gets missed in the mix.

McIlwain Moorings

Due to syncretism among the Palawanos in the Philippines, New Tribes Mission's (now Ethnos360) Australian Trevor McIlwain revised his evangelism by telling sixty-eight Bible stories, beginning in Genesis and concluding with the ascension. The modern-day evangelical orality movement in the missions world was born, although no one knew it at the time.[75]

Six other phases for maturing Jesus followers followed the evangelism phase. Few teachers, however, ever used phases 5–7. Nevertheless, McIlwain's model soon went beyond Philippine shores within New Tribes Mission beginning in 1981.

In 1983, Jim Slack of the Southern Baptist International Mission Board, accompanied by J. O. Terry and others, greatly expanded the evangelical orality movement well beyond both agencies. Multiple changes were made over the years, e.g., titles were added, the number of lessons was shortened, and the phases were contextualized for specific audiences.

We can thank McIlwain for giving us a structure that takes listeners through the entire Bible (phases 1–4). But there was a problem. There was

---

74. See W. Coppedge, *African Literacies*.

75. One of the major contributors to the modern-day evangelical orality movement was Walter Ong. His 1982 classic *Orality and Literacy* would soon be discovered by leaders in the infancy of the movement, thereby providing needed foundational theoretical support. See also Loewen, "Bible Stories," published in 1964 in *Practical Anthropology*, the precursor to *Missiology: An International Review*. See also T. Steffen, *Worldview-Based Storying*, for a succinct overview of the first forty years of the evangelical orality movement that influenced global ministry. Key players and their contributions are noted.

no initial story that provided the sixty-eight evangelism lessons of phase 1 at home.[76]

Following biblical theology, phase 1 built lesson by lesson as did all succeeding phases. The big picture that provides the little stories context as they incrementally add insights to an emerging glorious conclusion was missing. The holism, the global picture generally preferred by many oralists, was absent. It was up to the listeners to put the numerous puzzle pieces back together *without* seeing the finished picture on the box.

Sadly, for the most part, the grand narrative has been lost in the evangelical orality movement. Jennifer Jagerson discovered in her dissertation research of Oral Bible Schools in Ethiopia "there was an absence of mention. . . about how the biblical stories tied together or related to the metanarrative of scripture and its theological and historical developments." She continues, "While the Oral Bible Schools move through 296 stories from Genesis to Revelation, there did not seem to be strong understanding of the broader unfolding story and the key turning points that drive the narrative forward and establish the major theological markers in God's overarching plan."[77]

> What role should the grand narrative have in character theology curricula?

The authors propose that whether short-term or long-term ministries in evangelism or discipleship, whether in telling, singing, drawing, or dramatizing, one of the *greatest contributions* Bible communicators can leave behind with listeners is the grand narrative of sacred storybook. Every future Bible story someone hears/reads/views now has a home in which its room and role can begin to be identified. We must never forget that the micro-narratives find their home and meaning in the macro-narrative—the grand narrative.

Most Bible communicators likely come to Scripture with a systematic theology framework that covers the entire Bible—a fistful of pearls of different shapes, sizes, and shades retrieved from a beautiful, segmented jewelry box. Fewer come with a grand narrative framework—the entire pearl necklace, which prominently displays all the pearls held together by a strong string (another form of systemization). Early on, wise Bible storytellers encourage participants to enjoy the gorgeousness and grandeur of the *entire*

---

76. T. A. Steffen, *Passing the Baton*, 161.

77. Jagerson, "Transformation through Narrative," 237.

necklace, which is greater than any one piece. This requires knowing how and when each individual pearl makes its cumulative contribution.

What are possible ways to construct a grand narrative that takes us from alpha to omega? The Ifugao love to hear the sweep of Scripture or select slices of it, such as a whole book or letter, whether storied or sung. One example of this is the Bible story from creation to the ascension.

> Who comprises your "Who's Who" compendium of central Bible characters?

Using a traditional *Salidumay* tune, the lead singer (often female) composes the story in the moment (creativity within boundaries, which promotes mystery) with the first stanza being a short summary of the direction of the story (whole to part), and those listening sing the chorus (participation) after each of the 152 stanzas (repetition required; time is secondary). The familiar formulaic ending of the song demonstrates a high respect for the ability of the collective listener participants to discern truth absent outside pressure: *Ngenamung hu nemnem yu tep ag pepilit Jesus, ngenamung kayun tuu* (Your [collective] minds are free to decide, Jesus does not force, it's up to you [collective] to decide).

The traditional *Salidumay*-based, soothing song offers singer, participants, and searchers exposure to the Source of Truth through a strong emphasis on strategically placed significant Bible characters in the overall story. Not unlike what we find in the OT (e.g., Exod 15; Judg 5; Prov 144:9), inquirers sing their way to Truth. Similarly, Jesus followers sing their way to wisdom.[78]

Jagerson asks: "Is it possible to teach a paradigmatic story from each book of the Bible that makes clear to the oral learner what the big picture of the book is about? Might these paradigmatic stories be used to knit together the larger picture of God's overarching historical work to help ensure a strong understanding of the meta-narrative?"[79] In *The Epic of Eden*, Sandra Richter contends that if one can understand five characters and covenants—Adam, Noah, Abraham, Moses, and David—the OT can be understood. This linked time line from creation to the Jesus story offers a clothesline

---

78. See Arrington, *Songs of Lisu Hills*.
79. Jagerson, "Hermeneutics and the Methods," 260.

(linear or circular) on which to "hang our facts"[80] or, more relatable to oralists, "hang Bible characters."[81]

Wu offers another possibility based on how books or groups of books were ordered in the canon. "It is well known that the Pentateuch has pride of place within the OT, both in terms of position and influence. Accordingly, the entire OT should be read in view of the Pentateuch. A similar argument can be made that the Gospels serve a similar function in the NT."

Wu then reminds readers of something often forgotten: "What people hear or read first has a disproportionate effect on how they understand what follows."[82] Jumping from verse to verse tends to lose the grand narrative for the listener as does jumping from story to story.

What happens to the interpretation prowess of young Christ followers when *not* presented the grand narrative early in their spiritual journey? Written in 1992, which sadly remains true today, a Thai leader laments: "Thai Christians are unable to put events in the Bible into any sort of a timeline. This affects negatively their ability to understand both sermons and in their own personal study."[83] The followers missed it because their Thai pastors missed it because too many expatriate Bible teachers they studied under missed it.

In *Telling God's Stories with Power*, Paul Koehler believes Bible storytellers can capture the entire Bible through fifteen Bible characters along with their families and associates when "organized biographically." From the OT he mentions: Adam, Noah, Abraham, Isaac, Jacob, Joseph, Moses, Joshua, Samuel-Saul, David, Solomon, Elijah-Elisha, and Daniel. From the Gospels he includes Jesus and supporting characters, and from Acts, Peter and Paul. From these, one receives "a mastery of a large portion of the Bible."[84]

However one constructs the grand narrative, the effort will prove rewarding. One example would be as the stories play out episodically, listeners pick up "repeating patterns of actions and reactions" of characters. When a

---

80. Richter, *Epic of Eden*, 20.

81. Walk Thru the Bible offers an exceptional tool to help accomplish this *when adapted* to specific cultures. They developed hand signs to help teach both OT and NT, which is an excellent way to create a similar clothesline for memory. I (Ray) often use these when training oral learning pastors as it is a remarkably strong memory tool. I refer to this as a "kinetic table of contents." Once in place, storytellers can stop anywhere along the way to consider the stories that "hang" within that section of the grand narrative.

82. Wu, "Doctrine of Scripture," 325.

83. Jaengmuk, "Walk Through the Bible," 23.

84. Koehler, *Telling God's Stories*, 104.

lion attacks his sheep, e.g., David kills it. The same with a bear. When a giant humiliates David's God and nation, he kills him. Such repetition instructs interpreters "to begin to anticipate the outcome of characters." David's handling of tough situations will not go unnoticed by key players (Prov 22:29). Then, "perhaps they can imagine themselves in similar outcomes" and make appropriate choices and changes.[85]

The authors encourage keeping the grand narrative character-centric. Special focus is given to the Chief Character and his chosen characters (whom Ray calls "famous families" and "famous followers") as they advance the episodic event line (in contrast to a chronological time line) across various mountaintops of Scripture with special attention given to Mount Calvary.

Not only are Bible characters embodied in the grand narrative, they drive it as they demonstrate how Jesus's redemptive story (the red thread) unfolds. Keep the mystery ever present: Is Noah the promised savior? Moses? Joshua? David? John the Baptist? Jesus? Facts and fragmentism will constantly be looking over your shoulder offering contradictive advice (recall Facts Anonymous). We know which the oral reliant prefer. Whether a church, mission agency, Bible institute, college, or seminary, *is your Bible curricula framed, driven, interpreted, and communicated through the grand narrative?*

Not only have too many Bible storytellers overlooked the grand narrative, the same is true for complete books of the Bible. That is one reason why we chose to do the complete book of Jonah rather than a single chapter or four individual lessons.

To catch the full essence of a single story within a book requires, among others, knowing how the Author-author framed the individual stories and characters within the complete book.[86] Not only do Western theologians have a penchant for fragmentation, so do Bible storytellers.

Bible storytellers must constantly remind themselves that the full meaning of a story requires the complete story, the stories that frame it, and

---

85. Stringer and Stringer, "New Hope," 236.

86. The Gospel of Mark provides an example: "In addition to the formulaic connectives [e.g., 'immediately', 'and', 'and again'] and the various triads [e.g., Peter's three denials, Jesus enters Jerusalem three times] . . . the well-known Markan 'sandwich' technique of juxtaposing two stories, one framing the other. The scribes' charge that Jesus works in the power of Beelzebul is framed by Jesus's family's concern that he is possessed (3:20–35); the healing of the woman who had been hemorrhaging for twelve years is framed by the healing of the twelve-year-old dead young woman (5:21–43; Jesus's prophetic demonstration against the Temple is framed by the cursing of the fig tree (11:12–25); and Jesus's trial before the high priesthood is framed by Peter's denial (15:52–72). In this device of oral storytelling the core episode and the framing episode reinforce and interpret each other" (Horsley, "Oral and Written Aspects," 106).

the grand narrative that comprises all the individual stories. How representative are complete books or letters of the Bible in your overall curricula?

Looking Back and Ahead

As noted in chapter 1, if the church wishes to remain *irrelevant* in the twenty-first century to most of the world's population, it is easy—just keep advertising and offering linear, objective, abstract propositions as the main entrée on the menu at Old Faithful Fact Church and Buffet Seminary. Placing and advertising character theology verbally and visually as the top entrées on the menu will do much not only for the survival of the global church, but also for her advancement inwardly and outwardly.

Captivated by certain characters in a story, we easily shed our masks and become emotionally involved (laugh, cry, yell, love, swear) as they unrobed some aspects of their lives, *and* ours. Whether a well-lived life or a squandered one, it becomes personal. Reorienting Robert McKee's classic phrase slightly, *characters* (rather than stories) *are metaphors for life*.[87] We could go further—*characters are metaphors for revealing the Creator*.

Helpful Sources

Deen, *All the Women of the Bible*

Gardner, *New International Encyclopedia of Bible Characters*

Lockyer, *All the Men of the Bible*

Lockyer, *All the Women of the Bible*

Losch, *All the People in the Bible*

Resseguie, *Narrative Criticism of the New Testament*

Ryken, *How Bible Stories Work*

Tucker, *The Biographical Bible*

The truism that through others, we become ourselves, extends to all age groups. Life is a social process where others help us move beyond our capabilities of learning on our own. *The many others in our lives accelerate learning.* Paul serves as one of these "others," asking Christ followers to imitate him so they can blossom beyond themselves, thereby influencing a needy, lonely, insecure world.

---

87. *"Story is metaphor for life"* (McKee, Story, 25 [emphasis original]).

> *Is your Bible curricula framed, driven, interpreted, and communicated through the grand narrative?*

Self- or author characterization creates different types of characters with various personalities, which offers observers choices. Such human experiences vicariously can help dissipate the fog of life, opening hearts and minds to other value-moral possibilities; they make rattling noises, reminding us that our lives are not what they should or could be; or, yes, we are headed in the right direction, and to keep advancing full speed so that God is reverenced and a passion for people prevails.

Characters serve as the Great Disrupter's guardrails and guideposts. Conformity and fear turn to faith, which turns to eternal spiritual fruit. Pivotal people provide an incarnational avenue for Bible communicators to impact and influence others for Christ (the Word who became flesh). Characters paint pictures. Characters shape the significant.

Enfleshed people require embodied concepts. Such personification leaves lasting impressions on not just the heart, but also the mind. Like sticker burrs stuck to one's pants legs, characters continue to walk with us on life's journey. And they are a pain to dislodge. What keeps Bible communicators from allowing Bible characters to create a rainbow of emotions within us that wake us to the reality of our moment? Can we learn to trust characters to carry the content? The Creator they reveal?

This takes us to the third forerunner of character theology—orality. What is the role of *orality* in character theology?

Reflection Questions

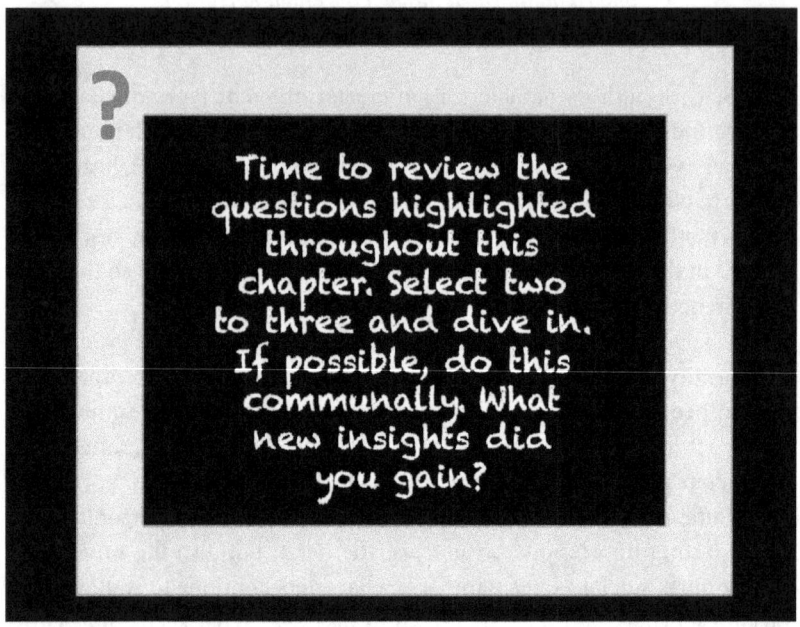

3

The Role of Orality

> The most difficult initial problem in the history
> of literacy is appreciating what preceded it.
>
> —M. T. CLANCHY

> We naturally, habitually, and instinctively work within a
> *literary paradigm*. We are, therefore, in no fit state to appreciate
> how a *non*literary culture, and oral culture, functions.
>
> —JAMES DUNN

> Orality-literacy theorems challenge biblical study perhaps
> more than any other field of learning for over the centuries,
> biblical study has generated what is doubtlessly the most
> massive body of textual commentary in the world.
>
> —WALTER ONG

A GRADUATE THEOLOGY STUDENT wrote the following for one of my (Tom's) classes: "At one point, it was mentioned that an overwhelming majority of Scripture is a story. Initially, that did not settle well with me. That completely discounts the poetry genre of the Bible. The prophets were primarily foretelling and forthtelling. The apocalyptic genre of Revelation is projecting an eschatological vision. The epistles are letters of instruction, completely removed from a story. At least, this was the first thought. Then I listened.

"The poets were very much an active part of a story. Job is nothing but one long story. The Song of Solomon is a romantic love story of a young man and his beautiful lady. The proverbs offer wisdom from a father to his sons. The prophets are foretelling and forthtelling, either pointing back to the earlier part of the story or looking forward to a future part of the story. This springs forth from the life story of Solomon. Even many of the psalms reflect on the stories from the past! In the NT, the epistles only make sense if we know the earlier story. And Revelation, of course, is one incredible end to the story, adding foreshadowing to every one of our stories. Apart from the stories, Scripture would make little or no sense."

Unlike knowing, learning requires listening.

After considering what character theology is and the role of characters within it, this chapter investigates some of the major implications of the "big forgot" and the "fatal flaw" in relation to canon construction (pre-, during, post-) and hermeneutics. We begin with the centerpiece that distinguishes and differentiates this book, the third forerunner of character theology—orality. If a Bible storyteller-interpreter misses or minimizes orality, Bible interpretation and understanding are destined to debilitation. Assumption blindness follows before considering the God who speaks and the spoken nature of Scripture. Orality is then defined and its influential identifiers isolated. We close with the role of orality in character theology.

Minimizing Orality Minimizes Meaning

Similar titles such as this—*He Gave Us Scripture: Foundations of Interpretation*—are common. Did anything in the title stand out? If you are a highly print-oriented learner, probably not. If you are a low to high oral-reliant learner, possibly.

What stood out to the authors? Two things. First, the false assumption that the foundation of interpretation is limited to text, and second, the first grace gift of communication God gave humanity was written Scripture. Both mischaracterize history.

Ironically, the above title quietly skips thousands of years of human history in God's world. Yes, God gave us Scripture in print, but his first written project did not emerge until Mount Sinai. This means something preceded print for a significant period. And what was that something? The psalmist provides a hint: "The breath of His mouth whispered the sea of stars into existence. . . . For he spoke, and all things came into being. A *single* command from *His lips*, and all creation *obeyed and* stood its ground" (Ps 33:6, 9 VOICE [emphasis original]).

Today, we know nothing was codified in the garden. Rather, the Creator gave our first parents essentially sufficient, non-textual revelations of himself, his will, and the meaning and purpose of life primarily through his *voice*.

The Spoken One used his *voice* in various tones—from intimate to scary—to communicate, e.g., Adam: "Where are you?"; Cain: "Why are you angry? And why do you look so despondent?" . . . "Where is your brother Abel?" . . . "What have you done?"; "*Jonah*, do you have any good reason to be angry?" (Gen 3:9; 4:6, 9, 10; Jonah 4:4 VOICE [emphasis original]). From hearing God's *voice* choices were made. These choices added depth of meaning to their calling to be "like God." Have we lost his voice? Have we silenced Scripture?

Sociologist Anne Karpf contends, "You can't really know a person until you have heard them speak."[1] It was strongly through *voice*[2] that Adam, Eve, Cain, Jonah, and many others learned about their Creator, themselves, and the material and spiritual worlds.

Interestingly, the Creator introduces himself to the world (Gen 1–2) with an art show (visual aspect of orality) where creativity, voice, color, movement, light, beauty, majesty, awe, order, critique, and power intersected. Where's the print? Or is there an unwritten assumption here that creation artistically introduces his highest creation to the Creator, the master craftsman through artistic theology? Is Michael O'Sheal correct when he asserts that art can "jostle the soil of the imagination"?[3]

No writing is found in the garden. Even the Ten Commandments were spoken before being engraved in stone (Exod 24:7). The Creator gave us the created world that mirrors and proclaims his glories. The Creator gave us his presence beginning with Adam and Eve. The Creator gave us voice, story, characters. Through word-pictured wisdom that embodied heart, head, and hands, the Creator engaged his first image-bearers. God communicated for centuries with his highest creation *before* his word became print.

Indeed, God's first written project, the Hebrew Bible, is considered by many to be merely a reduplication and republication of the Creator's abstract character revealed to our first parents through the speech acts that dominated their intimate daily relationship in the garden. Note, however,

---

1. Karpf, *Human Voice*, 4.

2. Hans-Georg Gadamer captures it this way: "Living speech [is] the spoken word interpret[ing] itself to an astonishing degree by the way of speaking, the tone of voice, the tempo, etc. but also by the circumstances in which it is spoken" (as quoted in McMahan, *Elite Oral History Discourse*, 7).

3. Price, "What Does Michael O'Sheal."

voice includes more than print. To hear his voice was to *experience* the Spoken One; it was a "reading" session; it was an event!

Our first parents saw (body language[4]), heard his voice, and "read" their Creator *without* reading print. And this extends to us. "The celestial realms announce God's glory. . . . Each day pours out more of their sayings; each night, more *to hear and more* to learn. Inaudible words are their manner of speech, and silence, their means to convey" (Ps 19:1–3 VOICE [emphasis original]). The visual is not inferior to verbal, nor is it mere decoration.[5]

The visual speaks without verbally speaking. But how? Following insights discovered studying the Bible as a young man, Neil Postman concluded the Second Commandment, which prohibits making concrete images to represent God, was because symbols carry a culturally tied message (blasphemy). Marshall McLuhan helped summarize this understanding for Postman in his highly celebrated axiom "the medium is the message." But the axiom required further amendment.

Symbols, images,[6] and other media forms speak, not in a way one can physically hear through the ear-gate; rather, they speak metaphorically through the mind's eye-gate. Postman proposes, "Media-metaphors classify the world for us, sequence it, frame it, enlarge it, reduce it, color it, argue a case for what the world is like."[7] Media images speak metaphorically.

This journey led Postman to conclude "the clearest way to see through a culture is to attend to its *tools* for conversation."[8] He uses the "word 'conversation' metaphorically to refer not only to speech but to all techniques and technologies that permit people of a particular culture to exchange messages."[9] These could include print, images, and certainly creation.

The Creator's broad oral communication modes, as well as his selected future authors, are key to Bible interpretation (including beyond the narrative sections of Scripture), even if some Bible scholars devalue this premise. *If Bible interpreters miss or minimize orality's reality and its hermeneutic implications within those texts, the robust appeal, impact, and meaning of the message will not be grasped to its fullest, thereby increasing misapplication.* We agree with Michael Brown who considers Bible authority "not . . . the

---

4. "*Body language can expose a person's intentions*" (Prov 16:30 VOICE [emphasis original]).

5. Filmmaker George Lucas of *Star Wars* fame wonders, "If students aren't taught the language of sound and images, shouldn't they be considered as illiterate as if they left college without being able to read or write?" (Daly, "Life on the Screen," para. 7).

6. See Colijn, *Images of Salvation*.

7. Postman, *Amusing Ourselves to Death*, 10.

8. Postman, *Amusing Ourselves to Death*, 8 (emphasis original).

9. Postman, *Amusing Ourselves to Death*, 6.

literal words on the page. It is . . . hearing the voice behind the words, the Word behind the words."[10]

The Creator's powerful and profound spoken words, whether in Eden or Sinai,[11] *preceded* his written word, and the living Word of God—Jesus. All are eventually present and integrated, but there was a sequence to the subsequent hybrid.

Just as text can be written or spoken,[12] so the spoken can be inaudible or audible. The world is *much more* than letters inscribed on paper. Kenneth Burke perceptively reminds the highly print-oriented, "The [written] record is usually but a fragment of the expression (as the written word omits all telltale record of gesture and tonality; and not only may our 'literacy' keep us from missing the omissions, it may blunt us to the appreciation of tone and gesture, so that even when we witness the full expression, we note only those aspects of it that can be written down)."[13] How oral-oriented is our perspective of text? How reductionistic is our perception of orality?

> The visual speaks without speaking. But how?

Script requires speech, and speech benefits from script. Each comes with its own advantages and disadvantages. One without the other, however, is likely to produce half-ripe fruit, bitter to the taste. How has our text centrism (not text) minimized God-intended apprehension and application? Does text serve as a stronger preserver of the message than as a living medium of the message?

We now consider some of the underlying assumptions that too many highly print-oriented Bible scholars and lay interpreters have failed to comprehend much less implement. Walter Ong, among other forerunners,[14]

---

10. M. Brown, "Hearing the Master's Voice," 11.

11. Note the ear-gate emphasis yet inclusion of the eye: "If you will listen closely to My voice—*the voice of* your God—and do what is right in My eyes, pay attention to My instructions, and keep all of My laws; then I will" (Exod 15:26 VOICE [emphasis original]).

12. See Finnegan, *Oral Literature in Africa*, 6.

13. Burke, *Rhetoric of Motives*, 185.

14. Ong (1912–2003) certainly was not the first to address orality. Whether predecessor or contemporary, some of his influential forerunners included Marcel Jousse (1886–1961), who believes he was the discoverer of the oral style, *Oral Style*; Albert Bates Lord (1912–1991), *Singer of Tales*; Eric Havelock (1903–1988), *Muse Learns to Write*; Jack Goody (1919–2015), *Domestication of Savage Mind*. For the convergence of the secular, sacred, and strategic story movements, see T. Steffen, *Worldview-Based Storying*, 25.

provided research that influenced the modern-day evangelical orality movement in missions. He warned: "One can be aware that texts have oral backgrounds without being entirely aware of what orality reality is."[15] Because of where the hermeneutic guilds have long pitched their tents—the written text world—the implications of orality have become the "big forgot" for far too many Bible exegetes and communicators.

Assumption Blindness

Every theory or model is driven by assumptions whether cognizant of them or not. These assumptions, however, are often difficult to recognize because they are like the air we breathe.

Millard Erickson believes, "A given hermeneutic will need to be understood as part of a much larger system of thought, and that system will have to be carefully evaluated."[16] Few, however, identify, much less analyze, the assumptions that drive their hermeneutic theoretical framework or resultant theology; too many blindly move forward with few if any apprehensions or alarms. After all, that's what we've always done.

> How has our text centrism (not text) minimized God-intended apprehension and application?

Five assumptions related to the role of orality in relation to the spoken words of God follow. But before addressing them, we will position them in the larger picture of history.

Dominant communications systems matter. Thomas Boomershine believes that whenever a new communication system emerges, a change in hermeneutics can be patterned. His dominant communication systems over history consist of: "oral to manuscript, manuscript to print, print to silent print, silent print to digital."[17]

Whether over centuries, or more recently decades, such communication paradigm shifts tend to project the inferiority of the former system. Rather than perceive such changes as inferior or even a break between systems, Boomershine refers to them as "watersheds." This conveys direction,

---

15. Ong, *Orality and Literacy*, 170.
16. M. Erickson, *Evangelical Interpretation*, 123.
17. Boomershine, *First-Century Gospel Storytellers*, 42.

energy, and past remnants evolving into new configurations influenced by different surroundings.

> How oral-oriented is our perspective of text?

Assumption 1: *The spoken Word preceded the written Word.* The spoken Word, God's Voice, was heard and lived long before it became the written words of God. "Before time itself was measured, the Voice was speaking. The Voice was and is God" (John 1:2 VOICE). God first breathed out words, not manuscripts.[18] And *both the spoken and later written were inspired.*[19]

Scripture in both Testaments began as shared oral tradition (indigenous transgenerational wisdom collectively preserved over time through eyewitnesses,[20] symbols, stories, rituals). This includes the Synoptic Gospels which "were handed down to us by those who from the first were eyewitnesses" (Luke 1:2 NIV). Luke writes: "I wrote about all that Jesus began to do and teach" (Acts 1:1 NIV). It also includes "the apostles' teaching" (Acts 2:42 NIV) and Paul's instructions (1 Thess 2:13; 4:2). Oral tradition preceded written text.

That Jesus wrote nothing down of his teachings nor asked anyone else to do so shows his strong faith in communal memory. For those groomed in individualist-oriented print media and reliance on technology for long-term memory, this is difficult to grasp. Eyewitness oralists, however, could remember his teachings after decades through the vividness of his voice.

Unfortunately, many Bible interpreters have a low view of voice. We appreciate Anne Karpf's keen insight:

18. "Hermann Gunkel was one of the first to recognize the orality of the Old Testament literature, and to posit that it was originally spoken and thus should be released 'from bondage to the printed page'" (Jakobson et al, *Verbal Art, Verbal Sign*, 150).

19. God-inspired voice (Deut 18:18–20; 1 Kgs 17:24; 2 Sam 32:2; Ezek 3:27, 30; Acts 28:25; 1 Thess 2:13; 2 Pet 1:20–21) and God-inspired script (2 Tim 3:16–17) coexisted. "Have you not heard?" and "Have you not read?" interfaced during first-century Christianity. No "great divide" then, nor should there be today between the oral, print, and digital. Sam Chan adds, "To insist that we must privilege one form of communication over another is to confuse orthopraxy with orthodoxy, form with content, method with message, and pedagogy with theology. It is also a failure to recognize that we are all influenced by our culture. The traditional expository Bible talk is a product of Western, logical, linear, Enlightenment, and inductive communication methods. So, when we accuse anyone else of 'selling out' to culture and 'trying to make the Bible relevant,' we must also be attuned to our own failure to see that we might be doing the same thing. Are we like the American who cannot hear his own accent, who laughs at the funny way everyone else speaks English?" (Sam Chan, *Evangelism in Skeptical World*, 194).

20. Did eyewitnesses include earwitnesses?

We have very little collective sense in Western societies of the importance of the voice.... We persist instead with the idea that the move from a primarily oral to a mainly literate society has made the voice much less important than the image and the written word, as if the voice belonged at the periphery of human experience, rather than at its centre.[21]

Kaarpf continues, "Literacy, however, downgrades intonation and our sensitivity to it, preferring to use grammar and syntax to help establish meaning.... The arrival of printing and literacy changed the voice's status—de*centred* it from official life."[22] How much thought have interpreters given to the role of voice and spoken words of the Spoken One? The sounds of Scripture? Have we marginalized voice?

How much time and practice are given to the spoken presentation of the Word in Sunday morning services? Bible studies? Devotions? VBS? Camps? Missions? If very little, at what cost in today's voice-saturated world?

Boomershine believes the cost is too high. He thinks today's literate interpreters have "read back our sensory system of silent reading into the ancient world." The result? "If the Bible was originally composed in a sensorium of sound, the Bible is not perceived when the Bible is read now as a 'text' (in silence with our eyes)." He insightfully asks, "How can we perceive and study the Bible in its original sensory medium, sound?"[23]

How different in ancient Israel and the first-century Mediterranean world with its strong emphasis on the nuances of oral-aural.[24] Susan Niditch notes, "Large, perhaps dominant, threads in Israelite culture were oral, and ... literacy in ancient Israel must be understood in terms of its continuity and interaction with the oral world."[25]

> How much time and practice are given to the spoken presentation of the Word in Sunday morning services?

---

21. Karpf, *Human Voice*, 3.

22. Karpf, *Human Voice*, 200–201 (emphasis added).

23. Boomershine, *First-Century Gospel Storytellers*, 127. See M. Lee and Scott, *Sound Mapping New Testament*.

24. "Studies of literacy in the ancient Mediterranean world place the number of people who could read and/or write at somewhere around 5%, with a somewhat higher percentage projected for urban males ... [Harris] suggests 15% for urban males" (Hearon, "Implications of 'Orality,'" 102). There was a reading and writing public.

25. Niditch, *Oral World*, 1.

Even when the spoken word dictated to scribes became the printed word of God, the resultant physical scroll became difficult to secure, store, and handle (Isaiah was around twenty-feet long and ten inches high), much less read. To keep it as short as possible so that it could be economically stored in the few existing public and private libraries, it purposely lacked punctuation, spaces between words, paragraph markers, verses, or separate chapters.[26]

Holly Hearon notes, "Since these 'written remains' were largely dictated, the 'remains' are, in fact, texts that began in oral expression and were 'actualized' in performance through the reoralization of the words." What results if storyteller-interpreters miss the "oral remains"?

Hearon continues, "To view them wholly as written texts, then, is to miss an important dimension of their function and to misconstrue how they were experienced in the ancient Mediterranean world."[27] In her classic *Oral Literature in Africa*, Ruth Finnegan adds, "Oral literature is by definition dependent on a performer who formulates it in words on a special occasion."[28] Richard Horsley concludes, "We cannot assume that texts were written to be 'studied' and 'interpreted' as in scholarly print-culture."[29] While the spoken word preceded and influenced the written word, the two interplayed, each influencing the other, and not without some tension.[30]

Assumption 2: *Literacy has blinded many to the oral features of Scripture.* In *The Return to Oral Hermeneutics*, the authors recognized the effects of centuries of literacy education and enculturation that produced a blind spot in the Western Christian world.

What was that blind spot? The neglect by most in the academies, agencies, and assemblies[31] of the foundational and influential role *orality* had on text and teaching. Generally, our strong literacy background (a minimum of

---

26. To illustrate, see how easy it is to read this familiar verse: FORGODSOLOVEDTHEWORLDTHATHEGAVEHISONEANDONLYSONTHATWHOSOEVERBELIEVESINHIMSHALLNOTPERISHBUTHAVEETERNALLIFE. Some degree of memorization of the manuscript was necessary.

27. Hearon, "Implications of 'Orality,'" 97.

28. Finnegan, *Oral Literature in Africa*, 2.

29. Horsley, "Oral and Written Aspects," 97.

30. John Niles identifies three interplaying contributive realms: 1) the "world of live performance," 2) the "world of elite literature," and 3) the "world of oral traditional literature that has been textualized." He then quotes Millard Parry, that each realm has "its own laws of operation and its own value." Each interacts with the others, offering its own subculture's nuanced contributions and complexities, all of which should be leveraged (Niles, "Introduction to Special Issue," 264).

31. We use this order to represent theological and hermeneutic influence, not significance.

twelve years in formal schooling in the US) has blinded many to the fact that the Bible is "a collection of sacred, religious texts orally composed for eventual oral articulation."[32] The highly print-oriented naturally tend to perceive meaning to be written words rather than heard sounds.[33]

> How oral-oriented is our perspective of text?

Werner Kelber correctly implores, "If [only] we can wean ourselves from the notion that texts constitute the center of gravity in tradition."[34] Bobby Loubser offers two reasons for the necessity for some *unlearning*: "Almost by default, most people living in modern literate cultures are 'media blind' . . . it [oral poetics] goes against the grain of our deep-seated literate inclinations."[35]

C. S. Lewis concurs: "The greatest barrier between us and our ancestors is the categorical barrier between oral and literary structures."[36] Robert Alter augments: "As modern readers of the Bible, we need to relearn something of this mode of perception that was second nature to the original audience."[37] Bible communicators often talk about knowing the context of antiquity. Part of that context includes knowing the variants of how oralists in antiquity interpreted, communicated, implemented, remembered, relayed, identified. On a scale of one to ten, ten being highest, where would you rate yourself in relation to oral literacy?

Assumption 3: *The spoken Word influenced the written Word.* The spoken word influenced the written word because Scripture was written primarily for the ear. Horsley therefore calls Scripture "oral-derived texts."[38]

---

32. Wendland, "Studying, Translating, and Transmitting," 6.

33. John Walton and Brent Sandy believe we have given too much attention to words over meaning. Three questions they raise related to the spoken and script include: "How could the texts of written forms be fluid like oral forms?"; "How would an author write differently when intending it for oral performance?"; and "How might an orally shaped text reveal clues to its meaning or non-oral readers?" (Walton and Sandy, *Lost World of Scripture*, 85, 5, 130).

34. Kelber, *Jesus and Tradition*, 163.

35. Loubser, *Oral and Manuscript Culture*, 4, 74.

36. C. S. Lewis, as quoted in Wuellner, "Where Is Rhetorical Criticism," 457.

37. Alter, *Art of Biblical Narrative*, 62.

38. Horsley, *Whoever Hears You*, 60. Such texts also aided retention: "The compositions were structured to facilitate the retention for the oral performer as well as for the hearing audience. Written text can be understood as memory aids" (Maxey, "New Testament," 12).

David Carr notes, a copied text "stood as a permanent reference point for an ongoing process of largely oral recitation."[39] Jan Assmann assumes, "Text is speech in the status of a mnemonic mark."[40] Ahmad Ibn Fadlan, played by Antonio Banderas in *The 13th Warrior* movie, illustrates when asked how he knows the twelve warriors' language. The dialogue goes like this: "Where did you learn our language?" "I listened." "You can draw sounds?" "Yes, *I can draw sounds, and I can speak them back.*"[41]

> How reductionistic is our perception of orality?

Scripture became a "sound print" hybrid as rhetoric (art of persuasion) influenced the written, and the written influenced the rhetoric. The written text, which "never exists without orality,"[42] protects the spoken-heard text. Sound and Scripture sync well.

Anne Wire distinguishes how this hybrid utilizes both the spoken and written. Wire believes writing "limits a story by recording only words, whereas storytelling depends for effective communication as much on the speaker's tone, volume, pace, gestures and embodiment of direct discourse as on the words spoken."[43] This means *every* telling requires a social-cultural

---

39. Carr, *Writing on the Tablet*, 4. Ben Witherington insightfully argues: "It is thus quite the wrong way around to talk about figuring out how rhetoric could be used in an epistolary mode. The issue was how letters could be written in a predominately oral and rhetorical culture that might faithfully reflect the rhetorical nature of discourse, and especially the various forms of public discourse" (Witherington, "Why Ignoring Rhetorical Shape," para. 3).

40. Assmann, "Form as Mnemonic Device," 72. Ernst Wendland notes, "A variety of stylistic devices within such ancient written compositions . . . were utilized for macro-structural design purposes and also to orally shape the text; among them are these: the recycling of major, culturally-relevant themes, concepts, key terms, and images; cohesive and strategic (boundary-marking) repetition, restatement, and paraphrase; the use of standard opening and closing transitional formulas; much parallelism and patterning in doublets/triads, or in terraced and chiastic arrangements; a preference for graphic, 'memorable' imagery, figures of speech, sayings, epithets, catch-words, familiar symbols, acrostic-alphabetic arrangements; citations of, and allusions to information that is already well-known; frequent dramatic, interactive discourse (real and rhetorical questions, interjections, imperatives, vocatives, etc.); periodic poetic or rhythmic, euphonic, sound-sensitive sequences of utterances; and as a general rule, the inclusion of as much direct 'character' speech as possible" (Wendland, *Orality and Its Implications*, 42–43).

41. Wisher and Lewis, *13th Warrior* (emphasis added; time stamp unavailable).

42. Ong, *Orality and Literacy*, 8.

43. Antoinette Clark Wire, as quoted in Hearon, "Implications of 'Orality,'" 100.

contextualization.[44] When the storyteller does not make such adjustments, the participating audience in the dialogue will be sure to let him/her know something is amiss (recall the abstract sermon presented to the Ifugao). Even so, the majority in antiquity tended to perceive this hybrid as strongly oral in nature. Rhetoric reigned in the texts, presentations, and hermeneutic.

"Thus *says* the Lord" is repeated over four hundred times in the OT. Jesus often repeated the phrase "you have heard it *said*." Loubser goes so far as to call Paul an "oral theologian"[45] because he generously interjected the oral within his written letters. Dean Flemming tells us why: "Paul's writings are less a collection of doctrinal studies than a series of theological conversations between the apostle and his diverse audiences with their life circumstances."[46] While most have identified Paul's epistles as letters, we tend to forget letters were written to initiate or continue a *conversation*. The epistles were encased in personal and/or collective stories even as the letters find themselves embedded in previous texts, e.g., Ephesians is embedded in Acts.

Scripture is strongly speech-sourced writing where personalities integrate with propositions, where characters integrate with concepts. Influenced predominately by oral audiences, Bible authors—including NT authors who found themselves within the 10 to 15 percent of minority elites in the first-century Greco-Roman world,[47]—rather than insist listeners move towards text, wisely adjusted the texts for the ear (heart and memory), not just the eye (mind and documents). The Spirit-inspired authors knew how to make the written assessable for oralists; they knew how to ease the symbiotic tension between text and the oral; they knew how to make the "written" word (which probably added credibility[48] and enhanced memory) the "spoken-written" word so that it became credible, comprehendible, applicable, memorable, and repeatable by the majority.

---

44. Whenever and wherever rhetoric reigns in the texts, presentations, and hermeneutic, the question arises—when is the "original" the "original" in the oral-reliant world? Is it not interesting how few differences are found in the Synoptic Gospels?

45. Loubser, "Orality and Literacy," 67.

46. Flemming, *Contextualization in New Testament*, 105. Dunn adds: "One cannot hope to write a theology of Paul except by listening to his letters as dialogue, overhearing, as it were, a great theological mind and spirit as it grappled with diversely challenging situations and questions. . . . Rather, in the letters we see and are privileged to overhear *theology in the making*, theology coming to expression, Paul theologizing" (Dunn, *New Testament Theology*, 15–16 [emphasis original]).

47. See Harris, *Ancient Literacy*.

48. Horsley, "Oral and Written Aspects," 98.

Again, Karpf: "Literacy didn't replace orality, only supplemented it."[49] The early Israelites and Christ followers were not given the *written* words of God on perishable parchments; rather, they (and generations later us) received the *spoken-written* words of God. Not to grasp the hybrid nature of Scripture is to demonstrate literary blindness to the significant and substantial role orality played in influencing, developing, and advancing Scripture.

James Maxey summarizes, "The Bible was for the most part created, transmitted, and received in a predominantly oral context."[50] From foundation to finish, orality influenced the formation and function of Scripture, thereby designing it primarily for relationship-based dialogue and action, not unlike the Trinity.[51]

> Does text serve as a stronger preserver of the message than as a living medium of the message?

Assumption 4: *Not only did voice precede text, it also followed text.* For centuries after the written text, voice still played a major role in interpretation and communication. Stock synthesizes: "The rules of oratorical discourse invaded the world of texts."[52] Hearon expands: "Alongside this perception of the text as 'written,' however, is the experience of the written text as, principally, a spoken word that is read aloud, received, and remembered. This is also how the text is most often employed: it is quoted in discourse and appealed to in debate." But there's more:

> Equally strong is both the perception and encounter of the text as a living voice that continues to speak to the present.... The Hebrew Scriptures, therefore, are representative of the complex relationship between written and spoken word. They are perceived of as both written word and spoken word (as having "voice"), yet they are most often encountered and employed as spoken word.[53]

---

49. Karpf, *Human Voice*, 204.
50. Maxey, *From Orality to Orality*, 1.
51. A good starter book is Rodrigues, *Oral Tradition*. For those wishing to dig deep, see Dunn, *Oral Gospel Tradition*; Eve, *Behind the Gospels*.
52. Stock, "Chiastic Awareness," 26. See also Winger, "Spoken Word."
53. Hearon, "Interplay," 65.

The spoken Voice *refused to* detach or distance itself from the written Voice.[54] The written script speaks because it is spoken script![55] Written scripts are living, speaking scripts; they speak metaphorically! How strongly has our literary background caused us to *undervalue speaking and listening* in relation to the spoken-written words of God?

Because most ancients assumed sound superior to script,[56] they therefore believed reputable teachers relied on memory, *not* written text when teaching. They also assumed reading should *not* be conducted silently or in solitude. Reading required: 1) the power of voice, which "intones the voice of God through vocal cords";[57] 2) the text *being read out loud* (Acts 8:30) to hear the "still small voice of the Holy Spirit";[58] 3) the text being read *in community* as a "shared experience" (Col 4:16; 1 Tim 4:13);[59] and 4) the text heard *in its entirety*.

> On a scale of one to ten, ten being highest, where would you rate yourself in relation to oral literacy?

Antiquity's equivalent for today's publishing a printed document was an oral public event where memory, performance-proclamation, and dialogue prevailed. Most first-century people of "the Way" perceived the words of God *not* as frozen "print on the page"[60] of a sacred text but rather as *live* embodied performance-proclamation.

Rhoads raises some poignant questions for high print-oriented interpreters:

---

54. The Bible ends not just with the written word, but also the spoken word from the throne: "I, Jesus, have sent My messenger *to show you and guide you* so that you in turn would share this testimony with the churches, I am the Root and Descendant of David, the Bright Morning Star" (Rev 22:16 VOICE [emphasis original]).

55. Marcel Jousse provides some nuance to the spoken and oral: "Spoken style is the style of everyday conversation. Oral style is designed to be heard, remembered, and transmitted by memory" (as quoted in Harvey, *Listening to the Text*, 56).

56. Third-century Christian Papias of Hierapolis claimed oral tradition to be superior to the printed page: "I did not suppose that information from books would help me so much as the word of a living and surviving voice" (as quoted in Gamble, *Books and Readers*, 30). See also Winger, "Spoken Word."

57/ Berger, *Oral Interpretation of Bible*, 38.

58. Berger, *Oral Interpretation of Bible*, 47.

59. Berger, *Oral Interpretation of Bible*, 99.

60. Rhoads, "Performing the Letter," 4.

> Can you imagine a musicologist who does nothing but sit in libraries and study the score of a composition without ever hearing a performance of it? Would it not seem strange for interpreters of drama, including ancient Greek drama, to analyze a play apart from interpretations of it in performance? Similarly, does it not seem odd that biblical critics interpret writings that were composed in and for oral performance—as gospels, letters, and apocalypses were—without ever experiencing performances of them and without giving some attention to the nature of the performance of these works in ancient and modern times?[61]

Teachers shifting from a high print-dominant culture in which telling reigns to become a storyteller means one has just now applied to become a text proclaimer-performer.

For unsuffocated imagination to transpire, some paradigm shifts may be necessary to begin to appreciate the powerful role of performance in the ancient world. Rhoads continues, "When we seek to imagine performances in oral cultures, we moderns need to shift our thinking from written to oral, from private to public, from 'public readers' to proclaimer-performers, from silent readers to listeners/audience, from individual to communal audience, and from manuscript transmission to oral transmission."[62]

Boomershine would agree with Rhoads in relation to performance not only in antiquity, but for today as well. "Based on a perception of the Bible as sound that was experienced.... Performance criticism is a foundation for the new paradigm of biblical interpretation for the communication culture of the digital age."[63] For Boomershine, "Biblical scholarship based on a silent reading of the compositions as texts is an inaccurate perception and interpretation of the Bible in its original historical context."[64]

> How strongly has our literary background caused us to *undervalue speaking and listening* in relation to the spoken-written words of God?

Once print existed, it was never a one-way street even when one communication system tended to dominate. Tension between the two was always present. "Oral texts," notes Pieter Botha, "depended on writing for

---

61. Rhoads, "Performance Criticism [pt. 1]," 119.
62. Rhoads, "Performance Criticism [pt. 1]," 123.
63. Boomershine, *First-Century Gospel Storytellers*, 19.
64. Boomershine, *First-Century Gospel Storytellers*, 13.

their survival while written texts were dependent on those oral aspects for their legitimacy."[65] The psalmist adds: "Write this down for the next generation so people not yet born will praise God" (Ps 102:18 MSG). The interfacing of the *spoken*-written Word prevailed in antiquity, thereby offering pedagogical relevance, preservation, and eventually the cessation for further transmission.

Nor did the transition to a stronger literate side happen overnight. As Ong explains, "Even after the development of writing, the pristine oral-aural modes of knowledge storage and retrievals still dominate. . . . Only during the last half of the second century did a scribal culture. . . . begin to dominate the transmission of early Christian literature."[66] Even then, "literacy was used to enhance and facilitate orality."[67] Karpf's summary for today rings true of antiquity: "The voice has remained . . . a weapon of mass persuasion."[68] Viva voice!

Any implications here for how today's communication medium may influence hermeneutics? Boomershine concludes, "To the degree that our goal is to understand the meaning of the biblical texts in their original historical context, we need to study and experience the texts in their original medium, namely, as sounds recited and heard at least in private but preferably in public."[69] Sounds were written to be *re*sounded publicly. Updating and maximizing sound for a digital world through performance-proclamation of a Bible story should prove captivating for today's audiences around the globe.

Assumption 5: *The narrative sections of Scripture require orality for fullest appeal, impact, and comprehension.* What perishes in print? Bible authors wrote not just for *cerebral clarity*, but also for *imaginative and emotional impact* (the enhanced experience feature)! Stories speak, offering a surplus of imaginatively-emotionally based appeal and impact.[70] Orality *layers meaning* in multiple ways, one being by adding the sensory, thereby increasing personal-collective impact. Bradt believes, "Story knows more as said than can ever be articulated—through indirection, suggestion, tone, and dynamics."[71]

---

65. Botha, *Orality and Literacy in Early Christianity*, xvi.
66. Ong, *Interfaces of the Word*, 214.
67. Joanna Dewey, *Orality and Textuality*, 45.
68. Karpf, *Human Voice*, 213.
69. Boomershine, *First-Century Gospel Storytellers*, 105.
70. "Spirit-led imagination, an imagination converted by the Word, is an essential faculty for the work of theological exegesis" (Hays, *Reading with the Grain*, 39).
71. Bradt, *Story as a Way*, 108.

Grounded in orality, Bible stories are inherently sensory in nature and therefore influence one's personality and relationships. As our friend Ricki Gidoomal would say, "Stories push us to personhood."

Few on the print side of spoken-written Scripture have been taught to engage in the cinematic nature of Bible *characters* to discover the sensory side of story. Rather—forget the footnotes for the moment—we have been taught to immediately identify the *theological headline*.

Ryken, however, reminds interpreters to *slow down*, to let the lives of characters develop in their fullness; let their lives capture us. Why? Because "truthfulness to life is an important part of the truth of . . . story."[72]

Can Bible interpreters learn to experience the experiences of characters before prematurely assigning propositional statements? "Truth is experiential," reasons Ryken, "as well as ideational."[73] Truth is more than *told* ideas; truth also consists of the *visualized*, i.e., the lived lives (actions) of biblical characters which includes the sensory.

> *What perishes in print?*

Ryken and Longman wave this warning flag: "Literary texts are irreducible to propositional statements and single meanings. A propositional statement of a theme can never be a substitute or even the appointed goal of experiencing a literary text."[74] Ryken adds, "A story does not have a unifying topic but a unifying *action*."[75]

Finnegan digs deeper: "The bare words cannot be left to speak for themselves, for the simple reason that in the actual literary work so much else is necessarily and intimately involved."[76] Truth goes beyond silent ancient scribbles of letters, written words, syntax, grammar; truth requires the actions of characters be played out in context.[77] Is it time to reconsider the role of activities of concrete characters in Bible interpretation?

Theology is conveyed most powerfully and most thoroughly when demonstrated through *living relationships* (*the heart of orality*). Until a storied event where relationships reign is grasped, theology tends to remain

---

72. Ryken, *How Bible Stories Work*, 22.
73. Ryken, *How Bible Stories Work*, 26.
74. Ryken and Longman, *Complete Literary Guide*, 17.
75. Ryken, *How Bible Stories Work*, 79.
76. Finnegan, *Oral Literature in Africa*, 17.
77. Which is easier to fool, the ear or the eye?

naked ideas having minimal imaginative, emotional, or transformative appeal or impact.

Focusing exclusively or even minimally on theological *ideas deplatforms, demystifies, deoralizes, devoices, denarratizes, deevents, deenfleshes, deembodies, deexhibits, decenters, and decharacterizes, and depersonalizes the dominant literary genre of Scripture—narrative. Worse yet, it deincarnates the Chief Character—Jesus—making him a philosophical Idea rather than a participating Person in the Trinity's ongoing story.*[78]

Robust theology revealed through a web of relationships focuses on relational formation rather than simply cognitive information. This helps explain why oral hermeneutics—intimately and intricately based on relationships (not reason alone)—matters, *especially today.*

Transformative transcendent theology has an inherently relational reflection. If Scripture is driven by a missionary God (*missio Dei*), one would expect to find theology to be missional in nature. This is evident of many key Bible characters whose lives intersected with those of different nations, e.g., Abraham, Moses, Paul.

Theology that deserves authoritative respect will communally express itself to the nations (Gen 12:3; Rev 7:9) through seeking and serving others, especially strangers (Gal 6:10). Such holistic ministries among the nations comprise a driving theme within the grand narrative.

Viable theology is relational theology that goes beyond the interaction between human and spiritual characters. This can happen by tying people's encounters with their Creator and others to places. Walter Brueggemann captures this when he comments on "the preoccupation of the Bible for placement"[79] (another orality feature—setting).

Such placement encounters began in the garden of Eden, moved to the promised land, to the exile, to the incarnation in Bethlehem,[80] culminating in the new Jerusalem. Each of these geographical placements could be associated with pivotal Bible characters. God's story is often tied to our story theologically through the geography associated with Bible characters. Geographical locations influence the actions of Bible characters, thereby providing interpretive clues. The Bible speaks geographically and visually (think Walk Thru the Bible) as well as verbally.

---

78. "The Voice took on flesh *and became human* and chose to live alongside us" (John 1:14 VOICE).

79. Brueggemann, *Land*, 10.

80. "It is clear from the incarnation that places are the seat of relations or the place of meeting and activity in the interaction between God and the world" (Inge, *A Christian Theology of Place*, 52).

> Is it time to reconsider the role of concrete characters in Bible interpretation?

Viable theology is relational theology that expresses the living voice of the Spoken One in geographical locations. Such theology is engineered to challenge our daily relationship with the Eternal One. Recapping: "The church is measured by how well it embodies the life of Christ, how extensively it welcomes and is constituted by the weak, and how prophetically it holds up the mirror of the gospel to an unbelieving world."[81]

Tasked by the Trinity[82] to guard and advance transcendent truth that transforms and liberates, the global covenant community (not just professionals), the recipients of grace, offer that same grace (*missio Dei* in action) through daily examples and explanations of "the Way." They demonstrate such so that spiritual blossoming (knowledge that leads to habitual, actionized wisdom) and numerical multiplication (individuals-groups and new churches) ensues globally. Viable theology of "the Way" is relationally expressed on the way as the called call out others through works and words. What spiritual beauty do others see in us?

Summarizing, orality connects not just people through stories, but hearts and places as well. This opens the door for an *army of amateurs* to interpret Bible stories, not just those formally trained in biblical and theological studies! The spoken-written hybrid Word (not just the written[83]) is foundational to a full-orbed, more robust understanding of the narrative sections of Scripture, including its Author.

> When does the oral submit to the written?
> The written submit to the oral?

---

81. Yong, *Theology and Down Syndrome*, 199.

82. "The formula of the Trinity is the shorthand symbol that encodes the story of the Christian community" (Haight, *Spirituality Seeking Theology*, 178).

83. God has chosen to build relationships with his highest creation through verbal and visual means. He accomplishes this through word-based relationships (the spoken Word), image-based relationships (symbols), print-based relationships (the written Word). All these find their center and core in an incarnation-based relationship—Jesus Christ, the Chief Character. The Eternal One utilizes multiple types of relationships to address the various types of learning styles around the globe.

These five assumptions raise some thought-provoking questions in relation to Scripture. When does the oral submit to the written? The written submit to the oral? When does the sacred text replace the spoken words of the prophets and apostles? What level of oral articulation does Scripture assign itself? The answers to these questions may not be as straight forward as many have been taught to think; it may be *much more* nuanced.

Karel van der Toorn correctly concludes, "The oral does not die, but its authority is subordinate to that of the written text."[84] As "literary tourists" blinded by our long literary history, it is that first part of the quote that most of us miss or minimize—orality's imprint and influence on Scripture *never* dies.

Why will the oral never die in Scripture? Sheer volume, for one. The narrative (connected events unpacked in stories that resolve conflict) and poetry (artistic imagery that emotionalizes language) sections of Scripture may comprise 90 percent of the Bible. Orality's influence throughout the pages of Scripture, including the ongoing conversations between Paul and the various covenant communities spread across the Mediterranean, focused strongly on the ear and eye, the concrete, the repetitive, the metaphorical. It was heart-oriented, imaginative, sensory, as well as rational. While there was definite respect and appreciation for the sacred text, the auditory dominated well beyond first century Christianity.

Yes, the authoritative word *was* delivered "once and for all" to the saints (Jude 3 VOICE). *But its oral influence ("the big forgot") must never be overlooked or minimized if we wish to experience a richer grasp* of the spoken-written words of God. Oral residue remains from Genesis to Revelation. It is after all, the *spoken*-written words of God.

Blindness can be much more than physical. Blindness can encompass the literary. It goes deeper—it encompasses our foundational assumptions. Too many Bible interpreters blinded by print bias have missed the oral-aural implications of how Scripture was conceived, composed, communicated, and communally discussed around the diverse ancient rhetorical-driven Mediterranean cultures. Loss of textual appeal, impact, and meaning result.

The God Who Speaks

Habakkuk asks: "What use is an idol shaped by its maker?" His answer? "*It is nothing but* an image cast in metal; it teaches deception. For a *foolish* idol-maker puts faith in his own creation." Then comes the clincher, "a god that cannot speak" (Hab 2:18 VOICE [emphasis original]).[85] While its maker

---

84. Van der Toorn, *Scribal Culture*, 218.
85. See also 1 Kgs 18:26, 28; Ps 115; Isa 46:7; Jer 10:5.

could talk to the powerless piece of pewter being fashioned, the breathless idol could *not* talk back to its maker.

How drastically different the Speaking One (Heb 12:25)! *He spoke and he speaks!* He desires to communicate to and through his highest creation. His spoken words—from whispered to roared (Exod 19:19) often tied to geographical areas, demonstrate not only his mighty creative power, but also his desire for an intimate relationship with us.

Moses writes, "*At first* the earth lacked shape and was totally empty, and a dark *fog* draped over the deep while God's spirit-wind hovered over the surface of the *empty* waters. *Then there was the voice of God*" (Gen 1:2 VOICE [emphasis original]). Moses later reveals how the Speaking One spoke with him "face-to-face, just as a friend speaks to another friend" (Exod 33:11 VOICE). The Speaking One voiced the *first* word *and* he will always voice the *last* word with lots of speaking in between.

The spoken word resulted in a world born to house his highest creation to the lowest. Even so, the Speaking One did not demand that his highest creation obey his voice. He left that up to them, and not just individually: "Now if you will *hear My voice*, obey what I say, and keep My covenant, then you—out of all the nations of the world—will be My treasured people" (Exod 19:5 VOICE [emphasis original]). This *speaking God* through a *talking Book* points to a *talking Person* (John 5:39) who offers an intimate relationship to all who heed his voice.

The Spoken Nature of Scripture

Many literates perceive the Bible as simply a written book of words. Just as the Western Christian world virtually edited out the spiritual world and its daily influence on humanity for generations, what Paul Hiebert called the "flaw of the excluded middle,"[86] so many have edited out the influence of the spoken word. Natural speech that conveys color and texture while enhancing sensory impact on the written text was set aside for perceived loftier grammar. We call this oversight the "*fatal flaw of the excluded voice.*"[87]

Like the "big forgot," the "fatal flaw" would include pre-canon, as the canon was being constructed, and post-canon.[88] One of the geniuses of Scripture is that it is composed of both oral text and written text.

---

86. Hiebert, *Anthropological Reflections*, 189–201.

87. The title of Hans Frei's 1974 classic offers another probable possibility—*The Eclipse of Biblical Narrative*.

88. See T. Steffen and Bjoraker, *Return of Oral Hermeneutics*, 63–102.

Pre-canon: Were Moses's words authoritative *before* written down? Job's? Jeremiah's? Jesus's?[89] The apostles' teachings? God initially spoke his inspired word to and through sovereignly chosen characters.

> Were Moses's words authoritative before written? Jobs? Jeremiah's? Jesus's? The apostles' teachings?

Canon construction: The Bible was written for the ear on permanent parchments. Note the litany of oral-related words that traverse the landscape of Scripture from Genesis through Revelation: call, tell, listen, hear, heard, ear, voice, said, say, speak, spoken, silent, sing, proclaim, preach, teach, word of mouth, remember, do, follow, watch, among others.

Since the ear and the eye are integrated in canon construction, also note the litany of words in relation to the eye (which speaks metaphorically)—the visual and sensory: taste, eat, touch, look, smell, pour out, drink, offer, see. Interesting, is it not, how most literates tend to read such words without detecting their oral suggestions or significance. Too many Bible interpreters have committed the "fatal flaw"—we minimized or missed the voiced (and visual) nature of the written text.[90]

Post-canon: This includes the public reading[91] (a performance-proclamation where message and messenger fuse[92]) of Scripture (Deut 31:11–13; Josh 8:34–35; Neh 8:8–9; Col 4:16; 1 Thess 5:27; 1 Tim 4:13; Rev 1:3) in its entirety, normally followed by teaching and communal discussion. Communal accountability was expected. From start to stop, Scripture was revealed, received, recorded, rehearsed, and relayed to others through oral-aural means. Not only did eyes "read," ears "saw." Voice and vision reigned together!

---

89. In Jesus's time oral teaching was considered by most to be superior to written text. The written was considered by most a great memorization aid, not a teaching crutch. Any teacher worth his salt should be able to verbally tell what he knows, not rely on substitutionary documents. When Jesus taught on the mountainside (Matt 5:1), he "taught as one who had authority" (Matt 7:29 NIV). Did this refer to his strong reliance on oral teaching?

90. Adapted from T. Steffen, "Saving the Locals," 14.

91. Even reading in solitude (self-involved event) was not silent (Acts 8:30). Thomas Winger notes, "A Gospel can be read in an hour; an average epistle in fifteen to twenty minutes. Throughout history, the first half of the Divine Service has been devoted to hearing God's Word read to the people (the sermon being subordinate to the reading)" (Winger, "Spoken Word," 149).

92. Wendland, *Finding and Translating*, 53. *Proclamation* focuses on the past, "the original setting," while *performance* focuses on a contemporary contextual presentation that matches the moment.

Thomas Winger raises this penetrating question: "Does not modern historical-critical (or even the traditional historical-grammatical) method render the text silent, dulling its character as *proclaimed* Word of God?"[93] Too many contemporary Bible exegetes, blinded by literacy, read the written Word without ever hearing its *spoken side*. Being literary-centric, we tend to miss the hybrid nature of the *spoken*-written words of God; we tend to miss the interplay of the oral and written that reveals the living Voice. For example, John writes, "Blessings come to those who read and proclaim these words aloud.... 'Let the person who is able to hear, listen to *and follow* what the Spirit proclaims to all the churches'" (Rev 1:3; 2:7 VOICE [emphasis original]). How well do we hear the Spirit's spoken-written voice?

> How well do we hear the Spirit's spoken-written voice?

Why such a great emphasis on speech and dialogue in Scripture? Alter offers this plausible possibility, "Everything in the world of biblical narrative ultimately gravitates toward dialog—perhaps ... because to the ancient Hebrew writer's speech seemed the essential human faculty."[94]

Maybe it is time to *stop reading Scripture*! Maybe it is time to *start listening to Scripture* in various translations *until* the aural sound effects catch up with our print influence.[95]

Did not the fishermen drop what they were doing and follow Jesus when they *heard* him call them (Mark 1:20)? Does not faith come by *hearing*? Does not salvation come if you "*voice* your allegiance by *confessing* that 'Jesus is Lord'"? (Rom 10:9 VOICE [emphasis added]). Do not his sheep know his *voice*? (John 10:27). "If you belong to God's family, then why can't you hear God speak?" (John 8:47 VOICE).[96]

Listening gives animated life to frozen print; it thaws out powerful words that the author never intended to become icy. To minimize the integral nature of spoken Scripture is to *minimize its full appeal, impact, and meaning.* Is it time to "listen up"?[97]

---

93. Winger, "Orality as the Key," ix (emphasis original).

94. Alter, *Art of Biblical Narrative*, 182.

95. See Sandy, *Hear Ye the Word*.

96. We wish Zondervan's *Books of the Bible* was in an aural format as it is laid out for the oralist—no chapters, no verses, no study notes or cross-references, no columns. Individual books are arranged to make it easier to capture the unfolding biblical drama.

97. For a dramatic oral performance of the Gospel of Mark, see McLean, "Mark's Gospel."

Everett Fox warns against excluding "the spokenness of the Bible"[98] in Bible translation, which has application for Bible communicators. He argues the OT authors took into consideration rhythm and sound, thereby producing a richer read of the text (God's verbalized revelation). By "using echoes, allusions, and powerful inner structurers of sound, the text is often able to convey ideas in a manner that vocabulary alone cannot.... Translating with attention to sound therefore may help to preserve the message of the text but also its ambiguity and open-endedness."[99] Does the text have an oral ring to you? If not, has the fifteen-century "Gutenberg galaxy" (unintentionally?) been read back into antiquity, thereby minimizing what those in antiquity experienced daily?

> Does the text have an oral ring to you?

The Bible was also written, as noted, for the eye, e.g., the OT prophets used drama (Isa 20:3–4; Ezek 4:1–4). In the NT, was there a degree of performance of the text (e.g., gestures, intonation, facial expression, reaction to the audience, possible humor) when the dispatched letter carrier arrived to communicate the complete text to a covenant community? Did sight complement sound? Not only do we "read" with our eyes, we also "see" with our ears.

For far too many Bible interpreters, orality is heard through a foreign accent. Can we begin to eliminate the foreign accent? For Bible interpreters to move beyond the "big forgot" and the "fatal flaw" to experientially internalize a deeper understanding of the spoken-written words of God, a firm grasp of orality without the accent will be *required*.

What Is Orality?

"Orality" is difficult to define.[100] Many situate orality's focus strictly on the spoken. But does the term incorporate more? We agree with Lance Strate when he posits that oral cultures go beyond the spoken to "employ multisensory mnemonics [including] ritual, poetry, music, dance, pictures [and]

---

98. Fox, *Five Books of Bible*, xv.

99. Fox, *Five Books of Bible*, xi, xx.

100. See Finnegan, "What Is Orality"; Madinger, "Coming to Terms." Lynn Thigpen prefers "connected" or "relational learners" (Thigpen, *Connected Learning*). See also https://i-ostrat.com/training/.

tastes."[101] This raises some strategic questions. Should a new term be coined? Or should additions be incorporated to broaden its current definition? We have chosen the latter.

What is orality? Simply stated, *orality includes multiple variants of holistic communication embodied in relationships that create social identities.* We will now expand and unpack the definition.

By choice or circumstance, multiple variants of orality include a natural, universal, living (socially embodied), holistic (appealing, impactful, multisensory, rational) modes of relating and communicating—receiving, reflecting, remembering, rehearsing, relaying—that wed ear (sound) and eye (sight), often in an indirect circular spiral or casual fashion, all of which create social identities and ideologies individually and collectively.

Expanding the Components

By choice or circumstance, multiple variants of orality. No one chooses their parents, place of birth, or status in life; everyone inherits their own reality. For some, this means growing up without or limited access to written text.[102] They become and possibly remain to some degree oral[103] in their thinking (ideology), communication, relationships, and identity. And they do so in various ways.

Common in biblical times, some relied on those who could read to be their readers. Lynn Thigpen refers to this as "proximal literacy."[104]

Others were born and grew up with access to text and the digital-virtual-AI world but preferred a more orally based way of relating, communicating, and identifying, thereby intentionally limiting the use of text. While these groups, individually or collectively, could be tagged oralist, some chose a particular outcome while others had it conferred. Remaining at status quo in any case, however, could result in dreaded shame.

---

101. Strate, "Time-Binding in Oral Cultures," 241–42.

102. Ong calls these "primary" and "secondary" orality respectively. "I style the orality of a culture totally untouched by any knowledge of writing or print, 'primary orality.' It is 'primary' by contrast with the 'secondary orality' of present-day high-technology culture, in which a new orality is sustained by telephone, radio, television, and other electronic devices that depend for their existence and functioning on writing and print" (Ong, *Orality and Literacy*, 10–11).

103. Ong calls this "residual orality" in that it never leaves anyone entirely during their lifetime (Ong, *Orality and Literacy*, 41). Lynn Thigpen prefers to call this "persistent orality" (Thigpen, *Connected Learning*, 158).

104. Thigpen, *Connected Learning*, 115.

Oralists find themselves on a continuum between high oral reliant (HOR) to low oral reliant (LOR).[105] There is *not* a single universal expression of orality. Rather, there are *oralities*.

Include a natural, universal, living (socially embodied), holistic (appealing, impactful, multisensory, rational) modes of relating and communicating. Everyone begins as an oralist (and remains so to some degree throughout life). Babies heard their mothers speak (fetal learning) long *before* birth and learned immediately to recognize their voices post birth. Post birth, children learn orally by listening, observing, and mimicking the multiple sounds and sights, among others, that surround them. While literacy tasks participants to spell things out, orality tasks participants to speak things out through voice and the visual. All these social exhibitions include the good, the bad, and the ugly. Growing up oral is natural and universal.

Oralist learn early in life to explain—to put meat on the bones, rather than dismantle the bones. On the flip side, becoming a reader requires, in many cases, a formal education which changes one's way of thinking (logic) and relating.[106] Fragmented (in contrast to holism) abstractness following linear pathways begins to feel natural and eventually assumed universal.

What some high to low print-bound interpreters perceive as contradictions within various textual accounts, oralists may perceive as expected uniqueness and ambiguousness.[107] Many tend to swim in an oral world without recognizing the significance of its oral surroundings, and therefore have a difficult time leveraging its power.

As a medium of thought and expression, orality not only encompasses but relies on at least the five senses—hearing, smell, touch, vision, and taste—when relating, communicating, and identifying. It calls for imagination, emotion, aesthetics, gestures, among others. All this carries with it some ambiguity, mystery, anticipation, enigma, paradox, subjectiveness, but not at the expense of the cognitive. Oralists generally live in a grey world (in contrast to a black and white print world) *and* feel secure in doing so.

Orality also carries with it appeal and impact. This holistic habit of the heart activates when hearing or seeing something, reflecting on it, remembering it, or rehearsing it to others; orality arrives in a holistic, multisensory package. Part of that package includes appealing beauty.

---

105. For an excellent orality mapping tool you can take to find your orality level, see the Global Orality Mapping Project (https://gomap.pro/).

106. "Writing, commitment of the word to space, enlarges the potentiality of language almost beyond measure, and restructures thought" (Ong, *Orality and Literacy*, 7).

107. See Dunn, *Oral Gospel Tradition*; Bauckham, *Jesus and the Eyewitnesses*.

The print-oriented often minimize the power of spoken words, and hence its appeal and impact. Recall Simon the sorcerer.

We often forget that those living in biblical times understood that *words create events*. Rhoads reminds us that for the Israelites, "Naming gives power over; prophesying generates events; blessing and cursing bring about what they pronounce; and pronouncements effects a healing in the speaking. In the Gospels, Jesus announces, proclaims, names, heals, pardons, exorcizes, prophesies, blesses, curses, and warns." And he did all these "speech-acts" and more "with words that are understood as actions."[108]

Central to orality is face-to-face communal relationships where discussion and dialogue (voice and sound) reign. Such human relationships include assistance, appreciation, appeals, alerts, alarms. And they are often initiated and maintained when centered around communal gatherings that include food and drink.

Unlike other forms of communication, orality relates to our personhood. This places its focus on the internal which requires embodiment.

Relationships extend beyond the human world to include the material (e.g., colors, trees, land) and spirit worlds. As a holistic mode of communication, orality goes well beyond sound to include a rainbow of senses, symbols, and rituals. Orality finds it foundation centered in relationships. But is there more?

In *Let's Start with Jesus: A New Way of Doing Theology*, Dennis Kinlaw considers seven characteristics of personhood, e.g., people are aware of their own identity and operate within a web of relationships which he believes leads us deliberately and directly to the embodied Jesus.[109] As a member of the Trinity, Jesus demonstrated the interconnectivity of relationships (no isolation) and interpersonal communication between the three-in-one (no lone wolves). And these characteristics intentionally extend *beyond* the Triune One to humanity. Could personhood along with a relational seeking (missional), speaking God suggest the remnants of a theology of orality?

The authors appreciate William Coppedge's insight that orality is *not* a "second-tier issue" but has its origin in the Trinity. Coppedge claims:

> Orality involves both the embodied and spoken word and Jesus is the embodied, spoken Word of God. This is a far cry from the generic stereotype that interprets orality as merely a pragmatic tool for relating with people who lack literacy skills; on the contrary, orality finds its origins in the very nature of God—a

---

108. Rhoads, "Performance Criticism [pt. 2]," 169.
109. See Kinlaw, *Let's Start with Jesus*, 71–106.

relational Triune God who has communicated Himself to the world as the embodied, spoken Word.[110]

With ties to the relationally based Trinity, should not orality be appreciated as a first-tier issue?

Coppedge concludes, "Orality involves not just the spoken but also the embodied word. If there are no bodies involved, you can have print media or digital media but you cannot have oral communication."[111] This is why the Chief Character entered the world stage—to make an invisible relationship visible and viable (Col 1:15) through the incarnation (embodiment) so that he could "demonstrate the power of truth" (John 18:37 VOICE) to the nations.[112]

Orality embraces and expresses remnants of the Trinity. It recognizes and relies on a web of intimate familial relationships (son, daughter, father, bride, bridegroom) even as it distinguishes individual identity and roles. Individuals require others as life is intended to be lived out communally even as personal choices are made to fulfill specific personal roles.

Human personhood finds it roots in the eternal relational interactions and intercommunication between members of the Trinity. It even finds itself in some names of God, e.g., Abba (Father [Gal 4:6]), Qanna (jealous husband [Exod 34:14]), and El Chuwl (the God who gave you birth [Isa 43:1–3]). Orality extends far beyond being a great communication tool or even a personal or collective identification—it expresses significant aspects of the intricate inner workings of the Triune One.

It should also be noted that while the printed biblical text is mandatory, *more is required.* Why? Simply put, textuality differs from natural speech. Textuality tends to be more abstract, more dense than concrete and clear, more linear then the episodic, less expressive (pace and articulation) and repetitive then the nimble tongue voicing the moment. What is that something more that is required?

The embodiment by a member of the Trinity is required to make up the above differences. In that humans are incapable of crossing the great chasm between themselves and their Sovereign, Someone else is needed. To redeem flesh, flesh is required. The embodied Seeking One who came and walked among and with us in time and space, who spoke (voice) and acted (visual demonstration), inaugurated the possibility for such an intimate relationship. Paul reminds us, "'For in him we live and move and have our

---

110. B. Coppedge, "Towards Theology of Orality," para. 28.

111. B. Coppedge, "Towards Theology of Orality," para. 24.

112. Jesus followed the same model when discipling his disciples. He preferred living among them and showing what it means to be a true disciple rather than teaching through a list of key kingdom principles.

being'" (Acts 17:28 NIV). And that redeemed relationship mirrors that of the Triune God!

Jesus Christ is the incarnate (embodied) Speaking One who demonstrated a model to emulate before the nations throughout the centuries. It included incarnation (relate concretely through service and sacrifice [be other-centric]); it used narrative logic to close the distance between hearing and understanding by igniting the senses which kindles reason; it called for the use of metaphors, stories, symbols, and rituals (focus on the experiential); it increased understanding by creating mystery that required discovery through multiple humble communal discussions over time; it added repetition to increase preservation. Modeling the Trinity, Jesus clarified truth through incarnation, thereby providing us a model to emulate.[113]

The Trinity serves as a prototype of relationally based orality in multiple ways; orality is rooted in the relational Trinity. We foresee a theology of orality emerging from a strong historical foundation.[114]

Orality weds ear (sound) and eye (sight) often in an indirect circular-spiral or casual fashion. It weds verbal power (voice and sound) with visual power (e.g., symbols, rituals, body language[115]). Mouth, ears, and eyes work together concurrently as people relate, communicate, and identify. Mouths speak. Ears hear. Eyes see.[116] As the psalmist reminds us, "Ears to listen, eyes to see—the Eternal designed them both" (Prov 20:12 VOICE).

---

113. In *The Return of Oral Hermeneutics*, the authors included "return" in the title to draw attention to ancient Hebrew hermeneutics. In other words, the topic under discussion—oral hermeneutics—is *not* new; it has an history that goes back to first custodians of Scripture, the Israelites. In contrast, orality ties back to the Trinity.

114. Besides the life of Jesus Christ, an interesting collaborative exercise would be to construct a theology of orality by investigating the bookends of the Bible—Gen 1–2 and Rev 21–22.

115. "*Body language can expose a person's intentions:* whoever winks the eye is planning perversity; whoever purses his lips is intent on evil" (Prov 16:30 VOICE [emphasis original]). See Prov 6:13.

116. Philip Yenawine defines "visual literacy" as "the ability to find meaning in imagery. It involves a set of skills ranging from simple identification—naming what one sees—to complex interpretation on contextual, metaphoric and philosophical levels. Many aspects of cognition are called upon, such as personal association, questioning, speculating, analyzing, fact-finding, and categorizing. Objective understanding is the premise of much of this literacy, but subjective and affective aspects of knowing are equally important. Visual literacy usually begins to develop as a viewer finds his/her own relative understanding of what s/he confronts, usually based on concrete and circumstantial evidence. It eventually involves considering the intentions of the maker, applying systems for thinking and rethinking one's opinions, and acquiring a body of information to support conclusions and judgments. The expert will also express these understandings in a specialized vocabulary" (Yenawine, "Thoughts on Visual Literacy," 1).

Both ears and eyes speak metaphorically. And each operates differently. Ong notes, "Sight isolates, sounds incorporate. Whereas sight situates the observer outside what he views, at a distance, sound pours into the hearer."[117] When blended, a richness emerges that far exceeds each individual medium. And it does so in classic narrative fashion—indirectly with a repetitive theme spread out over the discussion which helps maintain harmony thus avoid shaming anyone.

Renowned Filipina anthropologist Melba Maggay would say such blending tends to occur in a downward circular-spiral "to assure a soft landing." Less frequent is chronological as episodic installments tend to be rewarded. James's letter comes to mind.

All of which create social identities and ideologies individually and collectively. The inability to read can lead to catastrophic consequences. Shattering shame often suffocates some who cannot read or have difficulty doing so.[118] A stigma prevails over these individuals and groups often exacerbated by those who can and are quick to remind them of their backwardness. This sometimes is done directly through stinging statements, sometimes indirectly, e.g., diplomas displayed prominently on a wall. Many believe they figuratively wear the emblazoned social identity tag "Shamed Illiterate" for all to see.

As a medium of thought and expression, orality creates a way of thinking, a way of relating, a social identity defined by one's place on the orality-literacy continuum. This "way of life" operates intuitively, experientially, and concretely (in contrast to the abstract) in a nonlinear, holistic-global manner discerned through repetitive demonstration and participation (in contrast to recalling abstract theory in isolation). Strongly communal in nature, orality appreciates collective face-to-face processing through participatory discussion, debate, and action. The Creator sovereignly designed part of humanity's spiritual DNA to include orality.

Isolating Influential Identifiers of Orality

Orality's major influential identifiers will now be isolated. Orality is:

- A medium of thought and expression
- Universal
- Inclusive (everyone is oral to some degree)

117. Ong, *Orality and Literacy*, 71.
118. See Thigpen, "Dark Side of Orality."

- Takes place somewhere at some time
- Social (therefore oralities evolve)
- Communal (the "public eye")
- Face-to-face
- Relational
- Character-centric
- Honor-shame–oriented (expect envy)
- Driven by narrative logic (developed in ch. 4)
- Verbal and visual text
- Participatory discussion, debate, observation, and practice
- Concrete,
- Holistic (big picture, global, metanarrative)
- Performed
- Multisensory
- Imaginative and emotional
- Ambiguous
- Mysterious
- Imitative
- Repetitive and thematic
- Circular-spiral and casual
- An offering of beauty and impact
- An unleashing of an unquenchable thirst for deeper meaning
- A collection of shared oral tradition based on communal memory

The above components and identifiers will receive further illustration and elaboration in the forthcoming chapters.

The Role of Orality in Character Theology

The next time you read Scripture, read ten verses, skip the next nine, and repeat the cycle. Why? To gain a fuller respect for the oral nature of Scripture. The poetry section comprises over 30 percent of the Bible. The narrative sections comprise over 50 percent of the Bible. Combined, around 90 percent of the Bible has strong oral underpinnings and influence. Add this to how Bible authors oralized the text for a highly oral-reliant audience, which includes the ongoing conversations within the epistles, a very different picture of Scripture begins to emerge from what most of us were taught or thought.

The prophet Ezekiel provides an excellent example of the oral nature of God's communication to Israelites who perceived Ever Present as distant as the expatriate Israelites remained captive in a foreign land. Ezekiel experienced three visions (1–3; 8–11; 40–48) that made him fall on his face and that in a foreign land demonstrated the glory of God was not confined to a distant temple as the despondent Israelites believed. In each speaking vision, three things were reiterated as a memory enhancer for replication: 1) what was seen (visual), 2) what was heard (auditory), and 3) what Ezekiel was to say (telling).

> What level of paper and print is necessary for their formal and informal training to be respected in the local and larger communal contexts?
>
> What is considered *authoritative communication* in surrounding social settings?

Ever Present's oral communication (showing and speaking) with Ezekiel (required listening and interpretation) and the exiled Israelites (required listening and interpretation) no doubt brought hope amidst ongoing despair as they pondered the lessons being learned surrounding their exile. Ever Present had not forgotten his covenant people even as he required their restorative cleansing by those they were chosen to serve.

Ever Present answered Israel's question—where is Ever Present?—by answering the question *who is God* rather than *what is God*. Shared oral tradition emerged in Ever Present's methodological presentation of the visions rather than written words. Visions spoke.

To learn, some must sing, some must sit, some must dance, some must draw, some must touch, some must smell, some must cook, some must "taste and see" (Ps 34:8 NIV). These require the intuitive, the experiential, the sensory, the pageantry, the participatory—precisely what orality offers. Orality, having Trinitarian origins, layers the concrete, the multisensory side of humanity without bypassing the rational.

There is a reason why God chose those of an ancient Semitic language and culture to become the canon custodians. The language is rich, imagistic, poetic, relational, and eventually became the Bible Jesus read. The Hebrew culture is subjective, holistic, concrete, visual. Note the vivid imagery that saturates Scripture:[119] visions, covenants, the tabernacle, temples, memorials, symbols (trees, temples), and rituals (Passover, Purim, foot washing, the Lord's Supper). No wonder the Hebrew language-culture was chosen for around two-thirds of Scripture.

There is a reason why over half of the Bible is presented in narrative. Stories reign.

There is a reason for the strong focus on barrenness, genealogies, and the family of God. Relationships reign.

There is a reason why the songs of Moses, Miriam, Hannah, Jonah, among others, were incorporated into the canon.[120] There is a reason musical instruments are found early in Scripture (Gen 4:21). There is a reason why Psalms is the third longest book in the Bible (by Hebrew word count) and Jesus's most quoted book.[121] The emotional reigns.

There is a reason why Jesus became the firstborn (supreme status) and the God-man. A written announcement alone would not cut it. Rather, a vast heavenly choir descended from the heavens praising God, sending

---

119. "God is not a bundle of concepts, just as we human beings are not. God is not made up of ideas, and neither are we human beings. Concepts and ideas can be made and discarded in ways that stories cannot. Theology constructed on concepts and ideas can imagine because of their image-making power.... To deny the image-making power of humans is to deny the creation story of God creating, not in God's concept, but in God's image. The power to think in images, to construct images, is a God-given power" (Song, *In Beginning Were Stories*, 70). "The Bible is not written in terms of modern science or philosophy. Largely, the Bible is written in the pregnant language of imagery" (Jordan, *Through New Eyes*, 17).

120. "Tell *stories* of His great deeds through songs of joy" (Ps 107:22 VOICE [emphasis original]). The depiction of Scripture, creeds or confessions through instrumental music, drumming, chanting, singing, sculpting, dramatizing, stained glass windows, all add further levels of meanings as they offer powerful pictorial proclamation and sound.

Attempting to restore the dignity of the Lakota people, redeem his culture, and contextualize the gospel, Larry Salway, copastor of He Sapa New Life in Rapid City, South Dakota, says this about the power of drums: "Using the drum. Feeling the drum, the heartbeat of the Native American and the heartbeat as you feel the thud and thud of the drum down into your feet, and it reverberates into your soul and very spirit" (Salway, "General Conferences 2012" [time stamp unavailable]). See also Arrington, *Songs of Lisu Hills*, where Arrington discovered two books influenced the continuation of ministry begun by J. O. Fraser in 1914—the Bible and the hymnal. While the missionaries stressed *personal* Bible study, the Lisu learned and maintained most of their theology for generations through the *corporate singing* of hymns (Deut 31:19). Singing praises to God not only opens prison doors physically and mentally, it also multiplies learning (Acts 16:25–26). And it activates worship through songs for the journey (Ps 120–34).

121. See Kranz, "Word Counts."

some surprised smelly shepherds on their way to Bethlehem. Incarnation reigns.

There is a reason why God is called "Father." There is a reason why the Jesus followers are called "children of God" and "sons and daughters of God." There is a reason why large groups assembled on multiple occasions. Family and community reign.

What's the reason? The Creator reflects himself in and through his highest creation which is much more than the cognitive, abstractness, written words; it also includes the sensory, mystery, beauty, the concrete.

Characters expand meaning *beyond* written words as they are *experienced* events. As John Piper purports, "Words and the realities they signify are not the same. The word kiss in not a kiss. The word happiness is not happiness. The word faith or believe is not the experiential reality required for salvation."[122] Is this why the Preacher calls Scripture "words of delight" (Eccl 12:10 ESV)?

There is also a reason why God's word did not remain *only* oral. Time, culture, forgetfulness, stubbornness, rebellion, among others, have a way of eroding and erasing memories of his words. Written texts that could survive generations and geography were therefore necessary. Nevertheless, those with high print-privileged backgrounds, circling back to Clanchy's quote at the beginning of the chapter, have had difficulty appreciating what preceded literacy—the "big forgot"—orality.[123] Spreading the "speak" alone, however, was *insufficient*.

The spoken words of God eventually became the written words of God. A hybrid of oral and written, sight and sound, ear and eye, voice and vision, verbal and print, suggestion and statement, message and manuscript resulted. In God's wisdom, humanity received not just the *written* words of God, but rather the *spoken-written* words of God. Not only did this meet a need in antiquity, it also meets a need today—it provides contemporary Bible interpreters another sound way to consider hermeneutics and theology.

If present-day Bible communicators can perceive this hybrid *not as a rival but as complementary*,[124] the spoken-written Scripture and its Author, the Voice, will receive increased awareness and application. Such insight opens the door to the hallways of oral hermeneutics and character theology.

---

122. Piper, *What is Saving Faith*, 89–90.

123. Clanchy, *Memory to Written Record*, 4.

124. "So, brothers and sisters, *all you need to do now is* stand firm and hold tight to the line of teachings we have passed on to you, whether in person or in a letter" (2 Thess 2:15 VOICE [emphasis original]); "Blessed is the one who reads the words of this prophecy, and blessed are those who hear it and take to heart what is written in it, because the time is near" (Rev 1:3 NIV).

Figure 3.1 accentuates two major distinctives between the multiple variations of textual and oral hermeneutics in practice today—orality ("big forgot") and voice ("fatal flaw"). Where would you place your preferred hermeneutic model in this schematic? How well does it match the interpretation preferences of the host audience? The oral accents of Scripture?

Should Paper and Print Mix with Oral?

Coppedge's research in *African Literacies and Western Oralities?* raises critical questions for Western oral practitioners, particularly purist, when storying in the Majority World. What level of paper and print is necessary for the recipient's informal and formal training to be respected in the local and larger communities? Is a book more than a book? An outline more than an outline? What is considered *authoritative communication* in surrounding social settings?

The answer to such questions may become for some the "middle way" noted in the previous chapter. Ignoring such questions can easily be perceived by the Majority World as the Minority World advancing a new form of colonialism to deprive them of social status and potential material gain. Some in the Minority World, however, will perceive a press towards orality as a step backwards from the required printed text. Do your cultural homework and match the model to the moment.

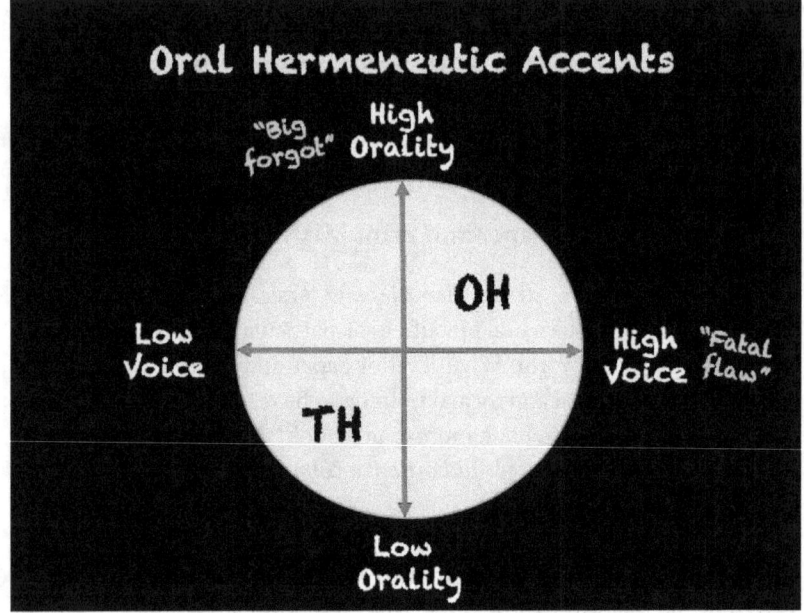

Figure 3.1. Oral Hermeneutic Accents

Looking Back and Ahead

How do you make God laugh? Tell him about your favorite hermeneutic and resultant theology. Has the broad and constructive role of orality and voice in Scripture, the third forerunner of character theology, become the "big forgot" and the "fatal flaw" within today's hermeneutic and theological guilds? Have interpreters minimized the value of the voice? How strongly required are the skill sets (oral, print, digital) for effective interpretation and communication in the twenty-first century?

> Has the broad and constructive role of orality and voice in Scripture become the "big forgot" and the "fatal flaw" in today's hermeneutic guilds? Today's theologies?

Since Gutenberg in the 1440s (with a mechanized version of the Chinese manual printing process some six hundred years later) made printed materials readily available, followed by the Scientific Revolution and

Western Enlightenment in the sixteenth and seventeenth centuries, how do we view orality? Have we joined with many others down through the centuries who considered oral-aural—the norm since creation—to now be obsolete, premodern, pre-logic, "an antique in the attic of a discarded past"?[125] What is your theology of orality? See fig. 3.2.

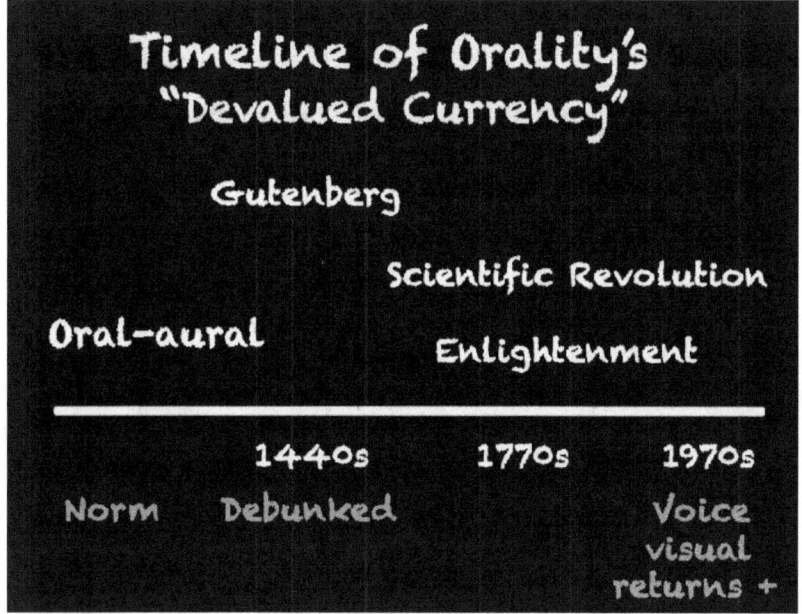

Figure 3.2. Time Line of Orality's "Devalued Currency"

Thanks to the debunked role of stories in much of the educational world, the oral-aural became perceived as "devalued currency," synonymous with fiction, for entertainment, for children, for the unsophisticated outside urban settings; it certainly was not related to objective, precise theology in any way.[126] Newbigin notes the West's capitulation to the Enlightenment resulted in a "shift from a way of seeing truth as located in a narrative, to a way of seeing truth as located in timeless, law-like statements."[127]

> What is your theology of orality?

125. Bradt, *Story as a Way*, 35.
126. T. A. Steffen, *Reconnecting God's Story*, 11.
127. Newbigin, "Gospel and Our Culture."

By the late seventies, early eighties, and driven by postmodernism, orality became the "comeback kid" in many major disciplines, such as psychology, medicine, theology, missions. The print barnacle build up was slowly being chipped away. Social media continues its unrelenting surge, returning orality (plus digital, virtual) to be the new norm. Even so, tensions continue. Present "propositions and pedagogy are based on more than preference; they are far too often based on unexamined underlying cultural assumptions."[128]

Can today's Bible interpreters learn from and allow for Scripture's sensory claims in antiquity to influence today's hermeneutics and theologies? Will Scripture make more sense to today's audiences when proclaimed-performed, heard/seen, interpreted, dialogued, debated, and retold as story-based characters?

Boomershine reminds us that "the sensory registers that were activated by the performance of biblical compositions were predominantly auditory throughout the period from 1000 BCE to 500 CE. Auditory address was the intention of ancient authors."[129] Today's audiences will also appreciate a return to the sensory.

Just as one cannot grasp the fullness of Jesus without a firm grasp of the OT, so one cannot grasp the fullness of the written Scripture without a firm grasp of orality. Why? Because of orality's major role in canon construction and communication.

Helpful Sources

Boomershine, *First-Century Gospel Storytellers and Audiences*

W. Coppedge, *African Literacies and Western Oralities?*

Ong, *Orality and Literacy*

Thigpen, *Connected Learning*

This takes us to the fourth forerunner of character theology—oral hermeneutics. What is the role of *oral hermeneutics* in character theology?

---

128. T. Steffen, "Saving the Locals," 23.

129. Boomershine, *First-Century Gospel Storytellers*, 123.

Reflection Questions

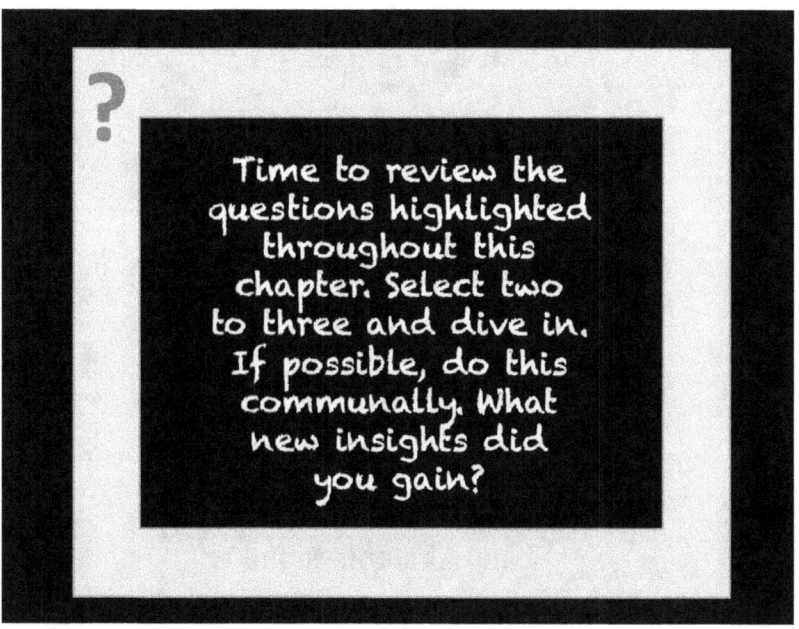

4

The Role of Oral Hermeneutics

What will be the hermeneutics of the electronic age? . . .
The underlying cultural hermeneutic in digital culture
is the priority of experience rather than concepts.

—THOMAS BOOMERSHINE

Orality studies represent an exciting, rapidly developing area
of research and application, one that is not just the "new
kid on the block" in the interrelated macro-fields of Bible
interpretation, translation, transmission, and reception.

—ERNST WENDLEND

Is hermeneutics static, or is it dynamic in the sense
that it can change as methods of interpretation
are adapted to different cultural contexts?

—ELIZABETH MBURU

A FILIPINA ASKED THE following of her expatriate professor in a nonformal class in Manila: "I have very benefited from exploring passages like Genesis 1, to circle important words and phrases about God's ways, to underline important ideas. . . . But how do I help them circle and underline since they cannot read?"[1]

A graduate theology student for one of my (Tom's) US classes wrote: "I have been taught how to outline and analyze Scripture, but I have not been taught how to capture the drama of story and communicate truth through it."

Have Bible professors done these students from two different and distinct parts of the world a great disservice? Those they serve?

Everyone interprets! Sometimes individually. Sometimes corporately. Sometimes the interpretation is in the ballpark. Sometimes outside. Sometimes in between. A Bible study is no different. But there are different types of Bible studies.

While interpreting requires telling, first and foremost it requires *listening*. For those formally trained in Bible, listening first to the text is necessary. Then it is time to tell, to systematically lay out the interpretation of the story—authorship, historical background, meaning of key words and phrases, headliners, outline, and so forth. This gives the green light to those with the spiritual gift of teaching and years of training to communicate the multilayered nuances of thought aggregated through the centuries as they watch heads shaking and smiling in agreement. Some call this "Bible study."

We propose a different model, one that does not reject the spiritual gift of teaching but is much more communal, much more participatory, much more oral-oriented. We prefer a different emphasis captured in part by "Bible discussion."

Oh, isn't that where everyone—the non-formally trained—pools their collective Bible ignorance? Isn't that where a bunch of amateurs gather to—well let's be honest here—insult the text through spreading theological hobby horses verified by prooftexts often taken out of context, reflect a certain doctrinal framework, and/or riding off into unfamiliar theological sunsets? Isn't that where the role of the spiritual-gifted teacher gets trampled or certainly minimized?

While all that certainly has resulted, it does not necessarily have to be the case. There are those who read Scripture but need someone to help them make sense of it—think Philip and the Ethiopian dignitary (Acts 8). Using the role of facilitator along with character-centric questions, spiritual-gifted teachers can turn Bible studies into fruitful, memorable, communal Bible discussions—a model that rings true for many in today's world who prefer to participate and contribute.

Can storyteller-interpreters see themselves as developers of storyteller-interpreters through character-centric questions? When should correction

---

1. Worthington, "Orality's Breadth and Depth," 12.

take a backseat to challenge? When should asking a question of their question replace answering it? Is this not the real business of kingdom business?

Could the terms "Bible discussion" or "Bible study" be more focused so that a specific emphasis results even while retaining communal discussion and debate? Could it be more contemporized for today's world?

We propose an alternative—"engaging Bible characters" (EBC). EBC discussion groups (EBCs) led by Bible interpreters encourages communal discussion *centered around Bible characters*. Its goal? Thick theologizing that glorifies God through actionized, godly wisdom.

Rerouting Routine

But have we missed a step? Such communal interaction and discussion will also highlight what Larry Caldwell calls "ethnohermeneutics," i.e., interpretation models that *already* reside in a specific culture.[2] Caldwell raises several questions we seldom ask, but should: What are their interpretation methods? How appropriate are these when interpreting the narrative sections of Scripture? These questions should be asked of the storyteller's interpretive models as well. What interpretive insights do the answers to these questions provide?

Interestingly, the older some get, the more stuck in ruts they become. Routine sets in. Unlike children who are constantly experimenting as they try to figure out life "under the sun," they tend to settle into their securities. This includes theology and religious tradition. They've had sufficient life adventures. Their sense of wonder wains.

Shepherding sheep in the backcountry of Bethlehem can easily foster routine as well. That routine was shattered one solitary night when an angel surprisingly appeared. Terrifying! So much for daily routine.

> Could the terms "Bible discussion" or "Bible study" be more focused so that a specific emphasis results even while retaining communal discussion and debate?

Standard smelly shepherds were about to be the *first* to hear the greatest message Yahweh had promised to the world centuries prior. But instead of cowering, conviction-based courage pushed them forward to visit where one of the smaller clans of Judah resided (Mic 5:2) but where the *biggest event*

---

2. Caldwell, "Towards the New Discipline." See also his seven-step model in *Doing Bible Interpretation*.

ever to take place in the history of the world had just occurred. Wonder, an invitation into the unknown, won the day over fear. And the rest is HisStory.

Entering an EBC discussion group can be a terrifying experience. Some may feel intimidated or too embarrassed to participate, especially for those from strongly shame-oriented communities. They must be reminded that worry cancels out wonder; that courage is not the absence of fear. Better to follow the example of smelly shepherds. Everyone benefits.

For the theologically tutored who think communal ignorance is sure to be perpetuated, we ask you to humor us for the moment to see if God will unexpectedly appear again. Like the shepherds, see if the reader can regain that childlike faith that breaks routine.

"Don't be afraid." After all, none of us knows or has experienced everything in life. None of us comes close to fully understanding God. But for those who continue to ask, seek, and knock, many surprises await.

Can we allow that childlike wonder—a faith invitation into the unknown—to again provide possible new avenues to experience actionized wisdom in work and worship? In ways to serve with diligence and devotion the underserved? Our formal theological education may even be expanded and deepened. Routine may be replaced with a new respect for Mystery's wonder (Eph 3:4).

Wendland asked this perceptive question in 2010: "*So why is research in orality (and associated fields) becoming such an increasingly influential issue in contemporary hermeneutics?*"[3] This chapter will begin to answer Wendland's question.

Other related questions that will help guide this chapter include, do people have to analyze grammar to be able to interpret Scripture? How could orality help improve Bible interpretation? How could characters? What are the limits of textual hermeneutics? Oral hermeneutics? What happens when the wrong hermeneutic model is used on a genre?

To answer these and related questions we begin with propositional logic, show why narrative logic and oral hermeneutics are required for Scripture's narratives, define and distinguish oral hermeneutics—the fourth forerunner of character theology—and isolate its influential identifiers. We conclude by contrasting the integrative nature of textual and oral hermeneutics. Character theology requires a new hermeneutic—an oral hermeneutic.

---

3. Wendland, "Studying, Translating, and Transmitting," 21 (emphasis added).

Propositional Logic Prevails in the Academy

Centuries ago, the integration of philosophy and science laid the foundation for a preferred hermeneutic in the West—the historical-grammatical. Influenced by science, the Enlightenment, the Information Age (mechanical, electrical, digital, virtual-AI), and Western modernity,[4] scholars and students through the ages have attempted to reduce speculative textual meaning through detached compiling, analyzing, propositionalizing, and classifying.

Not only is it a preferred hermeneutic in the West, many consider it universal for all cultures and all genres of Scripture. Will Brooks and Abner Chou are representative:

> It is only through the study of the words, grammar, and syntax used by the original author that readers can determine the meaning he desired to communicate. For this reason, the grammatical-historical method of interpretation is the one that is best suited to an author-oriented approach to interpretation.[5]

Chou, after analyzing how the OT interprets the OT and the NT use of the OT, concludes, "Their faithful hermeneutic provides us the certainty that the way we were traditionally taught to interpret the Bible is the method the Bible upholds. Literal-grammatical-historical hermeneutics is not a modern formulation but how the biblical writers read the Scriptures."[6] A short stroll down Western Hermeneutic Lane is essential.

> Can storyteller-interpreters see themselves as developers of storyteller-interpreters through character-centric questions?

Bernard Ramm helped lead the way in this theoretical experiment when he made two claims in his classic *The Christian View of Science and Scripture*. These theorems influenced generations of exegetes, including today's. They include: "Training in logic and science forms excellent background for exegesis. . . . Systematic teaching of Scripture is the Scriptures'

---

4. One wonders if inerrancy, based on a scientific model birthed in modernity, would be a moot point under orality?

5. Brooks, *Interpreting Scripture across Cultures*, 131. In relation to Bible stories, Brooks would combine narrative analysis with the grammatical-historical (134).

6. Chou, *Hermeneutics of Biblical Writers*, 23.

final intention."[7] Charles Hodge's and Lewis Sperry Chafer's multivolume works on systematic theology give testament to this theory.

Chafer defined systematic theology as "the collecting, scientifically arranging, comparing, exhibiting, and defending of all facts from any and every source concerning God and his works."[8] The dean of twentieth-century American evangelical theologians, Carl Henry, aptly summarizes, "As an achievement of the Holy Spirit's inspiration, Scripture presents us with the remarkable phenomenon of a canon concerned primarily with the propositional disclosure of God. . . . In brief, the Bible is a propositional revelation of the unchanging truth of God."[9]

The resultant systematic theology, morphing through various "criticisms" over the generations, continues to rule the theological guilds and Bible interpreters globally. This includes, sadly, the oral Majority World, not to mention a fast-growing population of oralists in the West due to social media.[10]

And why not? Objectivity, cause and effect, linear thinking, facts and figures, checklists, taxonomies, deductive analysis, granularity with specificity, clarity and predictability, measurability, compilation and categorization, individualism, verification and validation, propositional logic, truth, all aided by chapter and verse numbers, footnotes, cross-references, reigned. A perfect hand-in-glove fit for a specific era.[11]

Correct interpretation was guaranteed. If science is settled, so can interpretation that uses detached, objective scientific methods. Former president of Wheaton College J. Oliver Buswell elaborates, "Theology has its own laws, and the theologian merely observes these, confident that their observation will yield doctrinal fidelity to God's truth."[12] Some writers, podcasters, and publishers today continue to exult science's valuable, howbeit limited, praises. The "modern" mind has its limitations.

---

7. Ramm, *Christian View of Science*, 53, 155.

8. Chafer, *Prolegomena, Bibliology, Theology Proper*, x.

9. Henry, *God Who Speaks*, 96, 457.

10. See A. Crouch, "Return of Shame."

11. Brueggemann is helpful here: "Interpretation informed by historical awareness was such a close appropriate match for our context of modernity for the past two hundred years that *we have scarcely been able to notice that the connection is culture-bound and did not always exist*. That is, scientific positivism *did not always determine* the shape of knowledge" (Brueggemann, *Texts under Negotiation*, 1 [emphasis added]).

12. We have lost the citation for this quote.

Philosophy Prevails

Most of us grew up using propositional logic, a science-based philosophy that pressures the Bible interpreter to see all text as informational. From this perspective, evidence can be extracted and condensed into a discernible single, objective, abstract, theoretical idea that synthesizes the topic under discussion. Just as the authors of Western Enlightenment-based logic[13]—one that must be formally learned requiring regular usage to retain usefulness—assume it to be universal, singular, and normal, so we have been socialized to think the same. Usually taken for granted and unquestioned, the underlying assumptions are seldom considered much less challenged.[14] Most Bible interpreters have been steeped in rational debate.

In relation to the interpretation of a Bible story, it seeks a single, objective, compressed idea that captures the author's main concern, doing so often through contrasts and contradictions. "And the moral of the story is . . ." The idea becomes a timeless, universal divine truth or ethic in contrast to an immediate local truth that orality would propose. There is little to no room for local expression.[15]

Propositional logic driven by science and applied through textual hermeneutics with all its variants, digs deep into words, syntax, and grammar with the goal of distilling a single objective interpretation that results

---

13. Like the term "theology," we often use "logic" as if our understanding of it is the real thing—no need for a qualifier. Yet when referring to a different (think inferior) type of logic (and theology), it requires a qualifier; it becomes Asian logic or Latin logic or . . .

14. Not all, however, are impressed with such logic. Lin Yutang (1885–1976) writes, "Western men were born 'with knives in their brains'; the weapon of logic was too sharp; it cut up almost everything which came into contact with it and offended the truth, which was always whole" (Yutang, *From Pagan to Christian*, 105).

15. Referencing Stephen Toulmin, Brueggemann writes that the move from oral to written helped establish the perception that the written was more reliable. Why? Because it was "a move from the particular to the *universal*, so that real truth is what is true everywhere; a move from local to *general*, so that real truth had to be the same from locale to locale; and a move from the timely to the *timeless*, so that the real is the unchanging" (Brueggemann, *Texts under Negotiation*, 5 [emphasis original]). There was no room for local contextualization to be considered authoritative. Authority came from print now invested in the now powerful heirs of the Enlightenment. But is it an either/or? A culturally preferred rather than a norm? See Bradt, *Story as a Way*, 125–29. Paul Ricoeur adds, "When we discover that there are several cultures instead of just one and consequently at the time when we acknowledge the end of a sort of cultural monopoly, be it illusory or real, we are threatened with destruction by our own discovery. Suddenly it becomes possible that there are just *others*, that we ourselves are an 'other' among others" (Ricoeur, *History and Truth*, 278 [emphasis original]).

in the "plain sense"[16] of a text. This model assumes subjectivism, relativism, mysticism should and will be avoided.

> "So why is research in orality (and associated fields) becoming such an increasingly influential issue in contemporary hermeneutics?"

Something else happens. With a strong focus on siloed fragments, the big picture, the grand narrative (the narrative behind the stories), tends to get lost in the shuffle.

But has the world moved beyond science-based propositional logic that seeks atomized preciseness outside the hard sciences? Has a former era been replaced with a new era? Has postmodernism driven by social media in a world of connectivity cast suspicion on a former era—modernism?

Rather than the historical-grammatical and its favorite theology—systematic theology—being the basis for Bible interpretation and life, are there other distinguishing characteristics that mark the dawning of a new era? Among others, could these include: subjectivity, simulation, emotions, imagination, events, unified, circular thinking, characters, collectivism, ambiguity, coreness, aesthesis? Could such help to correct a deficient past hermeneutic? Add more life to present wooden theology? Is there a fading fascination with the facts on file? Of truth? Of trust? Could such an addition make Bible colleges and seminaries more inviting?[17] More relevant?

N. T. Wright advances the historical timeline to the present: "What happened with the Enlightenment is the *denarrativization* of the Bible. And then within postmodernity, people tried to pay attention to the narrative without paying attention to the fact that it's a true story."[18] Can Bible interpreters avoid the pitfalls of both eras yet take advantage of the complementary and corrective characteristics of each?

16. David Cooper (1886–1965), founder of the Biblical Research Society, wrote, "When the plain sense of Scripture makes common sense, seek no other sense; therefore, take every word at its primary, ordinary, usual, literal meaning. Unless the facts of the immediate context, studied in the light of related passages and axiomatic and fundamental truths, indicate clearly otherwise." See "The Golden Rule of Interpretation" at http://www.biblicalresearch.info/.

17. "More than a tenth of final-year students felt that their college experience reflected an 'over-intellectual approach to theology' and a 'lack of practical connection to life or ministry, with virtually no connection with the secular world which is a large part of the context of lived Christianity'" (Hibbert and Hibbert, *Training Missionaries*, loc. 3622).

18. N. T. Wright, as quoted in Stafford, "Mere Mission," 40.

If a new era now exists, and we believe it does, how has it impacted hermeneutics? Do moviegoers anxiously await the first conversation so they can begin to analyze the grammar to determine the movie's meaning?

> Has the world moved beyond science-based propositional logic that seeks preciseness? Has a former failed era been replaced with a new era?

What should hermeneutics look like in a postmodern, post-Christian world? Post-fact world? Will another form of logic emerge? Will another type of theology emerge in this era as systematic theology did in a previous era? Could there be an additional type of hermeneutic that offers today's world recognizability, respect, and routine, as the historical-grammatical did in a former era?

If so, what could replace a more orderly, scientific, rational, objective, comprehensive layout of Christian thought? What nuanced characteristics of God may emerge? Of the spirit world? Of humanity?

Narratives Require a Narrative Logic

As noted in chapter 2, the narrative genre dominates the landscape of Scripture. If that genre is to be respected, the propositional logic most of us have been trained in will require reconsideration.

It is difficult to shrink a story into a single one-liner. Why? Because stories are *not* typically designed for one-liners.[19] The nature of orality is

---

19. Leland Ryken and Tremper Longman conclude: "Literary texts are irreducible to propositional statements and single meanings. A propositional statement of a theme can never be a substitute or even the appointed goal of experiencing a literary text" (Ryken and Longman, *Complete Literary Guide*, 17). Craig Blomberg observes: "(a) the introductory or concluding statements usually offer only weak generalizations which can scarcely account for the detail and vitality of the parables themselves; (b) a good parable (like a good joke!) will make its point so clearly on its own that subsequent explanation is unnecessary and demeaning; and (c) as metaphors, parables are not able to be paraphrased propositionally—the meaning is inherent in the form and is lost when one-sentence summaries are formulated. . . . Parables as metaphors are *performative* rather than *propositional*—utterances which do not convey information but perform an action. . . . Each parable makes one main point per main character—usually two or three in each case—and these main characters are the most likely elements within the parable to stand for something other than themselves" (Blomberg, *Interpreting the Parables*, 91–92, 137, 163 [emphasis original]). Hosea 12:10 reads, "I've spoken to the prophets; I've given them many visions, and I've told you parables through them" (VOICE). And of course, Jesus spoke often in parables. Outlines, summaries, or distilled themes can never imprint a story or proverb fully on one's soul.

to expand through aggregation rather than contract through deduction. Meaning accumulates as characters drive the plot (main and subplots) from scene to scene in search of some semblance of a satisfactory solution; the *complete story becomes the meaning*.[20]

Also, story's metaphorical,[21] mystical nature prefers poetic space, constant revisits, and continual reevaluation. Additionally, it attempts to synthesize an accumulative plot-driven story propelled by characters with complex and often competing personalities (and sometimes different cultures, e.g., Joseph, Moses, Esther, Daniel, Paul). The distinctive narrative genre necessitates a drastically different type of logic—a narrative logic.

> What should hermeneutics look like in a postmodern, post-Christian world?

Narrative logic, which is clothed in relational characters, learned informally, and used naturally, challenges Bible interpreters to discern possible timeless truths of a story that are more subjective in nature.[22] It does so as listeners search for probability (coherence, i.e., the story hangs together culturally) and fidelity (the story rings true culturally).[23]

While numerous forms of logic exist,[24] we will summarize two (see fig. 4.1). One focuses on relationships, the other on reason. One focuses on mystery, the other on science. One focuses on ambiguity, the other on precision. One focuses on meaning, the other on words. One lands on *coreness*, the other on *correctness*. One allows for *multiple truths* within a single story, the other limits to a *single truth*. One directs attention exclusively to the

---

20. "In African storytelling, the whole story carries the message and every part of it has a role to play. In other words, there is no clear identification of the 'moral' of the story. One cannot merely seek out the punchline to understand the message of the story. Storytelling is therefore not linear but cyclical linear; the story does progress forward but not in a straight line" (Mburu, *African Hermeneutics*, 119).

21. For Paul Ricoeur, metaphor, which focuses more on sentences than words, creatively connects two known entities that morphs into a new unconventional but catchy outcome. This new outcome (metaphor) offers a "surplus of meaning" (oral layering of the sensory) to the written text or discourse (when someone says something to somebody about something) (Ricoeur, *Interpretation Theory*).

22. Securing "pure" subjectivity (or objectivity) may be a great goal but not typically possible through human efforts.

23. Fisher, *Human Communication as Narration*, 47.

24. See Hiebert, *Transforming Worldviews*, 39–44; T. Steffen and Bjoraker, *Return of Oral Hermeneutics*, 145–46.

narrative sections of Scripture, the other to *multiple genres*. One is *informally* learned, the other *formally*. One is more *multi- and interdisciplinary* than the other. In relation to hermeneutics applied to the narrative sections of Scripture, narrative logic is sadly stingily utilized.

In the application of narrative logic to Bible stories, the interpreter's goal is to discover the Divine Author's authoritative spiritual truth and/or ethics communicated through the interaction of the words and works of chosen characters. Such metaphorical, mystery-driven plots that demand personal-collective choices, when explored through narrative logic, lends itself to multiple associations and applications. Thomas Stallter accurately summarizes, "We can control information, but we cannot control mystery."[25]

Welcome to the ambiguous, obscure, creative nature of narrative logic. Is there any virtue in vagueness? Is ambiguity part of God's purpose to demonstrate his matchless distinctiveness and our limited humanness?

Yes, misinterpretation is *always* possible. While Scripture is canonized, not so our interpretations. Interpreter *beware*, be *humble*, be *tentative*, be *ever learning*, be willing to *share* the interpretive load, *not* shoulder it all.

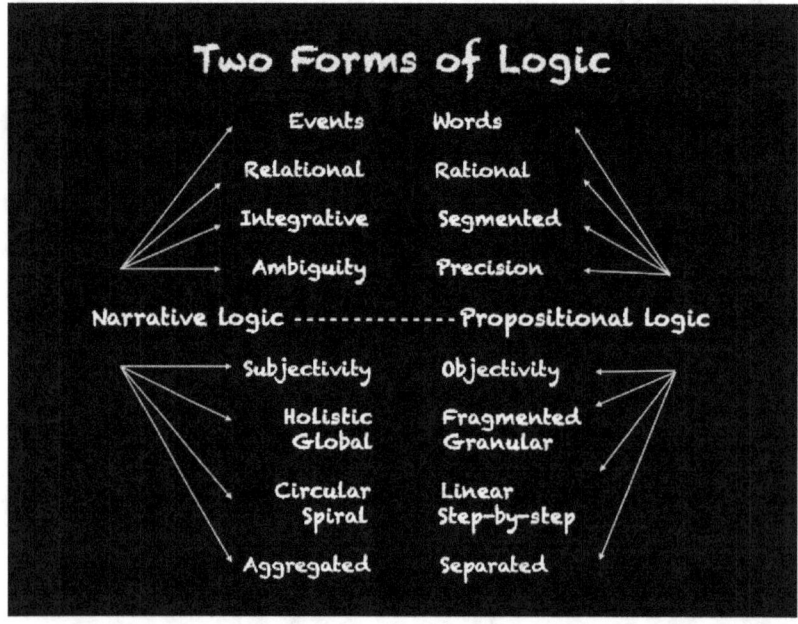

Figure 4.1. Two Forms of Logic

---

25. Stallter, *Gap between God*, 92.

Historical-Grammatical Plus

In the late seventies, and building through the nineties, the "historical-grammatical" hermeneutic received an additional descriptive—a greatly needed one—"literary." Bible interpreters were offered a "historical-grammatical-literary" hermeneutic. McGrath provides some backstory:

> The resurgence of theological interest in narrative since the late 1970s reflects many intertwined insights. Perhaps the most important is the realization that theologians and biblical interpreters who allowed themselves to be unduly influenced by the ideology of the Enlightenment suppressed what is actually the dominant and most characteristic literary form of the Christian Bible: the narrative.[26]

Many other scholars, such as Meir Sternberg, Hans Frei, Werner Kelber, Leland Ryken, James Wilhoit, Tremper Longman, realized the Bible was much more than a *code book*, it was also a *case book*; they realized genres, including narrative, must be respected if fuller, more appealing, impactful meaning were to emerge. Sadly, one does not hear much about the "literary" add-on today.

Narratives Require an Oral Hermeneutic

The narrative genre, when respected, requires not only a certain type of logic, but also a certain type of hermeneutic, the fourth forerunner of character theology—an oral hermeneutic.[27] Grounded in communal (leaders and led) oral exegesis, an oral hermeneutic will help secure its richest interpretive worth; it "*offers a fuller understanding of not only the cognitive but also the affective/cultural/psychological/motivational context the author had in mind.*"[28]

Genre must be respected if a text's fullest meaning, appeal, and impact are to manifest itself.[29] Genre, therefore, should determine the appropriate

---

26. McGrath, *Narrative Apologetics*, 39–40.

27. See T. Steffen and Bjoraker, *Return of Oral Hermeneutics*, 14–18. Related terms include: narrative hermeneutics, relational hermeneutics, heart hermeneutics, pedagogical hermeneutics. On the apologetic side—narrative apologetics, literary apologetics, experiential apologetics, cultural apologetics.

28. T. Steffen and Bjoraker, *Return of Oral Hermeneutics*, xxiii (emphasis original).

29. Jerome Bruner captures the broadness of narrative's persuasive potential often overlooked by Bible communicators when he proposes "it is not just the 'content' of these stories that grip us, but their narrative artifice" (Bruner, *Culture of Education*, 40). Leland Ryken's questions remain relevant today, "What does the Bible communicate through our imagination that it does not communicate through our reason? If the Bible

hermeneutic model for a text. For the narrative sections of Scripture, this requires an oral hermeneutic driven by narrative logic.

Multisensory-driven interpretation through oral hermeneutics (and the resulting character theology) is *not* a concession to limited or inferior cognition or the minimization of content. Rather, oral hermeneutics acknowledges our multisensory makeup, the same makeup that caused Moses to strike the rock twice (rather than speak to) and make this request, "Let me see Your glory" (Exod 33:8 VOICE); the same makeup that caused Sarah to laugh; *the same makeup that Jesus voluntarily acquired in the incarnation and appropriated in three years of ministry—while the Gospels offer no account where Jesus laughed,*[30] *they do show us he exuded, he laughed, exuded energy, became angry, grieved, wept.* Note also how Paul's emotional side comes through when he *grieves* over Galatians and Israelites who misunderstood the gospel (Gal 1:6; Rom 9:2–3).

To bypass the sensory is to exclude more than half of life, skew Christianity, and jettison around nine-tenths of the sacred storybook. Narrowing to narrative, Martha Nussbaum notes, "Stories first construct and then evoke (and strengthen) the experience of feeling. So, a criticism of emotion must be, prominently, an unwriting of stories."[31] Christianity is a way of life—an imaginative, emotional, rational way of life—based first and foremost on a relational story driven by concrete characters rather than a rational collection of theological truths.

Because the Creator is more than a rational Being, so is his highest creation. This requires utilizing everyday universal tools required in oral hermeneutics (in contrast to the sophisticated literary tools of textual hermeneutics) to mine narrative depths. In so doing, it empowers and equips the *average Jesus follower to become a skillful story interpreter*! The *"guide on the side"* (not unlike the driver's ed trainer) beckons the participant (student driver) to become the *"student on the stage,"* joining the decentered *"sage on the stage"* for some collaborative experiential theologizing that has the potential to transform the worldviews of *all* participants. This co-construction journey creates opportunity for critical-contextual ethnotheology to evolve.

---

uses the imagination as one way of communicating truth, should we not show an identical confidence in the power of the imagination to convey religious truth?" (Ryken, "God's Story-Book" 38; see also *An Unexpected Journal: Imagination* [2019]).

30. DeMarco, "Did Jesus Ever Laugh?"
31. Nussbaum, "Narrative Emotions," 226.

> Could there be an additional type of hermeneutic that
> offers today's world recognizability, respect, and routine as
> it did with the historical-grammatical in a former era?

Entering the story *is* required to gain its fullest impact and intent which will *not* happen by philosophizing alone. That is why high to low oralists prefer modeling over principles—they want to *see, feel* lived truth. They want actionized theology and ethics. Without such, what does one have? Vanhoozer answers, "The 'point' without the parable, the content without the form, the 'soul' without the body of the text."[32] Thinking abstractly is so deadening and ossifying for the oralist as life must be tethered to text. Personified principles sound the ring of truth.

Reconceptualizing the Ladder

In 1939, linguist Samuel Hayakawa coined the term "ladder of abstraction."[33] The integrative ladder illustrates how people think and communicate in relation to language. The lower rungs represent the concrete ascending to the top abstract rungs.

> Do moviegoers anxiously await the first
> conversation so they can begin to analyze the
> grammar to determine the movie's meaning?

All too often Bible communicators find themselves fixated on the top rungs of the ladder. It takes too much time to start at the bottom when attaining the top is the goal. What must happen for Bible communicators to begin on the bottom, concrete rungs *before* ascending (via concrete connectors) to the higher rungs of abstractions? To see the complete ladder as a necessary whole?

To reflect a more complete Creator, it becomes necessary for Bible communicators to not just capture minds but start where life changes begin. This means allowing the infinite Creator's transcendent mystery and majesty to arrest hearts and imaginations;[34] this means addressing the whole

---

32. Vanhoozer, "Drama-of-Redemption Model," 159.
33. Hayakawa, *Language in Action*, 96.
34. "The story of Christ is a feast for the imagination. Why not serve it this way to

154　PART 1: CHARACTER THEOLOGY DEFINED

person—body, mind, and soul; this means wedding entertainment and education.[35]

Wendland concludes, "It may well have been the primary intention of the original author to activate the expressive, affective, and aesthetic functions of communication to an equal or even greater extent than the cognitive function."[36] If so, this means entering the world of perplexing paradoxes and ambiguity that requires much more than a literalist interpretation. Says an old Scholastic axiom: "Nothing is present in the intellect that was not previously present in the senses."[37]

> What must happen for Bible communicators to begin on the bottom, concrete rungs of the ladder *before* ascending to the higher rungs of abstractions?

Lady Wisdom offers this sage reminder: "Above all else, guard thy heart; for out of it flows the *issues of* life" (Prov 4:23 JUB [emphasis original]). Reconsideration and reconfiguration begin with the imagination, which is the latchkey to unlocking faith, which simultaneously engages the mind to debate its acceptance, modification, harmonization, or rejection. Imagination is the electricity that sparks reason into actionized current. Focusing exclusively on reason or imagination is reductionism, which short-circuits heart transformation.

Some may argue, this is way too subjective. Or is it? Is the Creator a totally rational, objective, propositional Being? Totally comprehensible? Definable?[38] Controllable? Are we capable of implementing *any* hermeneutic apart from "an integrative act of the imagination?"[39]

Are we too suspicious of subjectivity? Is information or facts alone adequate? Can we become masters of imagination to the same degree we have of reason? C. S. Lewis hits the sweet spot when he insists that "reason is the

---

those who are starving?" (Mark Filiatreau, as quoted in Webber, *Younger Evangelicals*, 69). For an anthology on "imagination" by some of the best writers on the topic, see Ryken, *Christian Imagination*.

35. See Singhal et al., *Entertainment-Education and Social Change*.

36. Wendland, *Translating the Literature*, 94.

37. This axiom is often attributed to Thomas Aquinas (Stuart Brown, "Empiricism," para. 1). If you have ever attended a large assembly of thousands of people or even smaller gatherings, there is a sensory aspect of communal belonging with a collective focus that is never forgotten.

38. "Who has known the mind of the Lord?" (Rom 11:34 NIV).

39. Hays, "Scripture-Shaped Community," 45–46.

natural organ of truth, but imagination is the organ of meaning. Imagination . . . is not the cause of truth but its condition."[40] For Lewis, imagination goes far beyond the ability to dream up fanciful fables—it informs us.

For those who comprise oral-aural-visual–oriented communities, mystery, ambiguity, paradox, and contradictions are *not* typically feared, viewed as abnormal, or just tolerated. Rather, they are considered normal literary constructs that not only *enable* conversations but *enrich* as well.

> Is there any virtue in vagueness?
>
> Is ambiguity part of God's purpose?

While the literate mind may consider stories as messy muddles, not so the oral mind. The literate mind may also believe practitioners of such murkiness are unclear thinkers and totally disorganized; they beat around the bush; they take the scenic route. If true, why then did God entrust the Hebrews—who thought and "communicated in a narrative or holistic style"[41]—with authoring Scripture? How has our Aristotelian background blinded us to other possible legitimate thought patterns and modes of communication?

The creation of beauty, a reflection of the Creator (Ps 111:3), can and does lead people to the foot of the Creator's inviting yet intimidating throne. And it does so without bypassing cognition. Beautifully told or written stories driven by concrete characters are stimulating, sensuous, and seductive, speaking strongly to the soul, not just the mind.

Such beauty, whether nature or narrative, always points up. As Eugene Peterson perceptively notes, "Beauty is our sensory access to holiness."[42] Oral hermeneutics, among other hermeneutics, is designed to help unlock the meaning behind the beauty that the Creator long ago not only declared "very good," but wants enjoyed by all as well.

> How has our Aristotelian background blinded us to other possible legitimate thought patterns and modes of communication?

---

40. Hooper, *C. S. Lewis*, 570.
41. S. Lingenfelter and Mayers, *Ministering Cross-Culturally*, 40.
42. E. Peterson, *As Kingfishers Catch Fire*, 80.

Oral hermeneutics is an art that cherishes and chases meaningful metaphor, mystery, and imagination without diminishing or devaluing the mind.[43] It does so primarily through exemplary characters who tease our imagination through what they say and do. "In oral intercourse," claims Harold Innis, "the eye, ear, and brain, the senses and the faculties acted together in busy co-operation and rivalry each eliciting, stimulating, and supplementing the other."[44] The lives of characters in specific contexts ignite individual-communal imagination, excite emotions, physically move body parts, require steadfast faith, and call for participatory debate and reasoned reflection before implementation (see fig. 4.2).

Coreness or Correctness?

While textual hermeneutics seeks correctness (capture the concepts), oral hermeneutics is comfortable with boundaried fluidity[45] as it seeks coreness (capture the characters). Oral hermeneutics, based on orality (the soft yet strong music playing in the background),[46] allows for but does not require multiple truths[47] and multiple applications. As literates steeped in soulless science and frozen print, can we ever be able to hear/read the Bible like Jesus and his followers did during the first century? If not, what gets lost?

What if God's mysterious theological boundaries have more latitude then presumed? Stallter reminds us, "We must remember that theology is our description of God and his ways, not a relationship with him. . . . We

---

43. "A mystery, in the proper sense of the term, refers not to something that is irrational but to something that cannot be fully comprehended by reason, exceeding its capacity to discern and describe. The sheer vastness of God causes the images and words that humans craft to falter, if not break down completely, as they try to depict God fully and faithfully" (McGrath, *Narrative Apologetics*, 8).

44. Innis, *Bias of Communication*, 105.

45. Kenneth Bailey weighs in with this contribution: "informal and controlled." Anyone could tell a Bible story (informal), which would lead to some variation. But if the variation has gone too far, those in position of authority would correct (controlled) so that the core remains stable over generations (Bailey, "Informal Controlled Oral Tradition").

46. T. Steffen and Bjoraker, *Return of Oral Hermeneutics*, 65–72. Vanhoozer uses these terms: "creative fidelity" and "ruled spontaneity" (Vanhoozer, *Drama of Doctrine*, 129). We added "attractive or artistic accuracy."

47. Wendland, who seeks a singular point, offers this extension: "This is not to say that the main point should be considered the only point or the only important point. For example, though Romans 1:16–17 is the overall theme of Romans, literally hundreds of other theological and ethical truths are taught throughout the pages of this letter. The individual parts are best understood in light of how they contribute to the whole" (Wendland, "Interpreting the Bible," 61–62).

must never let our theological system become God."[48] One of the goals for any legitimate hermeneutic must be to *minimize misunderstanding* whatever one's theological tradition.

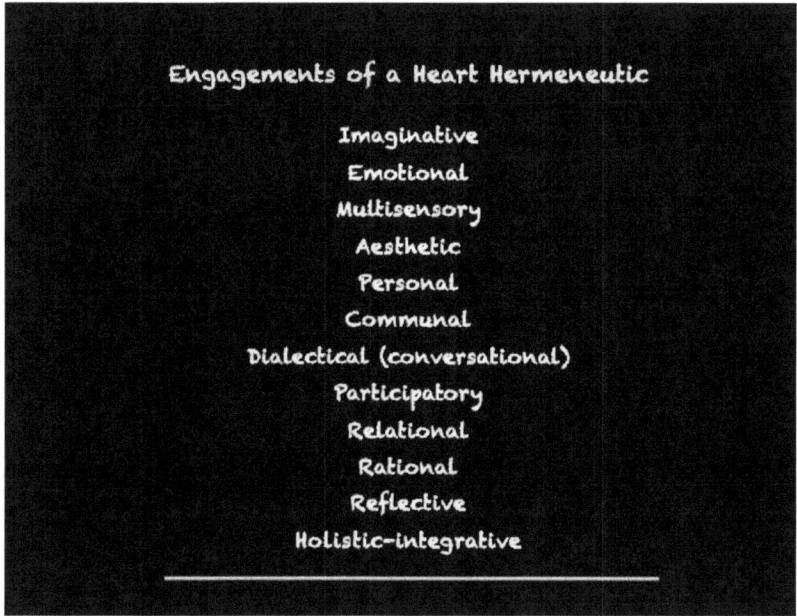

Figure 4.2. Engagements of a Heart Hermeneutic

For those enmeshed in oral-aural-visual cultures at home and abroad who seek the coreness (storyline) of a story, unlike those who seek correctness (fragments), tend not to question the authoritative nature of Scripture as it is typically assumed. While recognizing a step of steadfast faith is necessary, the coreness of a multisensory story centered on characters often fails to diminish the Author's authority for oral audiences.

While oral hermeneutics avoids what Paulo Freire and Antonio Faundez call the "castration of curiosity,"[49] it does *not* promote the postmodern subjectivism perspective that meaning is in "the eye of the beholder" or that *any* interpretation goes ("your truth"). Rather, oral hermeneutics follows principles that have internal (e.g., repetition,[50] rhythms, rhyme, alliteration)

---

48. Stallter, *Gap between God*, 92.
49. Freire and Faundez, *Learning to Question*, 36.
50. See "The Structure of Repetition: Strategies of Informational Redundancy," in Sternberg, *Poetics of Biblical Narrative*, 365–440.

and external (e.g., honor and shame[51] of the messenger and the covenant community) guide rails and guardrails to help ensure that an author's truths and ethics embodied in the characters in the story prevail. Oral hermeneutics offers communal seekers and servers a secure way as any to search for divine truths.

> What are the limits of textual hermeneutics?
> Oral hermeneutics?

While textual and oral hermeneutics can and should be integrative, there is a sequence to be followed *if* the story genre is to be respected. First, how to "read" people, voices, and the room is something learned informally, tends to come naturally, becomes second nature, and is therefore easily reproducible by the majority. Second, how to dissect text is learned formally, is unnatural, difficult to reproduce, and therefore tends to be limited to a few specialists. Guess which carries the most emotional impact making it memorable, retrievable, repeatable?

Recapping, textual hermeneutics establishes control through abstraction (e.g., grammar, categories, ideas) and persuasion through propositional logic. Oral hermeneutics establishes boundaried fluidity through aesthetics, concreteness, symbols (bread, wine), stories (echoes of the Passover), ritual ("as often as you do this"), and persuasion through revelation.

When interpreting the narrative genre of Scripture via the historical-grammatical hermeneutic method, things get overlooked, missed, and misapplied. Viv Edwards and Thomas Sienkewiez inform us why: "When the literate tool of analysis is applied to an oral context, a disequilibrium is created between the medium and the message."[52] It's almost like Bible story interpreters trying to catch mosquitoes with a chain-link fence. Most will naturally escape because the wrong tool was used for the job.

> What happens when the wrong hermeneutic is used?

---

51. If you don't understand the nuanced role of honor and shame during biblical times or within the host community, most likely you will have a difficult time grasping its role in preserving meaning.

52. Edwards and Sienkewiez, *Oral Cultures*, 147.

We can and must do better—for the Filipina and theological student quoted at the beginning of the chapter, and those God entrusts to us. It begins with respect for the genre.

Oral hermeneutics serves as a natural interpretative model for the narrative sections of Scripture while textual hermeneutics will prove more problematic as it was not designed to interpret narrative. Textual hermeneutics has its limitations. One's preferred hermeneutic can deepen or damage interpretation.

For many steeped in print, all this becomes an exceptionally high hurdle to clear. In "'My Tongue Is the Stylus of a Skilled Scribe' (Ps 45:2c)," Wendland proposes this challenge to Bible translators with implications for Bible communicators: "Translators must convince themselves of this fact, namely the excellent literary, indeed 'oratorical', quality of the original."[53] If the oral-aural character of Scripture materializes in the mind, not only will the sacred spoken-written word become more robust, respected, remembered, and repeated by Bible communicators, the same will most likely hold true for listeners/viewers.

For a richer, appealing, and impactful interpretation to transpire, today's wise Bible communicators will follow the example of the original authors—*they kept their audience in mind* as they delivered an intimate performance-proclamation. Do professors and practitioners think of their audience as *thinkers* (head focused) or as *imaginers* (heart focused)? For some 80 percent of the world, which includes a growing post-literate world, the answer to this question matters deeply.

> Can we literates who are so steeped in soulless science and frozen print ever be able to hear/read the Bible like Christ followers did during the first century? If not, what gets lost?

Oral hermeneutics, driven by narrative logic, is an interpretive process that leads to a product—character theology. Character theology—driven by Bible characters—purposely and painstakingly paints a portrait of the Chief Character in greater definition. It transforms dull dogma and doctrine into dynamic drama in a communal way. "Doctrine" becomes "*a rule for 'storied practice.*"[54] Rather than become an anchor, oral hermeneutics fills the nar-

---

53. Wendland, "My Tongue Is Stylus," 5. The CJB translates Ps 45:2: "My tongue is the pen of an expert scribe."

54. Vanhoozer, *Drama of Doctrine*, 93 (emphasis original).

rative sails with powerful interpretive winds. Not all hermeneutics are equal when it comes to the narrative genre.

What Is Oral Hermeneutics?

The oral hermeneutics that the authors argue for is *not* a new fad, nor is it anti-intellectual, nor is it just for children's ministry, nor is it just for tribal people. What is oral hermeneutics? Simply stated, *oral hermeneutics is an experiential interpretation model designed to grasp a more appealing, impactful, fuller sense of Scripture's narratives through collective dialogue.*[55] We will now expand and unpack the definition.

Oral hermeneutics consists of variations of an adapted ancient story-centric interpretive process that focuses predominately on the narrative sections of Scripture. Emphasis is given to the art of unraveling the relationships of the characters within a complete story and connected stories; it assumes theology and ethics are communicated through demonstration rather than definition. Implementation of this heart hermeneutic that ultimately reveals the Chief Character—guided by character-centric questions and guarded by the grand narrative and Holy Spirit—requires imagination, emotion, reason, and a different form of logic—narrative logic; it seeks life transformation, not simply plot resolution.

Expanding the Components

Oral hermeneutics consists of variations of an adapted ancient story-centric interpretive process. Oral hermeneutics takes its clues from the first custodians of Scripture—rabbis, scholars, and teachers of the Israelites. Scribes usually wrote the text after hearing it spoken. The text was written in an experiential manner for both ear and eye, communicated communally in a story-centric message with likely dialogue to follow, and perpetuated over generations through visual symbols and participatory rituals. Because stories—and the characters who drive them—take place in time and place, scribes took seriously the historical aspects surrounding the stories. Other current clues have been added and adapted for our present era and audiences. Multiple variants result.

That focuses predominately on the narrative sections of Scripture. The predominate genre of Scripture is narrative. The poetry sections (another

---

55. See "Hebrew Hermeneutics," in T. Steffen and Bjoraker, *Return of Oral Hermeneutics*, 135–63.

aspect of orality) and the more didactic epistles (letters that initiate or continue ongoing conversations) also include snippets of the stories of various personalities and groups, not to mention their connection to Acts.

With emphasis given to the art of unraveling the relationships of the characters. Bible characters serve as metaphors for human life. Standing beside the characters on the stage we watch as they live out their (and our) tangled lives. What they say, do, feel, wear, express, and desire, where and when things happened, the sincerity behind their words and works, whom they interact with, internal and external conflicts (actionized tensions) that emerge, *all* require attention. The same holds true for the use of symbols and/or rituals (pictorial rehearsals that remind). Unraveling the interpretive clues and putting all the pieces of the puzzle back together requires the role of an aware artist.

Within a complete story and connected stories. Oral hermeneutics is not interested in just the fragments of a story. "At least some of the time," claims Richard Platt, "'What does the verse mean?' should be replaced by 'What does this story, section, and book mean?'"[56] F. F. Bruce's definition of exegesis extends Pratt's second question, "Canonical exegesis may be defined as the interpretation of individual components of the canon in the context of the canon as a whole."[57]

For a story to make sense, the complete story is required. This applies not just to individual stories but also the surrounding stories in the book, outside the book, and the grand narrative. The individual stories are told in relation to the greater surrounding communal story. The whole story is the meaning because, as fiction writer Flannery O'Conner hypothesizes, "it is an experience, not an abstraction."[58] Just as people come in whole packages, so also characters and stories. In orality, holism and connections trump fragments and disconnections.[59]

It assumes theology and ethics are communicated through demonstration rather than definition. Unlike the more didactic sections of Scripture where doctrinal truths and ethics tend to be more explicitly stated seemingly in their abstractness (albeit often connected to ongoing local issues and personalities), the narrative sections reveal such truths through illustrations

---

56. Platt, *He Gave Us Stories*, 56.

57. Bruce, *Canon of Scripture*, 291.

58. O'Connor, *Mystery and Manners*, 73.

59. Elizabeth Mburu notes the point of a story is not something that is "made clear by only one part of the story—the ending—so that we can say at the conclusion 'and the moral of the story is. . . .' Rather, the moral is brought out throughout the entire story" (Mburu, *African Hermeneutics*, 61).

and demonstrations lived out through concrete characters in specific events in certain contexts and times.

To illustrate, while definitions are few in Scripture, e.g., faith (Heb 11:1), demonstrations of faith by a parade of personalities over the ages are multiple (Heb 11:2–38). Definitions tend to emerge from demonstrations, from human experiences, from exhibits. Stony, emotionless doctrines receive enrichment and explicitness through the dynamic drama of the lives of saintly saints as well as the not so saintly.

Implementation of this heart hermeneutic. Most hermeneutic models are head hermeneutics. Intentionally focused on objectivity, they try to eliminate or at least minimize the inclusion of imagination and emotions. Reason reigns.

A heart hermeneutic includes reason as well but much more. It, like the Hebrew understanding of heart (*lev*), integrates emotions and the mind. While not bypassing reason, a heart hermeneutic initiates debate through imagination and emotions. Representing healthy holism—feeling and thinking that influences choices—it offers a fuller, more appealing, more impactful understanding of Scripture. The sensory leads to biblical values. A heart hermeneutic braids together imagination, emotions, and reason. Holism reigns.

It ultimately reveals the Chief Character. Bible characters serve as vicarious signposts and billboards to point us to the Ultimate One who stars from the beginning of the revealed sacred story to the end, and beyond.

Guided by character-centric questions. Because characters are central to oral hermeneutics, so too should be the questions that unpack and expose the pivotal personalities and practices. Character-centric questions keep the discussion focused on the concrete rather than the abstract. Competent character-centric questions reveal more than the obvious; they take Bible interpreters on a deep dive to discover what's really going on in the lives of the pivotal people highlighted. For insightful revelations, unraveling the lives of characters requires focused character-centric questions.

It is guarded by the grand narrative and Holy Spirit. The Bible contains hundreds of stories. Strung together they construct a grand narrative (a panoramic pageant of the Chief Character); they weave all the little snippets into a single movie. This holism (the forest) provides interpretive boundaries for the individual stories (trees). The Author, the Holy Spirit, is always present to ensure clarity and credibility to the ethno-theology emerging through communal dialogue.

It requires imagination, emotion, reason. Oral hermeneutics approaches the Bible in a natural way that offers most faith followers (not just the spiritual mature or formally trained) an engaging on-ramp to Bible interpretation and application. Rather than analyzing abstract grammar,[60] it decodes concrete characters and contexts using imagination, emotions, and reason. Oral hermeneutics calls interpreters to *enter* the text rather than just *examine* it from afar; to be heart smart as well as brain smart; it calls for a *personal-collective heart encounter* rather than an *individual-intellectual encounter*.

It requires a different form of logic—narrative logic. Most readers grew up where propositional logic prevailed—A leads to B. And the educational system rewarded those who successfully implemented this objective, science-Enlightenment-based linear model.

Narrative logic, however, relies on coherence, truthfulness, interconnectedness, and identification (see yourself/family/community/nation in the story) to discover meaning; it is much more subjective, metaphorical, circular-spiral, casual. "Narrative logic is the logic of association."[61] The narrative-centric nature of Scripture requires a special and specific form of logic—narrative logic—this is like that (see fig. 4.1).

And it seeks life transformation, not simply plot resolution. While Bible story interpreters seek a resolution to resolve the conflict that surrounds the main characters, oral hermeneutics asks for more; it seeks to move participants beyond knowledge to habitual, actionized wisdom.[62] "Interpreted Scripture must be allowed to interpret its interpreters"[63] so that genuine transformation occurs individually and collectively. Oral hermeneutics insists the Trinity's imagers reenact the actions of faithful characters in the sacred story. God-glorifying transformation becomes the narratized bottom line.

Isolating Influential Identifiers of Oral Hermeneutics

The major influential identifiers of oral hermeneutics will now be isolated. These could include:

- Built on a strong historical foundation
- An art
- Narrative-founded and -focused

---

60. Language-learning methodology moved through this same process—from focusing on grammar to focusing on people and events. This methodological change made language learning so much more natural and enjoyable.
61. T. Steffen and Bjoraker, *Return of Oral Hermeneutics*, 120.
62. See Mezirow and Associates, *Learning as Transformation*.
63. Packer, "Canonical Interpretation," 43.

- Verbal and visual
- Relational (a heart hermeneutic)
- Interpreted through narrative logic
- Experienced through entering the story
- Requires the complete story and surrounding stories
- Treasured teachings demonstrated rather than defined
- Focused on characters, stories, symbols, rituals
- Focused on conflict, confusion, chaos
- Unraveled best through character-centric questions
- Communal dialogue and interpretation
- Resolution-bound
- Holistically based—imagination, emotion, reason
- Ambiguous
- Mystery drives meaning
- Focused on coreness rather than correctness
- Open to multiple truths in a single story
- Guarded by the grand narrative, individual-communal shame, the Holy Spirit
- Centered on revealing the Chief Character
- Focused on God-glorifying transformation globally

The above components and identifiers will receive further illustration and elaboration in the forthcoming chapters.

Oral Hermeneutics Focuses on Characters

Mieke Bal astutely asserts that "literature is written by, for, and about people."[64] At the center of any story—spoken, written, or visual—are characters who interact with each other and/or themselves. Through appearance, conversation, actions (positive or negative) characters arrest our attention. Sometimes they even cause us to re-symbolize, re-story, re-ritualize;[65] they

---

64. Bal, *Narratology*, 115.
65. See T. Steffen, *Worldview-Based Storying*.

follow us like shadows through the contours of our lives. Characters are central to literature and life.

Speaking from a shame perspective, Charles Cooley is convinced "we live in the minds of others without even knowing it."[66] Writers (who could be considered a character) utilize characters to change others through the "power of familiarity."[67] Bible characters offer new (often competing) directional possibilities. What *was* said becomes what *is* said. What *happened* becomes what is *happening*. Character connection with the audience is the ultimate intention of Bible authors.

Recall the classic story of Cain and Abel. While we may not have had a family member murdered by another family member, all have experienced something in the story: division of labor, sibling rivalry, religious division, favoritism, envy, anger, temptation, and have observed or experienced the pressures of parenting. These are universal, timeless behaviors faced by people around the globe and therefore relate to daily lives.

Great writers are talented mind readers; they get into our minds because they know what is on our minds; they make us—almost unconsciously—internalize[68] the spoken lines and actions of certain characters in the story without us even knowing it. Disarming inside-the-story characters connect with outside-the-story characters, thereby challenging or cementing centuries of cultural norms that color cultural traditions.

> What is the role of relationships in oral hermeneutics?

Enter oral hermeneutics. Oral hermeneutics begins *not* with abstract grammar, but with concrete characters, which can include humans, spirits, animals (e.g., horses, donkeys, goats, roosters), insects, elements, and a host of others—fish, frogs, worms (recall ch. 1). Unlike textual hermeneutics, which focuses strongly on the meaning of words, which leads naturally to definitions, oral hermeneutics focuses strongly on decoding characters, which leads naturally to demonstrated values.

Oral hermeneutics focuses strongly on the earthiness of human life embodied and enacted through characters (real or fictive) in time and space. Oral hermeneutics assumes that the virtual lives of a cast of characters (from the "great cloud of witnesses" [Heb 12:1 NIV] to those who deliberately denied or challenged their Creator) serve as the heart

---

66. Cooley, *Human Nature*, 11. Many Cubans live with a policeman in their minds.
67. Gunn and Fewell, *Narrative in Hebrew Bible*, 107.
68. Larry Dinkins prefers using "absorb."

hermeneutic to unravel the truths and ethics of Bible stories, thereby revealing the Creator behind them.

But what about words, word arrangements? Phrases? Grammar? Have they no role in Bible interpretation? Will Brooks assumes Bible authors "made conscious decisions to use specific words and specific grammar constructions. This act of will in arranging and organizing their material in a certain way is what we speak of when we discuss authorial intent."[69]

Yes, language does play an important role in Bible interpretation in *all* genres of Scripture and that is why conversations are so important in relation to meaning in Bible stories. Wise interpreters carefully consider key terms and phases, honorific terms, formulaic expressions, repetition, structure, among others, as they decode conversations. Words, whether spoken or their placement, carry meaning. Oral hermeneutics insists interpreters read words as well as read characters.

They also pay attention to appearance, age, sexual orientation, geography, and so forth. All key characters display their personalities as they operate within a sociocultural, geographical context, enacting their roots, roles, and relationships. For oral hermeneutics, unlike textual hermeneutics, the starting point is *not* the historical-grammatical but the historical-character.

> Who are the most significant characters introduced in said story?
>
> How do these characters relate to their Creator? To other characters?

As a relationally focussed hermeneutic, oral hermeneutics is character-centric.[70] Oral hermeneutics continually asks, who are the pivotable characters introduced in said story? How do these characters relate to their Creator? To other characters?[71] Oral hermeneutics tracks primary

---

69. Brooks, *Interpreting Scripture across Cultures*, 29–30. One wonders how intentional literate authors were in not only selecting and arranging words and grammar (the "rules"), but how intentional they were in adapting the rules for their oral audiences.

70. Jens Brockmeier and Hanna Meretoja note, "Narrative hermeneutics goes beyond the meaning of language and texts. . . . It deals with the human being in the world as a historical, social, and cultural condition, rather than only with epistemological issues of knowledge, thought, and cognition" (Brockmeier and Meretoja, "Understanding Narrative Hermeneutics," 6).

71. "The main characters of a parable will probably be the most common candidates for allegorical interpretation, and the main points of the parable will most likely be associated with these characters" (Blomberg, *Interpreting the Parables*, 166).

and peripheral characters through relationships, reactions, and reflections throughout the storied landscapes of Scripture.

Central to Creator-designed characters are relationships. This begins with three characters—actually, three-in-one. Reflecting the interactive and integrative relationships modeled in the Trinity, orality finds itself embedded and embodied in a web of relationships between people, the spirit world, and the material world. The same applies for oral hermeneutics.

Oral hermeneutics is a relationally based tool that focuses the spotlight on the words and works of biblical characters as they interact from scene to scene, episode to episode, creating a relationally based story that offers audiences choices and consequences. This intentionally Author-author-selected colorful cast of characters who are *never* neutral serve as living signposts, living theologies, living ethics. Like rumble strips on the side of the highway they warn drivers through sound and feeling (bumpiness) of imminent danger—change direction *immediately*; they disorient and reorient us; they provide covenant communities concrete demonstrations of determination, direction, detail, distinction, and destination as they interact geographically and culturally with those close and distant. Their lives not only educate, they *re*educate; they not only equip, they *re*equip.

Referencing parables, Klyne Snodgrass surmises, "These are stories *with intent*, the communicative intent of Jesus. . . . Communication is not about abstract meaning; it acts and seeks to change things. The question for each parable is: How did Jesus seek to change attitudes and behavior with this parable?"[72] The answer—*through characters*! Oral hermeneutics and character theology travel well together.

Characters Drop Breadcrumbs

Characters continue to drop breadcrumbs (recall ch. 2). Listen for conflict, note any changes made by the various characters for these become dropped breadcrumbs. See if you can discern what's going on. Pick up as many breadcrumbs as you can and begin to develop a narratized theme. Call on the Discerner of truth for insight and see what unfolds. Dialogue with others. Never stop learning as some truths tend to trickle out over time.

---

72. Snodgrass, *Stories with Intent*, 3 (emphasis original).

Contrasting Textual and Oral Hermeneutics

In the search for clarity and distinctiveness, this section contrasts textual and oral hermeneutics (see tables 4.2–4). We recognize variations exist as there are multiple versions of each hermeneutic model in use globally, and that some integration exists between the two. The following table contrasts focus, assumptions, application, and results.

Textual Hermeneutics	Oral Hermeneutics
Focuses on the *written* words of God	Focuses on the *spoken-written* words of God
Is applicable to all types of text found in Scripture	Is exclusive to the narrative sections of Scripture
Dances with science to minimize illegitimate surprises	Dances with mystery to maximize legitimate surprises
Calls for analysis of a text	Calls for entering and experiencing a text
Focuses on facts	Focuses on function
Focuses on topics	Focuses on actions
Encourages forensic faith	Encourages inferred faith
Finds interpretive boundaries internally in grammar and externally in history	Finds interpretive boundaries internally (e.g., repetition, rhythms, rhyme, parallelism) and externally in history
Focuses on the language and grammar within the text	Focuses on the words, works, and context of characters in the text
Focuses on structural contrasts	Focuses on character contrasts
Prefers content-centric questions for analyzing grammar	Prefers character-centric questions for "reading" characters
Tends to seek answers to "how" and "why" questions	Tends to seek answers to "who" and "now what" questions
Seeks propositional statements	Seeks narrative-expressed themes

Table 4.1. Focus Distinctives

Textual Hermeneutics	Oral Hermeneutics
Is a more deductive approach that relies on the leader's interpretation	Is a more inductive approach that relies on the facilitator-group's interpretation
Promotes expert interpreters	Promotes amateur interpreters
Focuses on proposition statements	Focuses on narratized statements
Prefers monologue led by Holy Spirit–engifted teachers	Prefers monologue led by Holy Spirit–engifted teachers
Privileges a philosophical and rational approach to interpretation	Privileges an imaginative, emotional, mystical, aesthetic, sensory, relational, rational, approach to interpretation
Concludes minds are first changed through reason	Concludes minds are first changed through imagination and emotions
Perceives interpretation as an engineering project	Perceives interpretation as an art project
Justifies divine truth through disproving the false	Displays divine truth through exhibiting the consequences
Calls for reduction of the text to its minutest	Calls for expansion of the text to its fullest
Is highly cognitive-oriented	Is highly action-oriented
Considers interpretation more linear	Considers interpretation more circular-spiral and casual
Is designed to mine, categorize, and store detailed information for eventual retrieval	Is designed to mirror relational behavior and moral values for immediate implementation
Orients interpreters to a single truth per story (science reductionism)	Orients interpreters to possible multiple truths per story (oral expansionism)
Relies often on the systematized pieces for meaning	Relies on the grand narrative for interpreting the parts
Requires stories/characters to *illustrate* discerned propositions	Requires stories/characters to *demonstrate* discerned propositions

Table 4.2. Assumption Distinctives

Textual Hermeneutics	Oral Hermeneutics
Promotes telling	Promotes asking
Promotes identification through a rational appeal to grammar	Promotes identification through a relational appeal with characters
Reads abstract printed text	"Reads" concrete characters and contexts
Nudges interpretation to sharper textual clarity	Nudges interpretation to sharper human experience
Finds it difficult to transition the historical message to the present	Finds it easy to transition ancient characters to the present
Promotes dissection—words, syntax, propositions, themes, summaries, outlines	Promotes holism—the whole character, whole story, whole book, whole Book

Table 4.3. Application Distinctives

Textual Hermeneutics	Oral Hermeneutics
Seeks coreness	Seeks correctness
Privileges abstract propositions	Privileges concrete characters
Accentuates a *head* hermeneutic	Accentuates a *heart* hermeneutic
Promotes a rational theology	Promotes a relational theology
Relies on print and collections to maintain fidelity	Relies on collective memory and shame to maintain fidelity
Encourages professionals to interpret Scripture	Encourages amateurs to interpret Scripture
Results often in dry dogma	Results often in dynamic dogma
Rarely provides the full appeal, impact, or truth of a text	Provides a fuller appeal, impact, or truth of a text

Table 4.4. Result Distinctives

For science to be science, descent is required. For science-based theology to be theology, descent is required. For science-based hermeneutics to be hermeneutics, dissent is required. Even so, "OH [oral hermeneutics] is *not* a rival to TH [textual hermeneutics], rather it is its source spring of living water. OH is *not* a substitute hermeneutic, rather it has a signature shared role in a specific sequence. OH is *not* a supplemental hermeneutic, rather it serves as a catalyst. OH is *not* just an addition to TH, rather it is its indispensable bedrock and cornerstone. OH is *not* a simplistic hermeneutic, rather it is equally as complex as TH. OH is *not* an inferior hermeneutic, rather it is a different type of hermeneutic that fills in missing gaps found in TH."[73] When processed properly, oral hermeneutics forges Bible interpretation that is both *faithful and forceful*.

Oral hermeneutics finds its foundational defense in the reality that God, Jesus, and the Spirit are persons who relate. They relate to one another in their respective roles as persons; they feel and thus love one another out of loyalty; they honor each another; they support each another; they defend one another; they spread the fame of one another; they serve collaboratively.

> Do Bible communicators think of their audience as *thinkers* (head focused) or as *imaginers* (heart focused)?

As God-created handiwork, humans are built and wired to communicate with their Creator in a person-to-person manner. To relate with one another in such a way reflects our communion with God—empathy, respect, and so forth. As we blossom into a more excellent likeness of Jesus Christ, that is, experiencing a new, growing godliness, we become more complete, more consistent, more like the likeness of what the Triune God has always been and will always be.

Our complex composition of intellect and emotion exists because we are God-reflective persons. Oral hermeneutics starts with and builds on this spiritual-human relational foundation.

Unlike other hermeneutic models that call for the participant's detachment from the interpretive process to ensure objectivity—which can easily morph into application detachment—oral hermeneutics calls for the participant's genuine involvement in the interpretive process to ensure the experiential and habitual application.

Orality shouts, "Picture this!" Oral hermeneutics shouts, "Experience this!" Character theology shouts, "Watch this!" Application shouts, "Routinize this!" Christianity shouts, "Erupt with thanks to the Eternal" (Ps 107:1 VOICE).

---

73. T. Steffen and Bjorker, *Return of Oral Hermeneutics*, 298.

> **Helpful Sources**
>
> Brooks, *Interpreting Scripture across Cultures*
>
> Caldwell, *Doing Bible Interpretation*
>
> Mburu, *African Hermeneutics*
>
> McGrath, *Narrative Apologetics*
>
> T. Steffen and Bjoraker, *The Return of Oral Hermeneutics*

Looking Back and Ahead

Wendland answered his question raised at the beginning of this chapter as to why the sudden strong influence of orality on hermeneutics this way: 1) "print-oriented scholars simply failed to consider the spoken word"; 2) "past scholars were too focused on documentary text-centered approaches, like source, redaction, and form criticism. . . . When scholarship began to pay more attention to the *reception* side of the communication cycle, the *phonological factor* of discourse began to be investigated much more seriously." Why was orality rediscovered? It "figured prominently in the initial *composition* of the biblical texts, which as it turns out, were actually articulated aloud while they were being verbally created."[74]

Recall what Richard Hays noted in chapter 1—during the Reformation, the chief hermeneutical challenge was to relate Scripture to *tradition*. During the Enlightenment, the chief hermeneutical challenge was to relate Scripture to *reason*. How do we perceive the future? Have we entered a new era that requires a different hermeneutical focus? We believe so. We have now "passed into an era in which the urgent question is the relative authority of Scripture and *experience*."[75]

This new era requires an oral hermeneutic—a visual-voice–based hermeneutic that interprets the words and works of Author-author chosen characters resulting in a relational theology (character theology) that expects worship and expands witness. Oral hermeneutics prepares Bible storyteller-interpreters not only for contemporary times, but figures far into the foreseeable future as well.

74. Wendland, "Studying, Translating, and Transmitting," 21–22 (emphasis original). Harvey would agree: "Even writing was done aloud" (Harvey, *Listening to the Text*, 56).

75. Hays, *Moral Vision*, 211 (emphasis added).

> Could oral hermeneutics be the mother of relational theology?

Not only does a new era require a different hermeneutic, so does the narrative genre. Long analyzed by an inappropriate tool (e.g., a screwdriver used to remove a nail), it is time to use a hermeneutic tool that respects the narrative genre—oral hermeneutics.

Oral hermeneutics, resulting in character theology, offers *a legitimate and life-giving means* to interpret the narrative sections of spoken-written Scriptures, the dominant genre. With strong historical Hebrew precedent,[76] oral hermeneutics *opens the door, too, for the average Bible interpreter to become a skillful story interpreter* as they "read" the actions of agents within a story. Through direct conversations and conduct of various Bible characters in specific contexts, observers learn how to emulate God-honoring words and works or jettison the dishonoring.

Oral hermeneutics assumes it generates a more robust interpretation because it goes beyond printed words; it adds voice. Few have thought through how wind inhaled and exhaled, influenced by emotions, becomes sounded words.[77] Note also how voices heard ignite the imagination and emotions into actions probed by reason. Scripture values the richness of voice.

Oral hermeneutics assumes there is *no* Bible translation, no theological institution, no Bible teacher, no theological system, no Bible commentary or curricula that is culture-free because *no* hermeneutic is culture-free. Why? Because someone of some gender from some geographical location of some age representing some ethnicity from some socioeconomic and education level with some pedagogical preference from some political persuasion from some religious tradition was involved in the interpretation process. This includes oral hermeneutics.

Oral hermeneutics encourages participatory, active learning which leads to participatory actions which leads to the internalization of new knowledge which leads to habitual, actionized wisdom. Horace Bushnell brilliantly concludes, "Truth must be lived into meaning before it can be

---

76. See T. Steffen and Bjoraker, *Return of Oral Hermeneutics*, 135–63.

77. Richard Ward provides some insight quotes from Quintilian's teaching: "The voice is the index of the mind and is capable of expressing all varieties of feeling" (Ward, "Pauline Voice and Presence," 99). Referencing the reciter's role in sparking interest in the text, he "stimulates us by the animation of his delivery, and kindles the imagination not by presenting us with an elaborate picture but by bringing us into actual touch with the things themselves" (100).

truly known."[78] Oral hermeneutics advances participants beyond the heart, beyond the head, to lived life.

Oral hermeneutics assumes a story provides its own set of literary boundaries that serve as guide rails and guardrails of interpretation for the more ambiguous nature of orality. As print specialists, we often miss what high to low oralists naturally hear and observe. How has our print orientation blinded us to what is so obvious to oralists?

> Have we asked and answered, what is *their* way of interpreting?

Oral hermeneutics assumes that both listener and text are required to ascertain the message the Author-author wishes to convey and have habitually lived out. One without the other is sure to result in lost or misinformed meaning and application. It also recognizes holism is central to interpretation. The complete story, not just atomistic parts, is necessary to interpret a story.

Four integrated and interactive components (listener/reader and whole/part) influence the meaning of a story (see fig. 4.2). With the aid of the Grand Interpreter who leads us into *all* truth, and the grand narrative centered on the Christ Jesus, communal interpreters can *minimize* (rarely eliminate) reading their own culture and traditions into ancient text and times.

Even so, oral hermeneutics *humbly* recognizes that not all aspects of a story may be discernible or defensible and is therefore willing to live with some ambiguity until more insights bubble to the surface. Oral hermeneutics also acknowledges the validity of other hermeneutic models even as it recognizes and champions its reasonable and required role in interpreting the narrative sections of Scripture.

Like a calico cat cuddled up to a cozy, warm fire on a cold winter night, have those in the hermeneutic guilds become too comfortable in its interpretative theory-based models? Is it time to open the door to allow in a cold blast of theoretical fresh air? Could such a climactic change become a newfound treasure?

Could oral hermeneutics be a process that leads interpreters to the foothills of character theology? Is character theology the mother of relational theology?

---

78. Horace Bushnell, as quoted in P. Shaw, *Transforming Theological Education*, 93.

Everyone interprets. Everyone tends to use *their preferred* hermeneutic model. Have we asked the question, what is *their* way of interpreting?[79] How extensive has our investigation been of *our preferred* hermeneutic model in relation to assumptions? In relation to the cultural values beyond innocence-guilt (e.g., honor-shame, power-fear, purity-pollution)? Is it time for some deep exploration and examination of the assumptions of not only *their* preferred hermeneutic model, but *our* preferred hermeneutic model as well? The unexamined hermeneutic is *not* worth implementing.[80]

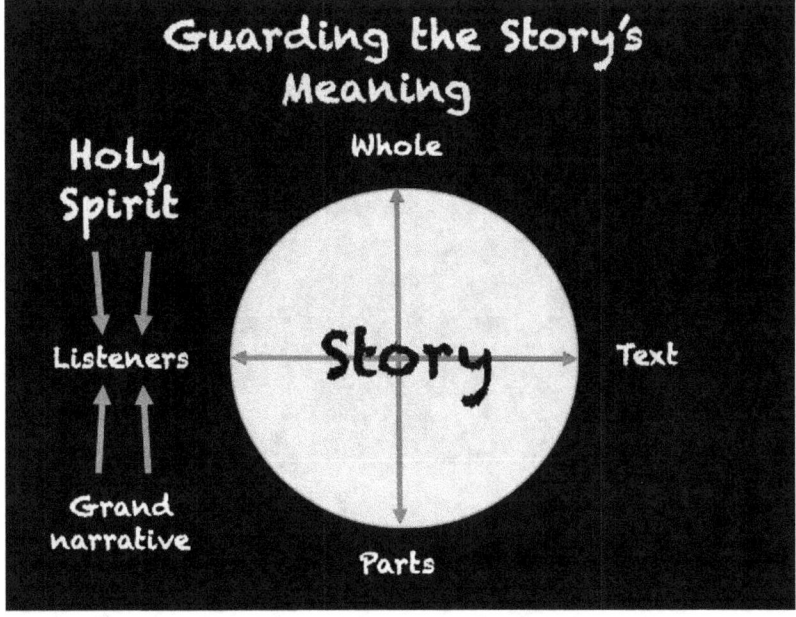

Figure 4.3. Guarding the Story's Meaning

Oral hermeneutics is relationally focused because it follows the relational model demonstrated by the Trinity. This results in a relational theology—character theology. But how does one unpack all this?

---

79. Referencing transformative learning, Jack Mezirow and Associates maintain, "Learning is understood as the process of using a prior interpretation to construe a new or revised interpretation of the meaning of one's experience as a guide to future action" (Mezirow and Associates, *Learning as Transformation*, 5). We would add, not only is current interpretation based on prior interpretation, it is also based on a preferred hermeneutic model.

80. An adaptation of Socrates: "The unexamined life is not worth living" (Plato, *Apol.* [38a5–6]).

This brings us to the fifth forerunner of character theology—character-centric questions. What is the role of *character-centric questions* in character theology?

Reflection Questions

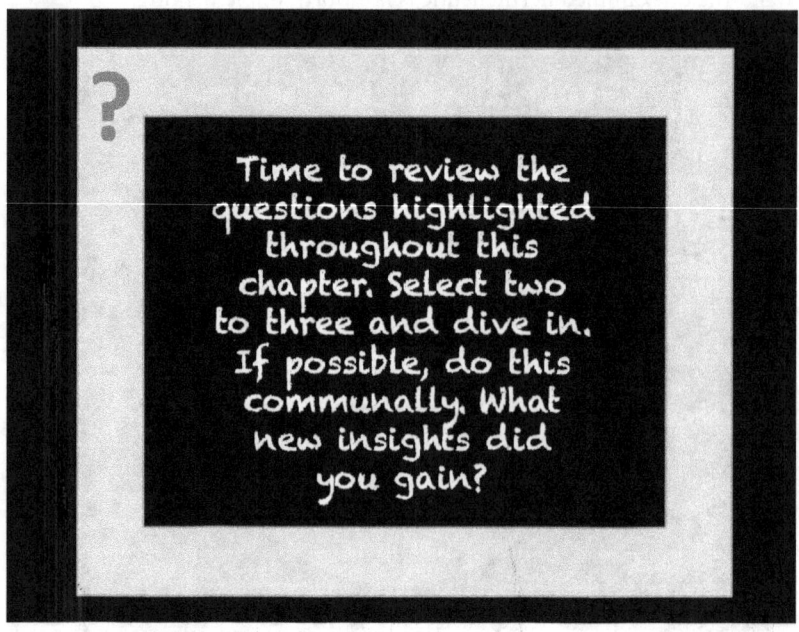

Time to review the questions highlighted throughout this chapter. Select two to three and dive in. If possible, do this communally. What new insights did you gain?

5

The Role of Character-Centric Questions

> Questions are the golden keys that unlock hearts and minds.
>
> —BOB TIEDE

> Answers are closed rooms; and questions
> are open doors that invite us in.
>
> —NANCY WILLARD

> Questioning is not the positing but the
> testing of possibilities....
> *A person who thinks must ask himself questions.*
>
> —HANS-GEORG GADAMER

> A conversation is only as good as the questions it entertains.
>
> —PARKER PALMER

WHY DIDN'T JESUS PLAY the role of the Bible Answer Man during his brief three-year tenure of public ministry? He certainly knew *all* the answers! No one had a stronger pedigree that qualified him to lay out what life is all about than Jesus. Yet rather than advance the answers (telling), he frequently reverted to parabolic stories and/or questions, many of which were rhetorical. What do stories and questions have in common? Before answering, we raise another question.

What is a parable? Note Bailey's emphasis on invitation and holism. "A parable is not a delivery system for an idea. It is not like a shell casing that can be discarded once the idea (the bullet) is fired. Rather a parable is a house in which the reader or listener is invited to take up residence. The reader is encouraged to look out on the world from the point of view of the story."[1] Parables are invitations to ongoing self-collective reflection.

Parables are powerful, probing puzzles that require relentless reflection and constant collaboration in that they are not normally designed to offer a simple, single, straightforward proposition. As parables play out cinematically in one's mind, they tend to raise more questions than answers. This again requires imagination. Not only is imagination required to get *into* the story, imagination is also required to get something *out of* the story.[2]

Behind each parable or teaching of Jesus lurked at least one seminal question. Sometimes he made the question obvious, "*Haven't you read . . . Don't you remember what the story of our creation tells us about marriage?*" (Matt 19:4 VOICE [emphasis original]). Sometimes he jumped right into a story, leaving the discovery of the seminal questions up to the listener. Jesus was not only the *quintessential storyteller*, often forgotten and of equal importance, he was also the *quintessential questioner*. Jesus serves as both message and model.

Back to our question, what do stories and questions have in common? *Mystery*. Mystery engenders discovery of an unfolding, unresolved conflict. Mystery *teases* listeners into truths rather than *tells* them, and it is often *not* in any hurry to do so.

> Why didn't Jesus play the role of the Bible Answer Man during his brief three years of public ministry?

Many, if not most, Bible teachers have been taught to give the correct answer up front. Tell them what it means. Provide definitions. The problem

---

1. Bailey, *Cross and the Prodigal*, 87. The same holds true for stories, proverbs, riddles, and so forth.

2. "These two acts of imagination can be clearly distinguished conceptually. In their operation they are likely to interpenetrate each other. Grasping the biblical stories' significance may enable us to see how to tell our story; bringing our story to the biblical stories may also fill out our grasp of their own significance. Interpretation involves the whole person—feelings, attitudes and will, as well as minds; it also involves us, not merely people 2,500 years ago" (Goldingay, "How Far Do Readers," 5–6).

is that meaning precedes mystery. Recall the student's quote in chapter 1 when he told the class that in all his undergraduate Bible classes he was "taught *what* to believe, not *how* to believe"; that he perceived all but one of the classes as "*indoctrination to conform* rather than *discovery to transform.*" Did rhetoric replace rhetorical questions?

Interestingly, this commonly used model flies in the face of most of Jesus's public teaching.[3] Why? Because telling all too often buries opportunities for learning by eliminating participation in collectively solving the mystery. Which lingers longer in one's mind—rhetoric or rhetorical questions (think Job)? Which enhances memory? Which causes ongoing, deeper self-collective reflection? What is your question-to-statement ratio?[4]

The greatest teacher ever to grace this planet provides an exemplary model to follow. Rather than be the consummate Bible Answer Man/Woman, no matter how high and heady it makes one feel, Bible communicators must add the role of questioner—the razor-sharp arrows in a questioner's quiver that ask rather tell.

> What is your question-to-statement ratio?

Tom Hughes quips, "Jesus does not have Q and A sessions. He has Q and Q sessions."[5] Jesus often followed up someone's question *not* with an answer, but with a clearer, more focused question that pinpointed the real issue, e.g., "Teacher, what must I do to experience the eternal life? What is written in the *Hebrew* Scriptures? How do you interpret the answer to your question?" (Luke 10:25–26 VOICE [emphasis original]). At other times he taught by asking a series of rhetorical questions, *not* by giving answers, e.g., he asked ten questions when the disciples forgot to buy bread (Mark 8:14–21).

Modeling the Model

Following Jesus's model, we must become quintessential storyteller-questioners. This translates into rarely answering the questions asked you; this

---

3. We recognize other modes of communication were used by Jesus. Jesus was also the quintessential image hanger, whether through baptism, healing miracles through touch, exorcising demons, multiplying fish and loaves of bread, writing in the dirt, praying, sharing food together, serving the Passover meal, being served with perfume, slow to speak to silence, and so forth.

4. See Mark Miller, *Smart Leadership*.

5. Tom Hughes, as quoted in Shearer, *Marketing Like Jesus*, 75.

means helping the questioner answer his or her own questions, sometimes via another question. How different from much formal training.

Counterquestions say, "Tell me!" They communicate, "You are important and have something to offer, let's hear it." Depending on need, it's time to notch and let fly some of those arrows found in your question quiver.

Which questions will draw storytellers and listeners closer to discovering the Author's/author's revealed truth? Unravel direct conversations, commitments, compromises? Expose gaps in our understanding? Raise unanticipated questions? Result in godly, habitual, actionized wisdom?

> Which questions will draw storytellers and listeners closer to discovering the Author's/author's intended truths?

Does repeatedly using the same set of six to eight questions, often replicated in multiple Bible storying models, limit the possibilities of investigating new ground? Digging deeper?

Challenging educational institutions teaching children in the late sixties, Neil Postman and Charles Weingartner maintained that the "art and science" of asking questions (the "inquiry method") should be taught to every student. Why? Because *"once you have learned how to ask questions—relevant and appropriate and substantial questions—you have learned how to learn and no one can keep you from learning whatever you want or need to know."*[6]

Postman and Weingartner then lament: "The most important and intellectual ability man has yet developed—the art and science of asking questions is *not* taught in school."[7] While *answering* questions is rewarded in schools, seldom rewarded is *asking* great questions. How can this be? Why do we habitually inhibit learning?

How many courses pertaining to questions has the reader participated in non-formally? Formally? For cross-cultural settings? This raises a seemingly missed question in the religious academy: If Jesus was the quintessential storyteller and questioner, *why have Bible students seldom been trained to model the Model?*

> If Jesus was the quintessential storyteller and questioner, *why have Bible students seldom been formerly trained to model the Model?*

---

6. Postman and Weingartner, *Teaching as Subversive Activity*, 23 (emphasis original).
7. Postman and Weingartner, *Teaching as Subversive Activity*, 23 (emphasis added).

In this chapter we will define and distinguish character-centric questions, the fifth forerunner of character theology, and isolate the influential identifiers before laying out the character-centric question process and potential questions for oral hermeneutics in relation to a story set.

What Is a Character-Centric Question?

Not all hermeneutic models respect genres. Not all theologies cover the bases of human needs. The same is true of questions. There are questions and then there are questions.

What is a character-centric question?[8] Simply stated, *character-centric questions seek participatory discovery of how biblical characters reveal the Creator through conversations, conflict, conduct, and context.* We will now expand and unpack the definition.

Character-centric questions promote participatory discovery by artfully and selectively framing the questions surrounding the setting and conflict between characters as shaped by the story. Following clues left by the author requires the participants' curiosity, imagination, emotions, and reason, thereby becoming powerful tools of interpretive discovery even as they foster sequential questions. The ultimate goal of character-centric questions is to reveal the Creator through the thoughts, actions, and interactions of the biblical characters within a story. Another goal is to facilitate the participants' identification with various characters in the story so that the Creator is glorified through transformed behavior that demonstrates truth or dodges error. Character-centric questions wave the welcome flag of participatory choice, change, and consequences.

Expanding the Components

Character-centric questions. Many questions Bible storytellers ask originate from a print culture, thereby resulting in a strong focus on facts. Character-centric questions, however, are orally based, thereby resulting in a strong focus on characters. Characters lead to characteristics, personal encounters lead to intellectual encounters, personalities lead to propositions, relationships lead to reasons, incidents lead to ideas, holism leads to fragments,

---

8. Douglas Estes defines a question as "*any utterance with interrogative force that asks not says, that always applies some rhetorical effect, and that invites a reply of some sort*" (Estes, *Questions and Rhetoric*, 20 [emphasis original]). He notes the Greek NT contains close to 1000 questions or roughly 15 percent of its sentences (*Questions and Rhetoric*, 18). Matthew has 169, Mark has 114, and Luke has 154, while John comes in at 172 (*Questions and Rhetoric*, 26).

demonstrations lead to definitions, what happens leads to an event encased with and entangled in meaning. What will it take to create a character-centric, questioning culture?

Promote participatory discovery by artfully and selectively framing the questions. Character-centric questions focus on having the participants discover the answers together rather than being told. As this takes place in an EBC group discussion, this requires the story facilitator to skillfully massage well-thought-through questions rather than follow a prescriptive one-size-fits-all canned list of questions. The story facilitator's job is to *steward the dialogue* through character-centric questions. This is an art and science because *one size fits one group*.

One of the greatest services professional theologians can do is to train students and members of the covenant community how to ask probing questions in mono- and cross-cultural settings. The same is true of storytellers. Why? Because the questions will help enlightenment to dawn more than an immediate answer would.

The answers to questions will eventually follow, as will long-term learning, because questions are the answers.[9] Most importantly, participants become wise interpreters of Scripture. What's worth knowing is what's worth asking about. This requires insightful questions that holistically engage the heart and mind *in the moment* as well as questions that encourage relationally based character reflection. The smartest people in the room are *not* necessarily those with all the right answers; rather, they are those with the most perceptive questions.

Not all questions are created equal. The right questions asked by the right person to the right people in the right sequence aid in the discovery of the right answers. But maybe it's not about the "right question" or "right people" or "right sequence"—too Western, too much certainty. Maybe it's more about the art than most realize. Doesn't a large puzzle usually end up with a few extra pieces? This art and science can be learned and developed, especially when intentionally modeled by great executors.

One of the most important things a storyteller can do is to learn to ask penetrating questions. Another is to also leave behind those who can astutely ask character-centric questions (2 Tim 2:2).

Surrounding the setting. All stories take place somewhere (urban, rural, suburbia) in some context (terrains—desert, mountains, lakes, oceans, tundra) at some time (morning, evening, seasons) within or between some cultural groups. Story facilitators can provide the sociocultural-historical background with strong character focus by beginning with a short story that

---

9. See Gregersen, *Questions Are the Answer*.

captures the setting followed by interjecting other aspects at appropriate times as the story unfolds. Setting sets the stage and tone for speech while speech reflects the setting.

And conflict between characters. In that conflict (plot) between characters personalizes and therefore drives stories, questions should focus and follow the story's engine within the cultural context of the story. This involves their conversations, questions, conduct, challenges, attire, among others, that emerge from the story. The main meaning tends to emerge out of the conflictive relationships and events surrounding characters. Crisis creates instructive connections as well as clues to interpretation. Wise questioners focus on areas of conflict.

As shaped by the story. Curious people tend to be disruptive people, which can make for good Bible interpreters. The questions the curious raise expand as well as constrict interpretational boundaries. They expand because they advance our thinking; they constrict because they sharpen focus. They may also run far beyond the text.

To help maximize interpretive integrity, here's one thing exegetes can do. Most have been taught to ask questions to discover what the text is *saying*. Few have been taught to ask questions to discover what the text is *asking* (stay tuned). Which question or questions initiated the author to tell said story? Knowing the answer to this question goes a long way in discovering the truths being demonstrated.

Through the interpretive lens we wear, the breadth and depth of interpretational boundaries are strongly determined by the questions raised. Identifying the author's questions behind the story early in the discussion will help establish interpretive boundaries. Wise interpreters constantly ask, how do my questions expand or constrict interpretational boundaries?

Following clues left by the author requires the participants' curiosity, imagination, emotions, and reason. Authors drop breadcrumbs along the path of the story for participants to discover; they also hide some, thereby requiring patience and persistence. Such clues activate the participants' curiosity, imagination, and emotions as well as the mind as they strain and struggle to unravel the mystery of what's going on and what will happen next. It should also be noted that the better one knows the author, the better one will understand the dropped breadcrumbs.

Some clues left behind consist of the author's intentionally interjected questions as well as repetitive words or phrases. For example, in the Cain and Abel story, "brother" is repeated seven times. The Creator asks, "Where's your brother, Abel?" and Cain responds, "Am I my brother's keeper?" (Gen 4:9 NIV). For ancient composers steeped in orality, Tverberg and Okkema remind us, word repetition and pattern matter, and "to repeat a word many times emphasized its centrality to the story."[10] The same is true for author-interjected questions. Curiosity seeks interpretive clues—obvious or otherwise—left behind by the author.

Thereby becoming powerful tools of interpretive discovery even as they foster sequential questions. Too often relegated to the back burner to make room for reason on the front burner, curiosity, imagination, and emotions are God-given entities that play major roles in Bible story interpretation. They also can help identify a sequence of necessary questions to ask as the scenes sequence, which includes building on participant raised questions.

Wise Bible questioners ask themselves early in the game, how do locals use questions? Who can ask what to whom? When? How? They recognize that Bible interpretation is a journey for each individual, each group, each ethnicity, each generation.

The ultimate goal of character-centric questions is to reveal the Creator through the thoughts, actions, and interactions of the biblical characters within a story. In EBC discussion groups, questions are never neutral; they are designed to reveal something, in this case, the Creator. By highlighting the words, actions, and interactions of characters within a story, the Creator's character and attributes are illuminated. Character-centric questions are designed to discover our Creator.

Another goal is to facilitate the participants' identification with various characters in the story. Character connection is key to individual and collective transformation. "I/we want to be like _____; I/we don't want to be like _____." The storyteller-turned-questioner will take every opportunity possible to connect the characters in the story with those in the audience. This is best accomplished through dialogue and debate rather than monologue. And these interactions are seeded by discerning questions. Do our questions fuel character curiosity?

The Creator is glorified through transformed behavior that demonstrates truth or dodges error. Facilitation continues as the participants seek to discover not just the answers to their personal-collective questions but also the answers to the author's questions that initiated the story. Some of these truths will require participants to establish new habits of the heart while others will require old ones to be altered or abolished.

Character-centric questions wave the welcome flag of participatory choice, participatory change, and participatory consequences.[11] Just as stories and their major characters are *never* designed to be neutral, the same holds

---

10. Tverberg and Okkema, *Listening to the Language,* 77.

11. The Ifugao often collectively sang traditional songs while harvesting rice. As Christianity spread, some of these songs changed to Christian songs, which sometimes brought ridicule.

true of character-centric questions. They go beyond the characters in the text to include the lives of the listeners. Inquiry-based learning driven by character-centric questions requires participants to collectively reflect on God's colorful cast of characters, make individual-corporate life-altering decisions, and live with the consequences.

Life transformation roots deep when accomplished through a collaborative process centered on character-centric questions. And the communal process of asking probing questions creates a culture of hermeneutic culpability.

Isolating Influential Identifiers of Character-Centric Questions

The major influential identifiers of character-centric questions will now be isolated. A character-centric question is:

- Focused on a character's conversations, conduct (actions), context
- Centered on conflict, chaos, controversy
- Participatory in nature
- Discovery-oriented
- An art and science
- Driven by curiosity, imagination, emotion, and reason
- Never neutral
- An accountability process
- The answer

The above components and identifiers will be amplified in the Jonah story in chapters 6 and 7.

Laying Out the Collection Process

Whether in Bible times or today, every community gathers to convey new information, but not necessarily in the same way. Who can initiate such gatherings? Where can they be held? When? Who can speak? What is acceptable attire? What type of topics are off limits? When? How are topics laid out? See fig. 5.1.

The answers to the above and related questions should be investigated for each Bible story, for our culture and for the host culture, *before* beginning an EBC discussion on a specific Bible story. Knowing *what* to teach is one thing. Knowing *how* to teach it is something entirely different. Have you become a curious culture watcher?

Laying Out the Question Process

In this section we lay out the oral hermeneutics process that is driven by narrative logic fueled by character-centric questions that leads to character theology. The backdrop is an EBC discussion group working their way through a story set. They have now reached the third lesson in the series of five. But there is a step often missed in the process, especially when the discussion group is conducted in subcultures or cross-cultural settings.

Don't Minimize the Preliminaries

Foundations have consequences. We will therefore briefly note some that will have tremendous impact on the outcome of the entire story-interpretative process.

Establish Relationships and Pray Frequently

At least two assumptions stand behind the story-interpretative process. First, when possible, relationships will have already been established with the audience, either personally or through respected intermediaries. These relationships tend to begin through questions and conversations in that they demonstrate genuine curiosity, care, concern; they also secure a speaker's credibility (necessary in many parts of the globe) once his/her faith story is heard. There is more than credibility of the text; there is also credibility of the communicator. Once credibility is secured, expect questions and story swapping to multiply.

Figure 5.1. Storytelling Cultures of Teller and Told.
Photo by Tom Steffen. Used with permission.

Second, prayer—before, during, and after—covers the entire story set presentation in that *"He is always listening"* (Ps 34:15 VOICE [emphasis original]). Why is prayer necessary? Because Bible storytelling between two combatant spiritual powers (angel armies vs. satanic armies) is spiritual warfare for story supremacy. Now to the story-interpretive process itself.

Do Your Cultural Homework

How well have we been trained to discern propositions? Form questions? Multiple question combinations? How well have we been trained to exegete what the text says for high to low oralists? What the text asks? Identify the author's questions behind the text? How those in different cultures ask and answer questions?

People in every culture ask and answer questions, although some appreciate this exercise more than others. Even so, people do not necessarily ask or answer questions in the same way, whether during Bible times or today. Nor can just anyone ask or answer questions. Who in a patron-client community can ask questions? How do strong honor-shame communities influence how questions are asked and answered? The answers to these and related questions should be investigated for our own culture as well as for the host culture *before* telling a Bible story at an EBC discussion group.

In communities where honor and shame remain strongly voiced and visualized values, answering a question can be dangerous. A wrong answer can be shameful not just for the responder, but for his/her family, and possibly the community as well. A circular relational seating arrangement (in contrast to watching the back of heads) helps, as does breaking the group up into small groups, then returning to the large group to offer collective findings.

To help encourage participation, Bible storyteller Jim Thurber offers this advice, "There are no wrong answers. Build on their answer whatever it is." We would add, honor the contributions of contributors publicly to build confidence. The goal is to create a safe, interactive question environment. Such adjustments can turn a dangerous, potentially shameful situation into a safe, beneficial event for all.

Why is doing one's cultural homework required *before* an EBC discussion begins? Because (speaking to Westerners) Richards and O'Brian warn, "We can easily forget that . . . reading the Bible is a cross-cultural experience."[12] Stallter adds this sobering insight: "If we ignore the cultural frameworks of the biblical world, we will default to our own with little question as to their relevancy to the tasks of hermeneutics and theology. . . . Our love affair may be spiritual adultery."[13] Worse yet we might not even know if spiritual adultery has occurred. The same could be true if Bible communicators neglect analyzing their own culture as well as the host culture.

Science has impacted not only our thinking, but by extension, the very questions we ask. We therefore tend to ask questions that seek content-based, quantifiable answers. *Culture drives our questions and hence tends to answer our expectations.*

> How well have we been trained to analyze how people tell stories communally?
>
> Have you become a curious culture watcher?

Culture also influences our research. The Greek New Testament, Douglas Estes explains, is "often consulted for what it says—and often poorly, in snippets" and "often seen as a book of 'answers' or 'information' or 'facts.'" Recall Facts Anonymous in "Setting the Stage."

12. Richards and O'Brian, *Misreading Scripture*, 75.
13. Stallter, *Gap between God*, 18–19.

Estes continues, long ago, moderns in their quest for certainty, as expected, focused on the "factual, rational, didactic, and *neat* truths." There was a problem however, "the NT writers were not very interested in modern, factual, rational, didactic, and *neat* truths." What was their interest? "Showing, persuading, encouraging, reasoning, and warning the reader."[14] This lands Estes on the role of questions in discourse:

> While propositions excel at communicating truth claims, questions excel at reasoning and persuading. In fact, while logic and reason in modernity focus on propositions, asking questions is truly "the first and foremost theory of reasoning." Thus, if reasoning and debate are to occur, questions must be a major component of the discourse.[15]

In contrast to modernity's focus on concepts and ideas, where should the storyteller-interpreter's questions focus? Knowing the answers to the above and related questions will aid in forming culturally relevant questions that convict and convince. Anthony Thiselton offers this warning and possible process:

> The interpreter brings his own questions to the text. But because his questions may not be the right ones, his initial understanding of the subject matter is limited, provisional, and liable to distortion. But this provisional understanding, in turn, helps him to revise his questions and to ask more adequate and appropriate ones.... The process continues until he is in a position to ask questions which have clearly been shaped by the text itself; so that he achieves a progressively more adequate understanding of its subject matter.[16]

Good teachers know when to suppress expertise. One way they can accomplish this is by *asking* penetrating questions rather than *telling*. Good teaching is not limited to offering content or correcting it. Good teaching requires an audience-attentive relationship centered on questions. Good teachers don't start with conclusions. The ancients remind us they were as "concerned about what they wanted to ask their readers as they were about what they wanted to say to their readers."[17]

---

14. Estes, *Questions and Rhetoric*, 22.
15. Estes, *Questions and Rhetoric*, 22–23 (emphasis original).
16. Anthony Thiselton, as quoted in Bartholomew, "Three Horizons," 126.
17. Estes, *Questions and Rhetoric*, 334.

> How do my questions expand or constrict the interpretational boundaries of the questions behind the text?

Good teachers are good questioners because good questions lead to the Author-author's core contributions for implementation. Wisely selected questions help bring clarity (and sometimes even consensus) surrounding the truths being communicated through characters in a story. This, however, requires doing one's cultural homework. When preliminaries are prioritized, *every Bible communicator can become not just a better storyteller, but a better questioner as well.* And they can leave behind a cadre of good storyteller-questioners (2 Tim 2:2).

Hit the Right Target

Conversations, by design, are reciprocal, risky, yet rewarding. To identify the appropriate questions to decode the conversations of characters and surrounding contexts within a story requires some homework.

Possibly the greatest mistake Bible interpreters make is to initially focus their attention on securing the right meaning of a story before identifying the author's questions behind the story. Have we put the cart before the horse?

Since questions focus the discussion and more easily persuade than telling, which critical questions might frame the story so that interpreters answer the author's questions? Challenge those who already believe they have the correct answer?

The easiest way to chop down a tree is to spend time initially sharpening the axe. The easiest way to interpret a story is to determine how best to frame the questions to ask so that the author's questions are answered.

> What will it take to create a character-centric, questioning culture?

When does giving advice and answers impede long-term understanding and spiritual growth? This is especially significant for Scripture presented to humanity as a mystery to be discovered. *Can we learn to listen not to just respond but to understand?* This may be challenging because listening can be dangerous to one's pride. Recall the broad implications for listening captured by the Chinese character in chapter 2—two ears to hear, ten eyes to see, undivided attention for focus, respect for the king in one's thinking, and an undivided heart to fully feel.

Can we learn to ask penetrating questions rather than just offer advice and answers? How could such an approach create curiosity that offers space to unleash constructive dialogue and debate? Promote long-term learning and spiritual maturation for both the recipients *and* the questioner? Create vividness that enhances memory?

Sage Bible storytellers recognize learning is a two-way street; they also know when to *ask* and when to *tell*. Why? Because they *listen*.

In relation to hermeneutics, questions can take Bible interpreters to different theological destinations, some appropriate, some not. The destination interpreters try to avoid is "faulty" theology (see fig. 5.2). Bible interpreters seek to respect the Author-author as they attempt to relate ancient history to current contexts (the two horizons).

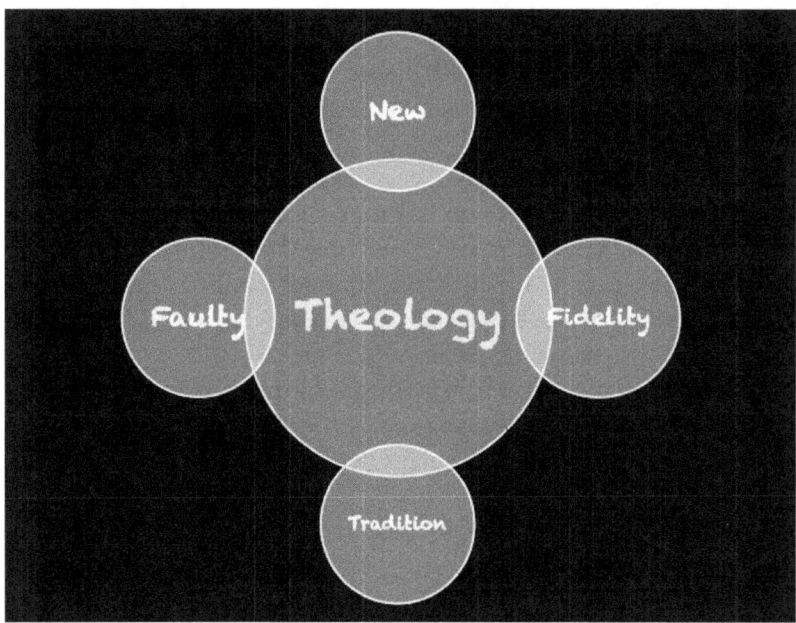

Figure 5.2. Appropriate Theology

Interpreters therefore strain for "fidelity" through more appropriate questions. This could place the interpretation in one of two spheres—"tradition" or "new." Tradition normally establishes the interpretation within acceptable church history over the centuries. New would place the interpretation outside of tradition yet biblically acceptable. For example, we remember when spiritual warfare caught the attention of many Evangelicals in the West during the nineties, and the flow of books that followed this theological novelty. Modernity's assertion that the supernatural did not exist received a much-needed course correction.

New in the West, however, did not mean new in Latin American, Africa, or Asia, which powerfully demonstrates how culture impacts one's theology. The same could be said of relational honor-shame influence on theology (in contrast to the legal innocence-guilt influence) that appeared on the West's missions radar screen around 2000. When was suffering added in the West? Who initiated it?

Such illustrations demonstrate that Western interpreters with the help of the Grand Interpreter and the Majority World can move *beyond* the total influence of their own culture in Bible interpretation. What will be the next "new" theology that derives from insightful questions?

When the storyteller-questioner asks a question, do who or what or where or why show up? We hope "who" becomes the first visitor, but *not* the last.

A Single, Timeless Meaning for Each Story?

One of the biggest critiques of oral hermeneutics is the possibly that a single Bible story could have more than one meaning.[18] We will use "truth" (theological and/or ethics) rather than "meaning" because many contemporary exegetes perceive "multiple meanings" to be synonymous with false ones as there can only be "one authorial intent" per story.

Starting points matter in that they tend to reflect the utilizer's assumptions. We are not suggesting one is right or wrong; rather, because of strong theological and/or denominational socialization we tend *not* to be cognizant of, much less scrutinize, the assumptions behind our favorite hermeneutic. *How aware is the interpreter of the assumptions that drive his or her hermeneutic?*

Questions originate from assumptions. Asking "What is the single meaning of this story?" is based on certain assumptions. Asking "What does the Holy Spirit demonstrate for us from this story?" is also based on different assumptions. One seeks correctness (capture the content) while the other seeks coreness (capture the character). One leads to information while the other leads to actions.

18. Is a "one main point" per parable partially the result of a knee-jerk reaction to the former allegorical interpretation?

> *How aware is the interpreter of the assumptions that drive his or her hermeneutic?*

Which sets in motion the best hermeneutic for the narrative sections of Scripture? Are these questions intentionally designed to discover different outcomes? Based on often hidden assumptions, storyteller-questioners frame questions to generate certain interpretive leverage.

Ever notice the "logical" in theo*logical* (education)? Note any assumptions behind this type of education? "God" studies are logical in nature, i.e., science-based systematics offered through formal and nonformal institutions. Recall our brief stroll down Western Hermeneutic Lane in chapter 4.

Science has influenced much of Western hermeneutics, socializing interpreters to funnel down to the finite. This sounds so correct to those socialized in the sciences. Recall Bernard Ramm's influential science-based definition of theology in chapter 4: "Training in logic and science forms excellent background for exegesis.... Systematic teaching of Scripture is the Scriptures' final intention."[19]

> When the storyteller-questioner asks a question, do who or what or where or why come to visit?

Orality socializes interpreters to inflate to its fullness. This sounds so right to those socialized in orality who think more holistically. Two different assumptions; two different types of questions; two different outcomes. Each begins with its "known," laying out an intentional path to discover the "unknown." Why? Because each question asked is driven by its own assumptions and logic.

Estes differentiates how people think about questions and statements (propositions). He believes the distinction lies between how people perceive "question logic" from "propositional logic." There is a problem, however— "their training only included approaches to the text using *alethic logic* (the thinking behind propositions)."[20] Estes offers an alternative:

> Gaining experience in the use of *erotetic logic* (the thinking behind questions) allows the Bible interpreters to approach the text in a whole new way. Instead of constantly thinking about what the

19. Ramm, *Christian View of Science*, 53, 155.
20. Estes, *Questions and Rhetoric*, 18.

text is saying, the interpreter with a background in *erotetic* logic can also think more precisely about what the text is asking.[21]

Should interpreters choose to utilize *alethic* logic, they can expect to find the spotlight focused on what the text is *saying*. Should they choose to utilize *erotetic* logic, interpreters can expect to find the spotlight focused on what the text is *asking*. Focusing on the questions the author is asking, Estes argues, aids immensely in interpretive integrity.

Let's briefly illustrate the thematic discovery process through the well-known and loved (especially in Asia) "prodigal son" story of Luke 15. The "asking" question Jesus seems to be answering goes back to the beginning of the chapter: *Should religious leaders hang out with sinners*? In that all stories are embedded in other stories, hints to the answer to Jesus's question can be found in the first two stories of the trilogy—the lost sheep and lost coin. Back to story 3.

Interpretation driven by different types of logic can result in different conclusions. Which type of logic shows the greatest respect for the narrative genre? Is ambiguity as bad as some print-oriented exegetes believe it to be? Could coreness for the narrative genre be the equivalent of correctness for other textual models?

> Which type of logic shows the greatest respect for the narrative genre?

What is the single theme of story 3? Forgiveness? Grace? Mercy? Inadequacy of works? God's love? Repentance? Vulnerability? Humility? Too abstract. Too boring. Too focused on what the text is *saying* rather than what it is *asking*.

Possibly a more concrete place to start is by asking, *Who is the hero in the story? Who is the antagonist*? How do the answers to these questions help focus and formulate a more character-centric theme? Do they help answer the author's question?

A possible theme that answers the question Jesus is asking and answering through the third story could be: *Celebrating humility requires spending time with outcasts*. How's that sound to the reader?

For some modern-day oralists, probably way too boring. More riveting and rousing would be something like: *Modeling God, true religious leaders who wish to celebrate humility will spend all their time, energy, and wherewithal necessary with those like the younger son in a distant land who*

---

21. Estes, *Questions and Rhetoric*, 18–19 (emphasis original).

spurns God's law (doesn't love his father) or the elder son at home who also *spurns God's law (doesn't love his father—refuses celebration invitation)* so that they have opportunity to experience God's loving grace and mercy and humbly restore their broken relationship with their Creator and others. How's that orally layered "narrative statement" sound? More character-centric?

For some of today's oralists, probably much softer, more sensory, more ascetic, more relatable, more memorable, more repeatable. And its length is not necessarily an issue. The strong focus on characters, symbols, and settings more than compensates for length in that they offer the participative audience *compelling and immediate* on-ramps to identify with one or more characters; it offers personified propositions. Since truths are embodied in relationships, who evidences self-righteousness? Retribution? Humble adoration? Legalism? Faith? Judgment? Grace? Mercy? Protection?

The focus on attitudes, actions, and artifacts advances beyond the meaning of abstract words frozen in print. Rather, it ties them to specific concrete events, symbols, rituals, and settings, thereby thawing them out. The melting process unleashes the integration of imagination, emotions, and reason, *not* just reason alone. Abstract concepts moored to concrete characters magnify not just meaning, but appeal and impact as well.

The participative audience will probably want to work their way through the entire story (not necessarily in scene sequence) considering the role and implications of *each* colorful character portrayed. For example, a despised God is mentioned as the single spiritual character. Human characters include: the restorative father, the dutiful hired servants, the partying guests, the repentant younger son, loose women, a pig owner, unhelpful locals, the law-keeping older son, the home community guarding her public reputation. Nonhuman characters serving as symbols include: a greedy inheritance, pigs, food, feast, the fattest calf, the best robe, a ring, shoes. Setting includes the family home and fields, a distant land experiencing famine, the home village.

> Could coreness for the narrative genre be the equivalent of correctness for other textual models?

Each character, symbol, and setting accentuates a different perspective of the story, thereby increasing identification possibilities for the participatory audience. In relation to characters, Gunn and Fewell conclude, "Because most stories involve more than one character, it is not uncommon to see several desires, often in conflict, working themselves out. There may be several climaxes and several resolutions."[22] That is why it takes the whole story (and, in this case, two previous stories [circular redundancy]) to discern the possible multiple truths being conveyed through the background question Jesus is answering.

All the above could be called "oral layering." Oral layering creates what Ryken calls "excess baggage."[23] Paul Ricoeur prefers a "surplus of meaning,"[24] i.e., nuanced understanding that goes *beyond* that found in objective print analysis alone, and *beyond* the present interpretive time when the story is later revisited.

To leverage the "surplus of meaning" (e.g., beauty, the experiential) to help discern the truth found in a story, which oral medium features contribute to the fidelity and forcefulness of the message? These social triggers could include such things as voice (volume/pace/pitch/tone), gestures, emotions, aesthetics, attire, repetition (interpretive and memory aids), body language, facial features and expressions, positions, and paraphernalia (see fig. 5.3).[25]

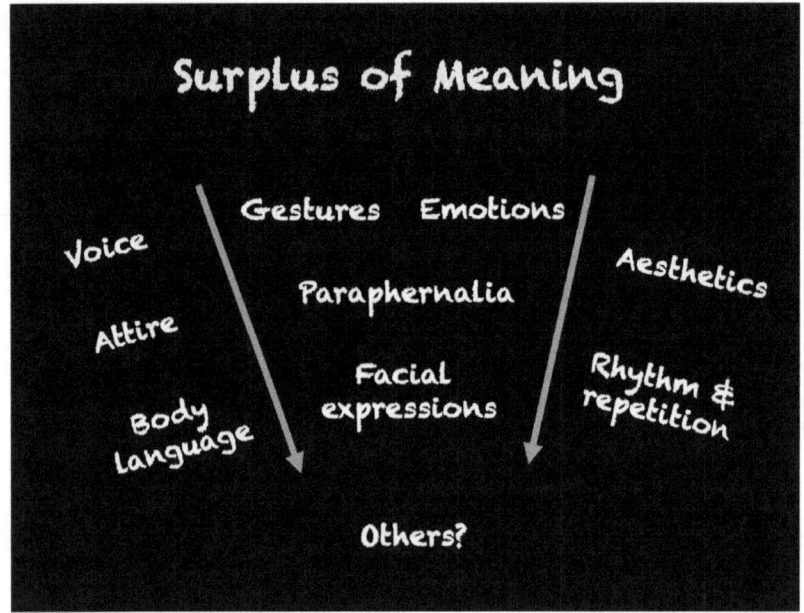

Figure 5.3. A Surplus of Meaning

22. Gunn and Fewell, *Narrative in Hebrew Bible*, 112.
23. Ryken, *How Bible Stories Work*, 26.
24. Ricoeur, *Interpretation Theory*, 57. See also Vanhoozer, *Drama of Doctrine*, 88.
25. For a rich, exhaustive, yet readable dissertation on orality and performance from a Bible translation perspective, see Dickie, "Zulu Song, Oral Art."

Matthews expands beyond the written: "Energy that is so much a part of a spoken conversation, especially when it becomes emotionally heated or intense, can lose a great deal in its translation to written form.... Written dialogue seldom includes the choppiness of normal speech patterns, the unconscious grammatical errors, or a true sense of the emotions that accompany a verbal exchange."[26] There is more than meets the eye!

But aren't these just window dressing, added embellishments to what is *primary*—the written words? Not so fast, interjects Finnegan. These are "not mere embellishments superadded to the already existent literary work—as we think of them in regard to written literature—but an integral as well as flexible part of its full realization as a work of art." She continues, we too often

> think of the *written* element as the primary and thus somehow the most fundamental material in every kind of literature—a concentration on the *words* to the exclusion of the vital and essential aspect of performance. It cannot be too often emphasized that this insidious model is a profoundly misleading one in the case of oral literature.[27]

What interpreters too often miss is the strong innate and immediate interplay and interdependence between print and the proclaimed-performed that takes storytelling (dialogue between teller and told), and hence meaning, to a much richer level. It also demonstrates the covenant community's concern for presentation, perception, and preservation. Those who want to make the spoken-written words of God—not just the written words of God—more relevant, more engaging to those living in today's world, must proclaim-perform it.

The influence of cultures and subcultures enters at every level of performance-proclamation. This places the onus on the storyteller to know how each aspect of the host's culture would differ from those found in the biblical text.

Proximity of the storyteller's culture and the host culture to Bible cultures can prove helpful. Most Westerners, however, find themselves distant from Bible cultures in countless significant ways, e.g., social hierarchy (patron-client), honor-shame, time orientation, orality. What are the criteria for Bible story performance-proclamation that doesn't *over-express or under-express* the story so that the author's questions are answered? How

---

26. V. Matthews, *More than Meets Ear*, 13, 21.

27. Finnegan, *Oral Literature in Africa*, 6 (emphasis original). Edouard Glissant, referencing Haiti with its heavy emphasis on the arts, replaces "literature" with "oraliture" (Praeger, "Edouard Glissant," 45).

does fidelity of the written text differ from fidelity of the spoken text? We have *much* to learn.

> Which oral communication medium features contribute to the fidelity and forcefulness of the message?

Not only do cultures and subcultures impact interpretation, so do gender, age, occupation, socioeconomic levels, geography, personal and spiritual maturation, current controversies (economic, political, religious). How will children, teens, adults, or seniors differ in their view of the twists and turns of the "prodigal son" story? In relation to occupations, how would an economist, government administrator, doctor, lawyer, veterinarian, businessperson, pimp, prostitute, pastor, theologian, or farmer perceive the story? Those of different socioeconomic levels? How would location offer different assessments of the story by those living in the desert, Arctic, mountains, seacoast, large cities, rural areas?

In relation to gender, many Western males (the dominant pool of theologians) tend to find themselves on a mission, therefore wanting to "get to the point." Many females prefer to see themselves on a *journey* with plenty of time to unpack details. What's the hurry? Gender colors the process and outcome of Bible interpretation in *every* culture.

Nor should one discount the level of personal and spiritual maturity of the participants or current controversies (local, global) reverberating within or without the covenant community. What life-situation questions are presently reverberating in the minds of participants? Would any of them offer a different title for the story? *No Bible story is heard (or told) from a blank slate.* Everyone arrives with interpretive interests. Is this not the genius of character theology?

Powerful and penetrating stories, like the three spiraled together in Luke 15, offer multiple levels of truths for different cultures, subcultures, age groups, maturation levels, occupations, locations. That is because good stories offer "representations of patterns of adaptive behavior."[28] This is the beauty, depth, and genius of great stories. We agree with Stephen Shoemaker, "Recognizing multiple meanings in a story is more reverencing to the holiness of God than straining after one meaning."[29]

Good stories keep listeners/viewers/readers coming back knowing *there is more to the story.* Is there more to the stories in Luke 15 that answers

---

28. J. Peterson, "Why We Remember Stories."
29. Shoemaker, *Godstories*, xxiii.

the author's questions? Is there more to be discovered or has the Minority World already nailed it?

All age groups are on a journey. Every family (nuclear or extended), every community (rural, urban, suburban), every nation (small, medium, or large) is on a journey. Each journey varies in level and diversity of need, which allows for the various characters in a story to meet *any* of these. In that our faith journey continues, we make new discoveries and gain new insights (that were always present) provided by the Author-author over time. God meets us where we are in the story, and then revolutionizes our story.

Does fidelity require a single, timeless meaning (principle) for each story? Not necessarily in an oral-reliant world or oral-influenced text where ambiguity and nuance are purposely at play. Assumed, anticipated, accepted, and appreciated by author and audience, ambiguity and nuance reigned then as it does now in a growing oral-digital-reliant world. Got ambiguity?

Even so, *no* Bible story is open to *any* interpretation. What are the questions behind the text? Which Author-author–dropped breadcrumbs provide interpretive clues (Acts 15:22)? Whose voices from the global covenant community throughout the centuries help provide some semblance of consensus (2 Pet 1:20)?

> *Can we learn to ask questions rather than just offer advice and answers?*

Through factors *within* the text, such as repetition and rhythm, and factors *beyond* the text, such as individual-communal honor and shame shared in the symbiotic world of tellers and told, all serve as *guide rails and guardrails* to a boundaried-fluid interpretation. The corporate church, i.e., "the saints outside our culture" and "down through the ages also plays a role in preserving written tradition."[30] And *behind* the text is the Grand Interpreter.

In the end, the individual-communal exegete-artists are responsible and accountable to the Author. Yes, in the oral world multiple truths are considered not only possible or plausible but probable, unless the author has stated otherwise. Intentionally told/written for the ear and eye, it was assumed the stories were an ongoing communal discussion. These are some of the many geniuses of story, oral hermeneutics, and character theology.

---

30. Hiebert, "Critical Contextualization," 108. Has the West's focus on individualism minimized our perception of the role the global covenant community over time should play in challenging beliefs and behaviors?

Encourage Participants to Ask Questions

Good storytelling is never a monologue. Rather, it's a dialogue where teller and told feed off each other. The same should be true for the use of questions. Good questions between storyteller and story listeners feed off each other; they become in-the-moment events.

When participants ask a question, for the most part the storyteller can be relatively assured they will be culturally relevant. They will also reveal the participants' level of comprehension about the story under discussion. Or they may be asked for the benefit of someone else in the audience, not uncommon in Ifugao.

> Does fidelity require a single, timeless meaning (principle) for each story?

Storytellers can leverage a participant's questions, thereby generating greater clarity to existing cloudiness. This also can provide opportunity for the storyteller to role-play one of the characters in the story to answer the question.

Asking in a conversational manner (rather than lecture mode) without cold calling also invites ongoing collaborative participation. Here's a possible conversation starter: "I've got this big question; can you-all help me with it?"

Question Your Questions

Seldom do storyteller-questioners ask themselves why they ask which questions. Simple lists of six to eight questions make it easy to follow. But what initiated these lists? Makes it easy for the listeners to repeat? Makes it easy for the storyteller-questioner to remember? How well do these questions match the flow of the conversation?

We offer this proposal for the review section of the story: let the questions *emerge from the text* rather than *superimposing a predetermined list of generic questions on the story*. This honors the text rather than one's predetermined theology with its possible limitations. As we move to the question categories, ask yourself for each category, *Why do I use the questions I use?*

Question Categories for the Storying Process

As the authoritative source of truth, sacred Scripture is our guide. The Grand Interpreter is our tutor. The goal is to become individually and collectively what God intends—honoring him by multiplying our talents among the nations.

The EBC discussion group is now ready for story 3. It's time for communal theologizing to continue.

A quick reminder of the backstory presented at the first EBC discussion (repetition) provides new participants some helpful background for the present story. Rather than systematically covering author, date, background, doctrines covered, outline, connection to the grand narrative, etc., tell a short story that covers these, then ask some questions.[31] "Do you remember who wrote this story and who were the recipients? Long ago Luke wrote this story to . . ." (other background information can be inserted appropriately as the story unfolds).[32] "Anyone remember any story that preceded this story?" This could follow, if needed: "Here's a brief overview . . ."

The EBC discussion continues with reflection questions related to *loyalty* (relational term rather than a legal term—*guilt*). See fig. 5.4. Note the emphasis on characters. Note also these questions are *not* meant to be followed sequentially or verbatim, but rather serve as possible character-centric examples. Nor are the questions against concepts; rather, they seek abstract content through concrete means—characters. Possible loyalty questions could include:

- Anyone like to summarize the story about _____ from last week?[33]
- Anyone able to tell someone our last Bible story about what _____ did/said?
- How did they respond? What questions did they ask?
- Anyone try to model what _____ said/did in our last story? How did people respond?
- Anyone else have something to add?

---

31. In 2023, some PhD students from Asia Graduate School of Theology in Manila taking one of my (Tom) classes chose for one assignment to write backstories to introduce certain epistles. Characters and conversations replaced the present typical sterile, systematic introductions (author, date, recipients, geography, focus, outline) into attractive and appealing stories.

32. For more ideas, see "Questioning Our Questions," in T. Steffen and Bjoraker, *Return of Oral Hermeneutics*, 196–29.

33. A great way to create confident Bible storytellers.

It's now time to *focus* on the story for the day. Not only do character-centric questions and themes keep things concrete and relational, so do titles for single stories and story sets. For example, "Today's story is 'True Fathers Never Stop Seeking Wayward Sons.'"

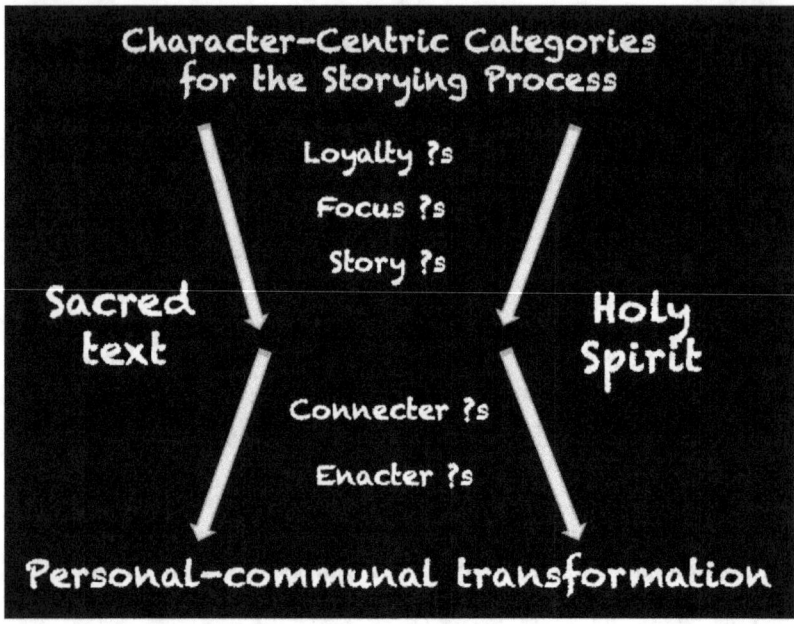

Figure 5.4. Character-Centric Categories for the Storying Process

The storyteller continues, "As I tell the story, imagine yourself in the story as a reporter or close bystander. What do you see? Smell? Hear? Feel? Taste? Who are the key characters? Who do you identify with?"

> What are the criteria for performance that doesn't *over-express or under-express*?

"While I tell the story, listen to how the author describes the main characters. Who tries to control whom? What were the consequences of their words and deeds? What questions do you think the author is trying to answer through the characters involved? Who is the hero of the story?"

These or similar questions begin to show the *interconnectedness* of Bible stories and possible *repetitive themes*. They also initiate the process of connecting characters and context to participants through imagination and emotions as authors drop breadcrumbs, challenging participants to abandon former ways of life and adopt new ones.

> *Why do I use the questions I use?*

When a participant arrives late, rather than considering this a distraction, use this opportunity to gather feedback and develop future storytellers. "Wendy, can you retell (rather than explain) the story for _____?" Others will no doubt chime in with additions and amendments. As the Yapese reminded the Lingenfelters, "Stories told orally are more accurate than those written down because a written story represents only one person's opinion, whereas an oral story is subject to the collective corrections of its hearers."[34] Collective feedback expands storytelling proficiency even as it cultivates future storytellers.

After telling the story the storyteller now turned story-questioner *focuses* the lesson through questions; it is time to see how the participants answered the general questions prior to hearing the story. Then walk through the story scene by scene, raising character-centric questions along the journey as well as building on the participants' questions. Questions could include:

- As a reporter or bystander, what did you observe about where the story took place?
- Any backstory we should be aware of?
- Any characters the author wants us to know?
- Who is the human hero of the story? Who challenges the hero? How?
- Who sides with whom in the story?
- Who influences whom in the story?
- Who made wise/poor choices? What were the consequences of his/her choices?
- What other options did _____ have?
- Who was shamed/honored, guilty/innocent, afraid/empowered, polluted/purified? What choices were made that resulted in these consequences?
- Who used their power in a constructive way? A destructive way?
- Who/what caused the conflict between _____ and _____?

34. J. Lingenfelter and Lingenfelter, *Teaching Cross-Culturally*, 28–29.

- What relationships were broken/healed/honored/shamed/feared/enjoyed?
- How did the space/place/timing influence _____'s conversations/conduct?
- How did the symbol/ritual influence _____'s conversations/conduct?
- How did you respond when _____ said/did this to _____?
- What would have happened if someone in our community/our family had done/said what _____ did/said?
- Who regressed the most in the story?
- How does God become the hero of this story?
- If you could ask any character a question, who would you ask what?
- What questions do you think the author is trying to get us to answer?
- Anyone else have something to add?

Note the focus on the more concrete questions: who, what, and how. Asking "why" questions requires more abstract critical thinking and tends to do best when preceded by more concrete questions.

No matter how good one's questions, heresy is the wolf always crouched by the door. We offer this *heresy buster* question: Who in/outside the story supports your conclusion?

One of the major weaknesses within the modern-day evangelical orality movement continues to be the focus on single stories or story sets without showing their connection to other stories or the grand narrative. All stories are embedded in other stories, as are all characters.

Connector questions help participants understand that the Bible is not just a collection of hundreds of stand-alone, subject-based stories (remnants of systematic theology). Rather, these stories help script a broader narrative as a series of related stories, e.g., the marriage supper of the Lamb in the new Jerusalem (Rev 19:9–10) is embedded in the Eden wedding, Luke's list of nations (Acts 2) is embedded in the Babel story, Mary's song (Luke 1:46–55) is embedded in Zechariah's song (Luke 1:68–74) and Hannah's prayer (1 Sam 2). *All* are embedded in the grand narrative. Questions could include:

- Who in the story reminds you of other people/events mentioned in other Bible stories?
- As a reporter or bystander, what did you notice about the present surroundings of the characters that mirror other Bible stories?[35]

---

35. God-ordained meetings at wells had long-term consequences, e.g., Isaac and

- Do any of the characters in the story foretell the coming of the Messiah?
- How do the characters in the story help advance God's grand narrative?[36]
- Anyone else have something to add?

No story, no main character, no well-crafted character-centric question is meant to be neutral. Advancing beyond awareness to application, the EBC discussion group has now reached the *enactor* questions that encourage Bible-based allegiance changes in attitudes and activities advanced throughout the story. This is key for low to high oralists who tend to prefer *immediate* application rather than tucking it away for later recall.

Osborne observes that "the actual purpose of Scripture is not explanation but exposition, not description but proclamation.... It is not enough to recreate the intended meaning of the passage. We must elucidate its significance for today."[37] In that light, possible "so what" character-centric questions could include:

- Do you know someone who experienced what _____ experienced? How did s/he handle it?
- Whose example in the story should the covenant community/your family/you imitate/avoid so God is glorified?
- What should the covenant community/my family/I say/do?
- Who in the story challenges us to advance God's mission (word and works, hospitality and hope) to those close and afar?
- If these characters represent truth, what would that mean for our lives today?
- Who would like to team up and review the story for us through a song/drawing/painting/drama/other?
- Who in the story do you want to emulate/shun this week? How will the covenant community/your family/you accomplish this?
- Starting today, what's our community/my family/my role in living out this story about _____?
- Anyone else have something to add?

Rebekah (Gen 24:10–61), Moses and Zipporah (Exod 2:15b–21), Jesus and the Samaritan woman (John 4:1–42).

36. For example, the Samaritan woman story shows God seeks *all* peoples.
37. Osborne, *Hermeneutical Spiral*, 12.

Note the progression from group to individually focused questions. Westerners tend to ask questions focused on you, the individual. Collective communities tend to ask questions that address the group ("you-all"). Ask an individually focussed question to a collective community, and one is likely to receive a communally focussed question in return.

Communally focussed questions can prove helpful in strongly honor-shame–oriented communities where spotlighting an individual could easily cause the entire audience to clam up. Wise storyteller-questioners know when to ask which type of question.

The above questions—which cover *behind, within, and beyond* the text—should be perceived as *idea stimulators* rather than used verbatim or sequentially followed. The storyteller-turned-questioner may also find himself/herself skipping back and forth across the landscape of the question categories as s/he continues to challenge participants to continue contemplating by asking: "Anything else?" All questions can serve as teachers with or without an answer heard from the storyteller or participants. Even Job and Jonah did not get all their questions answered. Is the question the answer?

Moral Value Categories for the Questioning Process

All cultures have at least four binary moral value systems: innocence-guilt (legal laws that seek obedience), honor-shame (relationships that seek loyalty and allegiance [expect envy]), power-fear (control that seeks forced/unforced submission), purity-pollution (hygiene that seeks cleanliness). See appendix A.

Not all cultures, however, give equal emphasis to each binary. Many tribal cultures, like the Ifugao, give strong emphasis to power-fear associated with control and honor-shame that is relationally based. Some Hindus, First Nations, Jews, and Christians give strong emphasis to cleanliness highlighted in purity-pollution. The West, built strongly on the predicate of law and order, tends to give strong impetus to legally based innocence-guilt.

The percentages of the four moral values in any culture vary and continually change—some fast, some slow. For example, social media is quickly moving many Americans from innocence-guilt toward honor-shame or honor-fame.[38]

Why are these binary moral values so important for the storyteller to know? Because they intuitively influence how one interprets, teaches, remembers the Bible. Because they intuitively influence one's resultant theology. For example, Westerners tend to read Scripture through legal eyes.

38. See A. Crouch, "Return of Shame."

Think Romans and the legal aspects of justification by faith found in most Minority World commentaries. Jackson Wu's *Reading Romans with Eastern Eyes: Honor and Shame in Paul's Message and Mission* offers a more culturally appropriate way to understand Romans.[39]

Which social moral values drive Scripture? Probably not those we think. Timothy Tennent compares two value binaries which some of the prominent systematic theology textbooks miss or minimize:

> A survey of all of the leading textbooks used in teaching Systematic Theology across the major theological traditions reveals that although the indexes are filled with references to guilt, the word "shame" appears in the index of only one of these textbooks. This omission continues to persist despite the fact that the term guilt and its various derivatives occur 145 times in the Old Testament and 10 times in the New Testament, whereas the term shame and its derivatives occur nearly 300 times in the Old Testament and 45 times in the New Testament.[40]

The three binary moral values have dominated since first promoted by United Bible Society translation consultant Eugene Nida in the 1950s.[41] I (Tom) added a fourth—the hygienic values of purity-pollution.[42] Even though purity-pollution rarely shows up in our evangelism and discipleship models, both Testaments place great emphasis on these values, as do many cultures outside the Minority World. Note also one of the major efforts of the Holy Spirit is to purify. Did we miss something? Have we missed other social values?

Which social values drive your questions? How closely do they relate to those of the host audience? Great questions align with the social values of the host culture.

What Makes a Good Question?

What makes a good question? Kevin Kelly offers fourteen insightful possibilities. From those, here are our top eight. A good question:

1. Cannot be answered immediately

---

39. See Flanders and Mischke, *Honor, Shame, and Gospel*; and Georges and Baker, *Ministering in Honor-Shame Cultures*.
40. Tennent, *Theology in the Context*, 92.
41. Nida, *Customs and Cultures*, 154.
42. T. Steffen, "Clothesline Theology."

2. Challenges existing answers
3. Is one you badly want answered once you hear it, but had no inkling you cared before it was asked
4. Creates new territory of thinking
5. Is the seed of innovation in science, technology, art, politics, and business [we would add theology.]
6. Is a probe, a what-if scenario
7. Is one that generates many other good questions
8. Is what humans are for[43]

Good questions go beyond asking *leading* or *closed* questions; they ask *open-ended* questions that invite participates to answer from their perspective. Good questions, argues Liz Wiseman, cause people "not only to think but rethink."[44] Good questions cause people not just to state, but to *re*state; not just to calibrate, but to *re*calibrate. Good questions clear the clutter of confusion.

Better questions lead to better answers. Like a hot knife cutting through cold butter, focused questions cut through interpretative paralysis. And they validate answers. Does your Bible teaching's engine run on questions or answers? To be a good storyteller requires one be a good questioner as well. Good questions can remake not only the Bible communicator but the world as well.

Tying Up Loose Threads

Oral hermeneutics is relationally centered. Characters are relationally centered. Questions, therefore, should follow suit, especially in this orally-digitally-virtually-AI reliant era where some five billion digital natives spend around two and a half hours a day on social media.[45] This is why character-centric questions relate well with today's orally-digitally reliant audiences.

Where does the interpreter begin? Note the following contrasts in table 5.1. By these distinctives we are not claiming one to be superior to the other. Rather, we wish to convey one is more natural, more concrete, more appealing, more impactful, a much closer match to the narrative genre. For

---

43. Kelly, *Inevitable*, 289.
44. Wiseman with Mckeown, *Multipliers*, 116.
45. We Are Social, "Digital 2022."

today's global audiences, more memorable and reproducible, and therefore in respect to the narrative genre should be utilized first.

Topic-oriented title vs. Character-event-oriented title
Discern the text's questions vs. Discern the author's questions
Objectively discerning the information of the text from offstage vs. Subjectively discerning the mystery from onstage
Ask questions of the text vs. Ask questions of the characters
How do I break down the passage? vs. How do I break up the scenes?
What are the supporting points/subpoints? vs. Who are the supporting characters?
What are the missing pieces? vs. Who comprises the missing relationships?
What are the key words spelled out? vs. Who are the key characters acting out?
What do the words mean? vs. What do the character's words and works demonstrate?
What is the flow of thought? vs. What is the flow of events?
What drives each segment? vs. Who drives each scene?
Conflict resolution assured through reason vs. Conflict resolution possibly delayed due to mystery
What is the author's "big idea"? vs. Who demonstrates the author's big idea?

Table 5.1. Contrasting Two Models

The main goal of Bible interpreters is to land somewhere within the traditional spectrum or create new categories of theology that remain faithful even as they nuance and expand understanding of Scripture. Scripture fidelity is the aim. How does one avoid faulty theology (review fig. 5.2)? Possible ways include communal discussion of selected character-centric questions (that can act as community correctors) asked by a humble group leader or participants as *all* listen for interjection from the Grand Interpreter.

> How does one avoid faulty theology?

The flow of the conversation requires a flow of questions, some to *rein in* the conversation, some to *dig deeper*, some to *dissipate the fog*, some to *build on* the previous question or comment, each edging to a higher level. As modeled in the book of Jonah, don't be afraid to end the story with a question without supplying an answer. Keep the suspense hanging; keep the audience anticipating; keep them coming back for more. Good questions keep the full hungry.

> **Helpful Sources**
>
> Estes, *Questions and Rhetoric in the Greek New Testament*
>
> Gregersen, *Questions Are the Answer*
>
> Tiede, "339 Questions Jesus Asked"
>
> Tiede and Davidson, "262 Questions Paul the Apostle of Christ Asked"

Looking Back and Ahead

In summary, there is not only something innate within us that necessitates resolving a conflict raised in a great story, but also offer answers to queried questions. We can't seem to just brush these aside. That includes those representing strong shame-oriented societies. While participants may not articulate a possible answer due to possible public shame, they hope someone will so they can mentally compare answers to see if anything new has emerged. Questions serve as one of the most natural ways to gain new understanding that can enhance one's life. Paraphrasing a rabbinic saying, "One who is easily embarrassed cannot learn."

Mediocre storyteller-interpreters tell listeners the meaning of a story. *Good storyteller-interpreters* ask questions, allowing the listeners to discern the answers. *Great storyteller-interpreters* ask character-centric questions tied to the text and ongoing discussion; they facilitate the moment, which they can do because they *listen*, not just *tell*.

> Does your Bible teaching run on questions or answers?

Bible storytellers-questioners have tended to underestimate the power of questions. *Never* take your questions for granted. The unexamined question is *not* worth asking.[46]

We conclude this chapter with more insightful advice from Lin: "Asking good questions, flexibility and a listening ear are keys to leading effectively."[47] Note all three can be considered action, which portrays one aspect of orality.

EBCs utilizing character-centric questions (oral hermeneutics) leads to character theology. Character theology highlights the Chief Character through carefully Author-author–selected Bible characters living out the messy ups and downs of real life. These highlighted raw biblical characters publicize the exploits and essence of the Chief Character, thereby making a compelling case for global Story superiority (Hab 2:14).

Switching Pedagogies

How better to grasp the concepts of character theology than to see them demonstrated in the short scroll of Jonah. It is time to grab your backpack and head to Nineveh with Jonah.

Before so, how comfortable did you feel with the layout of these initial chapters? If you felt relatively comfortable, e.g., with the definitions laid out, the linear flow of ideas, the emphasis on fragments, resourcing of ideas, we intentionally worked with your pedagogical preference. We purposely presented the material in a very Western linear format from definition to demonstration with a lot of repetition thrown in to begin to introduce a more oral pedagogy.

---

46. An adaptation of Socrates: "The unexamined life is not worth living" (Plato, *Apol.* [38a5–6]).

47. Lin, *Losing Face*, 66.

In part 2 of the book, we switch pedagogies, moving to a more oral orientation—from demonstration to definition, from voice to statement. Part 1 focused on the cognitive; part 2 focuses on the experiential—human experience.

Some readers may feel less comfortable with this type of presentation. Too many gaps in the flow, too much ambiguity, less linearity then preferred, too broad a theme, too many themes, insufficient fragmentation, too much repetition.

Note the generous use of alliterations in both parts 1 and 2. As a feature of orality, similar sounds in succession focus the spotlight on specific themes. Through this thematic, sometime emotive means of communication, alliteration enhances mood and memory. Also note the liberal use of rhetorical questions. These create mystery even as they respect the listeners' ability to answer them rather than quickly being given teacher-initiated answers.

Can we become comfortable with what 80 percent (and growing because of social media) of the world appreciates? Tri-communicators, those who can teach through the "middle way"—a hybrid of oral, print, and digital—will reign in the twenty-first century.[48] This will require Bible storytellers to grasp the interplay between the forest and the trees through digital means.

A Ticket to Ride

Before you decide to discard this book in the nearest trash bin, we ask one more favor. *Try it*. It's one thing to read and think about character theology; it's quite another to experience it—to hear voices; to see body language; to read characters and rooms (contexts). It's time to return to the communication medium used in antiquity (adding contemporary enhancements); most were talkers and viewers rather than readers. This allows us to experience the story more like they did; it's time to experience an EBC gathering.

To help prepare yourself for the Jonah story, *don't read* the four chapters. Rather, gather some friends and *listen* (don't follow the written text) to the story. Why hear it? Because "silent reading encourages psychological distance and a high degree of dispassionate objectivity."[49] Then watch the story presented and debriefed by Ray at Cross Bridge Church in Rockledge, Florida.[50]

48. See W. Coppedge, *African Literacies*.
49. Boomershine, *First-Century Gospel Storytellers*, 111.
50. See https://www.youtube.com/watch?v=1weH8zLAklk. Also available are presentations from the Philippines (https://youtu.be/Wbfy5pWwJUE) and Africa (https://

It's now time to board the boat with Jonah. *No*, not remain on shore to watch from offstage but rather to experience the entire journey with him onstage. Do you smell the saltwater? Dead fish? Hear the seagulls? The splash of waves hitting the boat? Background conversations and noises? Feel the heat of the sun? What does the dock look like? The boat? The weather? The crew? The expression on Jonah's face as he nears the boat? Does Jonah look tired after his long trek to Joppa? Time to buy your ticket to ride.

Reflection Questions

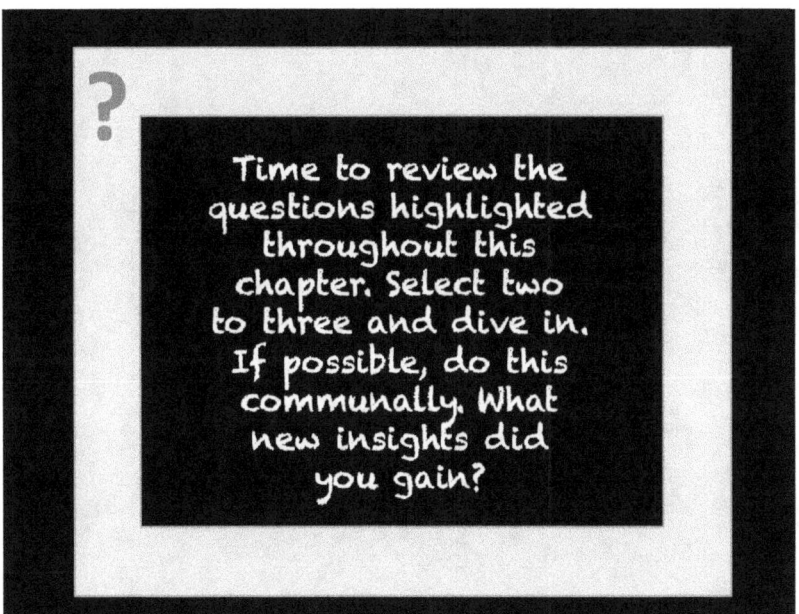

Time to review the questions highlighted throughout this chapter. Select two to three and dive in. If possible, do this communally. What new insights did you gain?

---

youtu.be/pkLtfXDPX2M).

Part 2

Character Theology Demonstrated

6

Participant Responses to the Jonah Story

> When we want mood experiences, we
> go to concerts or museums.
> When we want meaningful emotional
> experience, we go to the storyteller.
>
> —ROBERT McKEE

> Our responses are the fingerprint of our
> heart and the DNA of our conscience.
>
> —CRAIG LOUNSBROUGH

IT'S NOW TIME TO listen to the voices of those who participated in the three EBCs surrounding the Jonah story. Participants will tell us not just what was interesting but what they experienced, felt, whom they identified with and why, how these characters in Jonah impacted them, and because of all this, what they intend to do about it. We begin with a brief description of each of the participating EBCs before listening to their voices.

Description of the Three EBCs

Brief descriptions of the three participating groups in the Jonah story follows.[1] All the Jonah presentations took place in 2023. The Philippine EBC discussion group was the youngest group, with only one member being considered near middle age. Most participants were in their twenties. This group consisted of one male and eight females.

These Filipinos are very familiar with orality as all are trainers whom I (Ray) have been privileged to work with. They are very active in training others through a rigorous orality model designed for an international partner of Spoken Worldwide. While all are literate, some even highly literate, they have all learned the value of oral learning.

The second EBC discussion group includes Africans. This group consisted of seven males and three females. Many in this group are highly oral reliant even while maintaining a mixture of literacy levels. Their long-standing cultures continue to find expression strongly in oral modes of communication. Most in this group have also participated in various orality training workshops from basic to levels of pastoral training. We did struggle with internet and even connectivity issues at times and therefore missed out on fully appreciating some of the rich comments shared.

The final EBC discussion group occurred in Florida in the US. These hearty volunteers answered a "last-minute" call to create this opportunity. They had no experience with orality and represented the widest distribution of ages. This group consisted of three males and five females. Some were seasoned believers with decades of experiences in Christianity while others were much newer to the faith. One could be considered a novice, yet a very keen learner.

Our three EBCs were incredibly valuable to help assess and evaluate character theology as a model and method. We are deeply indebted to them and very grateful for their contribution. Check out figs. 6.1–4 for some of the artwork that helped convey the story.

Feedback Responses from Participants

The authors have argued in this book that character theology provides participants a richer, fuller, more impactful understanding of the story then other models when applied to the narrative sections of Scripture. Do their comments agree or suggest otherwise? Let's find out.

---

1. YouTube videos are available of the Filipino group (https://youtu.be/Wbfy5pW-wJUE), the African group (https://youtu.be/pkLtfXDPX2M), and the Floridian group (https://www.youtube.com/watch?v=1weH8zLAklk).

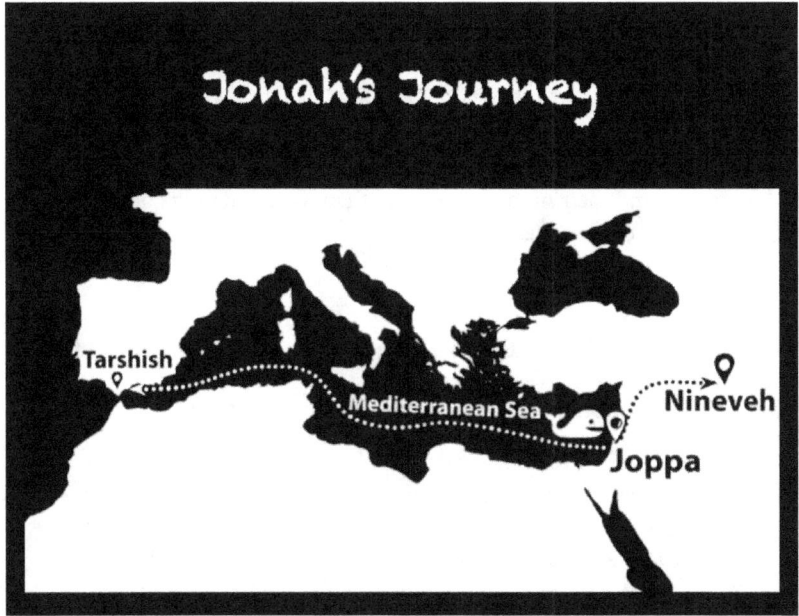

Figure 6.1 Map of Jonah's Journey (by Sarah Drobnack)

Covering Jonah in One Setting

Tackling the full story of the scroll of Jonah in one setting, especially limiting it to ninety minutes, was daunting yet delightful. Daunting in that there was so much that could have been explored more fully and yet delightful as discussing the full encounter at one time brought more clarity and a deeper appreciation for the larger story. When asked what it was like to experience the whole book of Jonah in one setting, here are some Floridian responses:

> The story felt complete. I'm mind-blown that it doesn't feel like it took up so much time to tell the whole story.

> It felt natural and comprehensive. I felt like I had completed a deep dive into the Scripture surrounding the truth of Jonah.

> I enjoyed it. I needed the storyteller to refresh some of the specifics for me though.

> I think it made the whole story more comprehensive since it wasn't spread out, so you didn't really forget details from certain parts of the story.
>
> It's great to experience the story as a whole because we get to see the resolution of the story, and we get to understand the characters and their motivations more than if we had only gotten a glimpse of their life.

God's Sovereignty

All three groups noted God's sovereignty throughout the story:

> God is still sovereign over all our lives. He specifically chose Jonah despite his character because God wanted to display his glory in the life of Jonah to the sailors and the people of Nineveh. Regardless of his attitude and character, God knew he could use him exactly the way he needed. God could have chosen someone else but he knew what Jonah was like and so he chose Jonah for the work.
>
> We should do what God wants us to do because God is sovereign, and God is working through Jonah's disobedience. At some point if we will just look at God's perspective, we cannot measure the sovereignty of God. It's not really about Nineveh but about Jonah's character, character building, to show to us as well that there might be times when we experience something like that, but the sovereignty of God will always prevail in our lives.
>
> We cannot pick and choose for God's character. It is he who decides. And I see in the story that Jonah just wants to focus on judgment for the people, but God wants to show love, mercy and grace. So, it's not up to us, it's up to God.

Jonah's Negative Attitudes and Behavior

Disobedience was pointedly explored in many thoughtful comments. One that stood out came from an East African:

Jonah's heart was so hardened that he could not discern the voice of God any longer. Then on the other end, he's having a struggle within his mind over a negative outcome that these people should be destroyed. When one disobeys God, the heart becomes so calloused that it is difficult to discern the compassion or the goodness of God. That's how I see it.

Several of the Filipinas focused on Jonah's disobedience as well and were strongly affected by what they saw. They viewed Jonah as a prophet, evangelist, and messenger, but as not fulfilling any of those functions. Here's some of their dialogue:

> Disobedient, stubborn, doing it his way, rebellious, running away from God. He thought he could do it . . . very intentional about doing it his way.

> I'm so shocked that Jonah was able to sleep! Did he have peace not obeying God in the midst of the storm?

> He's [Jonah] indifferent. A lot of people are already suffering with the storm but he is able to sleep. They're shouting but he's sleeping.

> He's also self-confident, stood by his own decision.

> Jonah wasn't aware that he was already drifting away from his relationship with God.

> I think when Jonah was sleeping it was also his way to run away from God. I'm going to sleep through this and when I wake up, I'll be in a different country and away from all this.

Jonah's hard-heartedness surfaced often in the discussions at various places throughout the story:

> I want to judge Jonah himself. God gave him a gift. When he delivered the message, people responded! That's a gift!

> The desperation [of the sailors] crying out to their gods, compared to one person who is self-righteous, selfish, confident of their salvation, but has a totally different view of the world. At times we can be like Jonah, not caring about those around us, which makes me sad.

Another Filipina added, "They [sailors] have a god, but their gods are not answering. There is one guy who knows the real God but is so indifferent that he's only sleeping." The huge contrast in faith, yet staunch indifference, had a visible impact on the participants.

As Jonah's journey progresses, other reflections on his attitudes were noted: "He is unwilling to accept the fault that he did. His entire prayer did not ask forgiveness for running away from God." Several saw this sad reality in that he never said he was sorry or repented. "His prayer picks up with him being thrown into the water and not what got him into the water—no confession. And why wasn't he praying while he was sinking?"

One participant from the African group asked, "Is this similar to Adam pointing his finger at God and saying, 'It was the woman *you* gave me that got me in trouble. *You* threw me into the water. *You* have driven me from your presence.'"

A man in the group agreed: "He is the one who fled away from the presence of God. God did not chase him away." Another surmised: "It's interesting that Jonah points out that others have turned their backs on God, but Jonah does not see that he literally turned his back on God. Praying but pointing out what other people do wrong. Still not taking personal responsibility for his actions."

A couple of participants highlighted that Jonah had no idea what happened on the ship after being thrown into the sea. I acknowledged that he would have been unaware of the sailors worshipping his God! I suggested a potential clue—Jonah may have heard the prayers of the sailors to God *before* they threw him overboard. Did Jonah hear the sailors praying to his God?

One Floridian had an interesting perspective that perhaps Jonah was making a concession more than a full acknowledgement of repentance. Perhaps Jonah thought:

> Okay. I'll do it. I can't run away, I guess. Like concession. Desperation. Let's get over with it. Almost like the spirit of a wild horse being broken, Jonah finally puts his own ego aside and says, "Okay, I will acknowledge the Lord, the one who will provide me with salvation."

Wow! Breaking the spirit of a horse. It's the first time Jonah yields to God's will. The entire time he's completely trying to impose his will. Then there's that little moment. It might be very self-serving, but he yielded. And God did follow through, breaking Jonah's spirit so that he will yield. Fascinating. Sadly, Jonah didn't maintain humility for long.

One Filipina thoughtfully commented:

Jonah had experienced mercy when in the belly of the fish, so he has been shown mercy for his plea to God, yet he sees these people crying out and yet he's willing to wait for forty days to see their destruction. His anger is so much that he sees the same things as when he was in the belly of the fish. They are even more crying out because they are fasting. Not only them but the animals also are fasting as they cry out to the Lord!

Figure 6.2. Sailors Throw Jonah Overboard (by Sarah Drobnack)

Ninevites and the Message

Following are some observations the participants made about Jonah delivering God's message to the Ninevites. They were not complimentary:

> He did not deliver the complete message, no compassion.

> I call this duty. He responded out of duty, not out of heart.

> If I'm Jonah, I already did what I'm supposed to do, now I'm done.

> He's giving the bare minimum, not the good news, not the mercy of God, "You told me to go say this, this is what I'm going to say."
>
> He's pronouncing judgement, not a warning. If it's a warning, he would include for them to repent, but there's no mention of repentance.
>
> It's because in the first place he didn't want to go there.
>
> So, what's missing in Jonah? The love, compassion, concern, mercy, grace.
>
> Seems that he [Jonah] has such a deep root of bitterness himself that it is poisoning him.

As participants thought about the people in Nineveh, the mood from all EBCs shifted dramatically. Here are two representative responses:

> The people are in remorse. These people know they did something to God. In contrast to Jonah, they accepted that they did something [wrong]. It must have been hard for young children to understand or for nursing mothers or young mothers but there was a sacrifice, I'm not going to answer the cry of my young baby for food because it will save him. They hoped that this would work.
>
> The Holy Spirit is working in the midst of the people in Nineveh. But the Holy Spirit left Jonah because he grieved the Holy Spirit so much.

The participants did not believe that God wanted to destroy the Ninevites, but Jonah wanted it because, as one Filipina said, "In the beginning if God wanted to destroy the people, he would not have sent Jonah." Keen insight.

When asked specifically about grace being received by others who cross paths with Jonah, the insights from all groups were uniform:

> Jonah made the cover and God provided the shade. Then after the worm, it's all about blaming God again. How quickly can we do the same things.
>
> This is a story about grace. The sailors got grace; the people of Nineveh got it; everyone did but Jonah. He didn't see it.

Nineveh represents those areas who need the word of God. Jonah represents messengers of God with excuses. But if they receive the message, God will use it to cause transformation.

This is a story of humankind and God, how God is pursuing us, how God is chasing us, the more we want to go away from him, the more he is chasing us, to bless us, to give us a chance. He's chasing us from the darkness to the light.

Repetition

When asked if there was any repetitiveness that was noticeable in the story, two areas were noted. The first was God's calling and purpose to send Jonah as a messenger to people who needed God's message. The second was Jonah's persistent pleas for God to take his life, to kill him, to allow him to die, that given the circumstances, death was preferable over life. These nonstop negative notions strongly shaped how the participants perceived Jonah! It indicated that the struggle inside Jonah was deeply rooted and not easily dismissed or surrendered. Here are a few responses:

> God continually reaching out to Jonah.

> God showing up wherever Jonah was, whether at home, in the ship, in the sea or the belly of the fish, or outside the city.

> Jonah said repeatedly that he would rather die and in *all* the occasions he misunderstood the mercy and grace of God.

Characters Reveal God

When I asked how the author of Jonah's story used characters to teach us about God, we were treated to a variety of insightful responses. Note the following:

> Through the character of Jonah, I am able to see how God can use just about anyone regardless of who they are and what is in their hearts. I am able to see contrast between man and God and who he is.

> Using the character Jonah to teach us about God was through evaluating his actions, interactions, and conversations made.

> He used characters like Jonah who truly depicts the real nature of mankind and how God is merciful, no matter how far we are from him.
>
> I'm surprised he [Jonah] didn't fear God enough to do what he asks.
>
> Not valuing that he heard from the Lord. Not everyone got that direct connection with the Lord and yet he did not value it.
>
> He [Jonah] is more concerned about what people would say about him if he was shown to be a false prophet rather than all those people who might die.
>
> He may have been willing to go away from his family permanently to avoid going to those people. He was vexed and angry at God, so he had neither value nor integrity towards God, yet God manifested integrity towards Jonah.

It was not a surprise that many comments were made about Jonah. Reviewing these I realized that Jonah was indeed quite the teacher and example for us, though not often in a positive way. One Ethiopian suggested a bit more lenient attitude towards Jonah:

> Maybe Jonah had a bad story prior to this, which caused his harsh feelings. Maybe he had trauma and so he had bad feelings. He had trauma and lots of bad thoughts against that nation. We don't see any love at all, so he must have had a bad background story with this nation in order to come to this heart decision against these people—120,000 of them.

Others from different EBCs shared varying perspectives:

> The author shows us through the characters how God interacts with different people in different circumstances. We also see his consistency in his dealings with people.
>
> The characters reacted to their circumstances by acknowledging God, arguing with God, getting angry with God, and even turning towards God in songs of praise and thanksgiving.
>
> A god was offended. Something was wrong and a god had been offended.

Gods could cause storms. The cast lot pointed to the only one who wasn't up there praying. They would pray to any god. They would abandon their god to save themselves.

The author took us on a journey of the life of faith and showing us the challenges that come with disobedience.

Figure 6.3. Jonah Prays (by Sarah Drobnack)

As we explored the various characters in this story, we also investigated the idea of learning through decoding characters. This is different from being told what ideas, truths, or concepts are found in a story. The highly participatory nature of character theology challenges such.

I often comment that people will likely forget things that are told to them from sermons, Sunday School lessons, small groups, and so forth, but that they will absolutely remember the observations they voice themselves! This is one of many major benefits of this style of inductive learning.

Some additional comments regarding characters revealing God included:

> I always focus on God, what he is like towards us, that seeing what we are towards God opened my eyes to see more and learn more.

I have always thought that God was always personal in terms of his interaction with the people in the Bible. Sometimes, some stories don't mention much of his name but he's always in the details.

When I read Scripture, I accept it as the truth it is and constantly am thinking about what message is being sent to me through the characters, words, actions and outcomes in his word.

God doesn't change. I find it interesting to see how God continues to pursue people in so many different ways. Individually.

It is true that we know God through his word and his word is full of interactions. What makes this story different is that every interaction between the characters points to God.

God was working in the hearts of those people. The king himself realized that they were sinners, that there was something missing in their lives. That was the Spirit of God manifesting in their lives! The message itself did not sound motivational but the effect was powerful.

I hadn't given it much thought, but looking back, I always learned something about God from looking at his interactions with people. I can always draw a parallel between myself and the characters that I'm reading about, so it shows me who God is in my life. And through the interactions of characters among themselves, I see how God responds to them in different scenarios.

Ending with a Question

Other questions I asked were: Why did God end this story with a question? Why would God not wrap this story up with a good Western happy ending? Why leave us in suspense?

Some felt very strongly that this was dissatisfying, urgently wanting to know "the rest of the story." Others pondered a bit before sharing. Note the ever deepening and rather intimate personal revelations from various EBCs:

> To make an impact; to make us reflect on the question.

> Our God wants us to reflect on his word. God wants us to think deeply about the possible outcomes of Jonah's story and how these may apply to our lives and our outcomes in life.

I think it's so that we continue to think about what God asks of us and how we respond to him. Maybe so that we continue to look at ourselves and our behavior.

To show Jonah and all the readers that he has the final say and we don't have the answers.

Jonah wants a God who will punish evil. The question that the book asks the reader then is this, can we accept and love God as God is?

Perhaps to let us recognize ourselves in it.

The persistent pursuit of God towards humanity. No matter what, I will pursue you, the choice is up to you. Reward or consequences.

It helps me to see myself where I am. Am I those who see myself in the mercy and grace of God? Or receives his mercy and grace every day and when I see someone else, I become very judgmental against them? So, it helps me see my attitude towards sinners. What would I do if I were in Jonah's place?

Figuring Out God

Another topic that arose in all three EBCs was what does one think when God doesn't make sense. The following quotes are representative:

> First, God humbles the prideful and uses grand gestures to do so. Second, without humility, the men of God can be like Jonah sometimes—unwilling, mad, and confused.

> God will always teach his people how to be humble. I think God succeeded with that because God has the last word, the last question, and Jonah had no reply, nothing to say back to God.

> God wants to spare us from the life of Jonah. God wants to search us, our hearts, to see if we are like Jonah. I should always check my heart. What part of my character would you like me to change because I don't want to disobey you. It's hard to obey God if our heart is not right before him.

> I learned that God can use anyone. If he hadn't called Jonah, what about those sailors? Maybe that's why God chose Jonah, because he knew he would run and he wanted to save those sailors. Even the message to people of "forty days till destruction" may sound scary to us but it was just what the people of Nineveh needed. They didn't need to hear a message about mercy, they needed to hear about destruction and God used that to save them.

Another Filipina added:

> I see how God works in us as he works through us. Just as God was teaching Jonah how to be merciful to his enemies, God will also place us in uncomfortable and even painful situations to perfect us. He may even isolate us, just as Jonah had been isolated in the belly of the fish, to draw us to him. I also see God's faithfulness through the life of Jonah. Though he was disobedient and even rude at times, the Lord continued to be patient with him and use him to proclaim his message.

Summary Statements

When asked if one could give a summary statement of Jonah, one participant responded: "Too many to list. It was interesting to hear all the feedback from the others in the room and how different our perspectives were."

That statement speaks to what many have observed about character theology. It defies the idea that there is only one main idea in every story which once discovered means you have deduced it's singular meaning and can now move on to decode other stories.

There is no question that seeking a primary meaning from a passage is very beneficial, especially when narratized. However, how much is lost if the investigating person is limited to that single perspective? Another participant shared: "There is so much more to learn as each story is quite literally a buffet of observational hors d'oeuvres waiting to be discovered and applied to our lives."

The type of questions—character-centric—used in character theology were found to be quite beneficial in corralling coreness. While the open-ended questions promote a lot of room for discussion, varying viewpoints, and further insights, they also serve as a means to maintain a level of control over potentially rampant thoughts. They do this by continually centering everyone on the observable actions, words, and responses of the characters in the story. Character-centric questions limit exploratory thinking to the choices and consequences of the characters in the story.

Potential Ministry Involvement

I found the following comments surrounding some participants potential ministry involvement riveting. Several comments follow:

> Disobedience is costly and will always lead one to be in a compromising position.

> God is working and I can fight it or join it, but his purpose will be accomplished. Need to focus on the lost.

Striking responses, are they not? What is missing for the reader is the feeling that persisted in each of the three EBCs during these open discussions. There were many who thought deeply before responding. Their responses were not the replies of a student seeking to pass an academic exam. These were the heartfelt responses to a tragic tale that had the potential for yielding wonderful results. The wonder was also found in the hearts, minds, and souls or the participants as the Spirit nudged some to take very strong personal action plans.

When asked if processing this story communally caused anyone to find a character they would want to emulate, we received some interesting responses. A couple of people wanted to be the king of Nineveh, yet for slightly different reasons:

> The king, who could tell others to repent.

> The king. The king was in a position of authority and power, however, he humbled himself, subdued his pride in full view of his people to pray to God and seek redemption.

It is significant to point out that one of these simply wants to tell people the right thing to do while the other wishes to demonstrate by personal behavior what should be done. Very character theology. These sentiments were followed closely by several who focused on the behavior of the people of Nineveh. Here are three representative comments:

> The people of Nineveh who repented over their sins when they heard God's pronouncement against them. They didn't know if God would relent from disaster, but they still fasted and mourned over their sins. I want to have the same character, to

be submissive and teachable. I will choose to emulate them by submitting to God's authority and bringing to mind his character, how he always works things for good and not evil, and by remembering his great love for me.

Another popular choice were the sailors:

> The sailors, because their prayers were heartfelt and so sincere. So much so that even at first, they prayed to other gods, eventually they had an encounter with the real God.

> I can turn to God and pray to him as the sailors, the captain, and the people of Nineveh did.

Figure 6.4. Fish Vomits Out Jonah (by Sarah Drobnack)

At times, people will make a connection with a nonhuman character because they recognize something virtuous about it. These can be humorous yet at the same time often reveal spiritual sensitivity not immediately grasped or recognized by others. Note the following:

> Maybe the fish? I'd like to be a vessel to someone who needs to go back to God.

I wanna be like the worm! I wanna do what God tells me to do and be filled.

Listening to their increasingly personal comments and keen insights caused me to ask: What if this story *is* about us? Here's an African response:

Is God calling us to share this message with our neighborhoods? Am I really obeying God's word to obey to share the good news? We want to live in a comfortable place, nothing uncomfortable. I never put myself in those situations, so sometimes I judge them for their situations. I see God is calling me for my response. We have a calling for different opportunities.

I asked the question a bit differently in Florida: Okay, so the $64,000 question is: If God sent a message to you to say, "I want you to go to *them*," how would you feel? Follow along as several voices expressed what their hearts were processing. Each quote is a different person sharing in rapid succession:

Maybe? Hesitant? Uncomfortable? Almost like a suicide mission?

If you're being sent to your enemies to give a message that, hey, you guys need to behave, or the city's going to be gone. That's not a . . . you can't expect that that's going to be a sequel. I think this is one of the most warmest, encouraging parts of the story for me personally. Because if God could use someone like Jonah to reach 120,000 people, you know, that he didn't even care about, it was like, well, then *what can he do through me*?[2]

I'm thinking Russia. That's what I'm thinking. Yeah, I'm not thinking like . . . Can I go to Russia? I really think though, in this political atmosphere that we have right now, I'd see more of that than anything else, because it's them against us, you know, and they would be the hardest people to have to witness to. People that are just really, really way out there on the left side, you know, because they just basically stand for everything that I don't. But they're the hardest people to reach, but you have to realize that Jesus died for them too.

But they hate you. Yeah. They're trying to kill you. Suicide mission? Is that okay?

---

2. This took me to tears then and again now. Wow!

> They did the same thing for Jesus.

> Well, now you gotta go make it all spiritual! But yeah, that makes sense. The way you describe what, you know, how he might be thinking of it. These were his enemies. I always have a little bit of empathy for him.

For the Philippine group, I phrased the question this way: If this were happening today, and God sent a message to the Philippines and it came to you, would there be a people that you would *not* want to go to? Once again, each quote is another member of the group, yet it was fascinating to experience as the conversation felt so blended as if they were of one mind. Here's what they said:

> God works in us, and he works through us. We are all called to speak and bring the good news to people. God will work in us and at times it will be painful. Let's not respond like Jonah and waste time to be isolated for three days and three nights so he can speak to us. My takeaway is to humble myself and obey.

> Yeah, there are people—those of other faiths who are different. When I was younger I was told by my relatives not to go there [to a certain island] because I'm a woman, and that is a Muslim part of the country and as a woman I will no longer be able to go out. So, growing up I had that in my mind. Later I was asked if I was willing to go there because there was a church there—one church in the midst of all the mosques. Even when the government was against the mosques, this church stood strong. Honestly my answer was, I don't know. I have to pray and ask God.

> There's a call for me since last year to work there at their college. Why would I go there? We have different faiths. My mentor would say, "Don't go to the place of our enemy." But they're not my enemy. I'm trying to wrestle with God. There are more who are still lost. I've asked for three months more to contemplate and hear loud and clear from God. Even now at the college, they are talking about this story and it reminds me of a phrase we use often, "Letting go and letting God." So the Lord has answered this prayer. Thank you so much. I'm so blessed.

> My daughter had showed me a map of all the places I'm not able to go to to show them this method of oral Bible study. This man asked why I had not come to one place on the map. I said, "We haven't gotten an invitation." He said, "I'm from there." What

this story teaches me for God's call to all of us is that we have to obey. If my concern is for safety, Jonah did not get safety. The call is upon you to go. God says, "My call is to move through you, the safety concern is on me. Not that I want to give judgment but to give salvation. I want to give them a chance. I want their hope to be placed on me." The same people that God wants me to go to Tawi-Tawi are the same people who are on the boat. They worship the god who is different but they are looking for the just God who can give answers.

Simple, personal, spiritual, practical. Can't argue much with these reflections. For me, the best part is that each of these statements were made *by* the participants. They were not spoken by a teacher and parroted back. They did not select clever comments or wise witticisms someone else developed. Each statement came from the heart and mind of a person engaging Bible characters through this interactive, collaborative, inductive learning style.

The discoveries in each EBC were different as they represented different personalities, cultures, and stages of life. This is normal. One thing that is consistently present and astounding to me is the depth of insights frequently resulting in communal ahas! These moments trigger adrenal and endorphin spikes as we are greeted or confronted with unanticipated discoveries.

Unanticipated discoveries are addictive. Finding such gems creates the desire to find even more. Even if someone else found the last treasure, the collective response is that the group and individuals in the group now want to unearth their own hidden gems which are embedded in the stories.

It will not be possible for the reader to capture the full experience through passive reading of their comments. I encourage you to watch the videos; they will help. Better yet, participate in an EBC discussion group so you can experience it for yourself. It's always better to experience a great meal at a fine restaurant than read a food critic's comments about how the meal is so great. I think you will find, like these participants in the three EBCs, that, yes, character theology does provide participants a richer, fuller, more impactful understanding of the story then other models when applied to the narrative sections of Scripture.

We conclude part 2 with an interview with my coauthor.

7

An Interview with the Jonah Storyteller

> All stories have a curious and even dangerous power. They are manifestations of truth—yours and mine. And truth is all at once the most wonderful yet terrifying thing in the world. . . . It is such a great responsibility that it's best not to tell a story at all unless you know you can do it right. You must be very careful or without knowing it you can change the world.
>
> —VERA NAZARIAN

IN THIS CHAPTER TOM interviews Ray about his experiences telling the Jonah story in multiple cultural contexts—African participants, a mix of metro and island Filipinos, and Floridians in the US. There's nothing like hearing about the recent involvement of a Bible storyteller utilizing character theology in an EBC. This is especially true when the whole book of Jonah—all forty-eight verses—is told and discussed in one setting.

Does character theology offer a richer, fuller, more impactful message from the storyteller's perspective? Let's find out.

Interview with the Jonah Storyteller

TOM: In the last chapter we highlighted the comments and questions of the participants in the three EBCs, all having different cultural backgrounds. In this chapter we want to hear *your* perspective, so I have some questions for you. Here's the first: When beginning to tell Bible stories, what teaching habits did you have to break or modify? What interpretive habits?

RAY: Great question. Your question has an embedded, firmly rooted idea that "teaching habits" are about the teacher doing the *telling* while the students do the *listening*. That's how I was taught. That's how most of us learned to teach as well.

A major paradigm shift occurred when I moved into orality-based teaching/learning. Teaching this way is akin to leading sheep to a pasture or a cool stream. The shepherd may lead the flock to the location, but the sheep decide when and if to eat, drink, and rest.

In the orality-based character theology model, I become the storyteller and facilitator of an exploration into a Bible story. First, I faithfully deliver the Scripture story, which I memorized, internalized, and delivered with personality and passion. This is storytelling at its finest—person to person.

Then I switch gears and move into an active learner mode as I facilitate the group discussion. As a teacher I have ideas about what should be discovered and some good starter questions to initiate the journey. Yet, it is inevitable, that far, far more insights will be discovered through thoughtful group reflection. These reflections usually go considerably *beyond* my ability to fathom the depths of what each story, each character, could bring to the conversation.

Forcing ourselves to be patient enough to allow the group to formulate their own thoughts is vital. This takes time, patience, trust. Time because people need time to think, to relive and reflect on the story. Patience is mostly for us—learning to become comfortable with the necessary silence while others are thinking. A wise teacher creates an atmosphere where thoughtful reflection amid silence is not awkward but welcomed because the teacher knows what is developing. Trust is needed for the process as well as for the Spirit to speak through others. When it all comes together, incredible shared experiential learning results as we saw in the last chapter.

The element of the *unknown*, yet anticipated and hopefully new insights, can make traditional teachers nervous because its *unscripted*. I used to feel that way, nervously anticipating some difficult question for which I alone would be responsible for offering an acceptable or even awesome answer. When I finally released that unfounded burden and realized that the story has the answer embedded inside it, everything became easier. All that was required was to patiently reflect further and work *with* the group to find the answer. I cannot tell you how *freeing and fascinating* it has been to discover the many times answers have been faithfully found from within the characters in the story, usually by one of the participants!

Figure 7.1. Ninevite King and People Call on God (by Sarah Drobnack)

Allow me to mention another area that can be of concern, that of accurate interpretation. Whenever I am asked about this model, I agree that it is possible for any group to come up with some less than stellar theology. However, my experience has been that when we follow the guidelines of sticking to the story, insisting that observations come from inside the boundaries of the story, i.e., the words and works of characters, rich theology emerges. When we carefully check each other, we have never wandered into poor theology.

On the rare occasion when someone suggests an "interesting" observation that doesn't appear to align with traditionally recognized theology, we use some facilitation tools to help examine the idea. First, we don't respond with anything harsh, such as "Well, that's just *wrong*!" We need to keep the participant engaged in the conversation and not defensively shutting down due to a rebuke from the "teacher." I usually say: "That's interesting. I've not considered that before. Could you help me see which characters support that in *this* story?"

Oftentimes, this gentle pause for clarification is enough to indicate that the observation could use a second glance. In response, they may say, "Oh, it's not really in this story, it's just something that I think of." Or "I don't really think it's in there, but I heard it in a sermon and wanted to share it here."

If the participant persists with their potentially errant line of thinking, I then enlist the aid of his/her peers by asking, "Does anyone else see this also, or do you maybe see something a bit different?" This opens the door for wider examination, which is being shared by the others in the group rather than coming from the perceived *authority figure* leading the discussion. This is very important to our goal of keeping people engaged and talking.

In one of the EBCs, we were discussing the endlessly fascinating story of Zacchaeus's encounter with Jesus. You know the one, where Zacchaeus could not see over the crowd of people, so he ran ahead, climbed a tree, and was later asked by Jesus to return together to Zacchaeus's home. During the conversation while dining, Zacchaeus makes a bold proclamation of giving away large sums of money. One woman in the group suggested that this was a clear example of *works theology* since Zacchaeus earned his way to heaven by giving away money.

After thanking her for her input, I followed the process described and was quite pleased to see that she saw the need to rethink her suggestion. This was made clearer after several of her friends in the group pointed out other factors in the story that indicated this was not an example of earning one's way to heaven.

When we as teacher-facilitators embrace the soon to be revealed mysteries of learning Scripture stories together through incredible colorful characters, as guided by the Holy Spirit, we are launching out on an epic journey of endless discovery. At least, that's been my experience and I love it!

TOM: How does teaching a single short story differ from teaching the complete book of Jonah in one setting?

RAY: Depth. Breadth. Big picture versus snapshot. We all have favorite scenes from movies or books which we can recall and momentarily relive that scene. Yet, the reality is that the very scene we enjoy so much is made significant because of the metanarrative, the surrounding story, the bigger picture. The context surrounding our favorite bits breathes life, incredible insights, and fascinating revelations into the experience and the knowledge of the story.

The "elephant in this room" could actually be the length of this whale of a tale. Many Bible stories are a very manageable ten to twelve—which are relatively easy to master. It is not as easy to memorize and internalize forty-eight verses!

My approach was to learn the full story as four shorter stories. The transitions at the end and beginning of each chapter were perfect places to stop, then restart each section. The action in each section of the scroll made it natural to follow the development of the journey.

The biggest challenge was the poetic prayer in chapter 2. The repetition there was a bit challenging as the similar phrases did not follow an easy-going pattern that we would comfortably follow in English. Noticing the patterns, creating visual and kinetic cues for myself, along with perpetual practice made it possible.

TOM: How did your understanding of orality help communicate the Jonah story?

RAY: Orality is a *heard* experience. It is *felt*. Knowing this and having experienced storytellers from many countries sharing Bible stories with their *full* self, reminded me of the importance of owning the story, letting the story own me, and telling it well.

First, owning the story means that I have indeed memorized it; it has become a part of me and so it will flow out when I tell it to others. I need to spend a lot of time internalizing the entire story as presented in God's sacred storybook so that I can faithfully reflect what was preserved and presented to us. Part of internalizing the story is meditating on it.

Then, after spending hours upon hours reflecting on what I think the story felt like, sounded like, smelled like, and looked like, I can begin to share it in such a way that it may transport people back into the story itself. Recall proclamation-performance.

Years ago, I created an orality model called Bible Trekking.[1] The byline is "Walking *into* the story, then taking it to others."

That's what we want to still do—use our sanctified imaginations to walk *into* the story. Look to your left, look to your right, see who is next to you. Listen closely to what is being said to consider the effect it would have on those people, *and* the ones next to you. Are they nervous? Angry? Excited? Confused?

They had emotions; we do too. *Read the characters; read the room* to gain insights into the atmosphere of the moment.

I must consider the *setting* as well. What did it feel like in that place in those moments? Hot? Cold? Dry and dusty? Moist and musty? How do such factors affect the characters in the story? How should that impact my storytelling preparation and actual performance?

TOM: How did the Jonah story spark your/their imagination? Emotions?

RAY: Wow, how much time do we have? This story is absolutely packed with sensory scenarios from the divine imperative at the beginning through

---

1. See www.bibletrekking.org.

several hair-raising, heart-wrenching encounters, intense emotional outbursts, life or death dramatics! And an ending that leaves a lingering question long after the camera has faded to black and the credits are rolling.

Spending time trying to imagine myself in Jonah's sandals was messy, maniacal, and moving in many ways. The gall to try to run from God! What was Jonah thinking? The careless attitude when the lives of others were in danger. The hesitancy to take ownership for his own actions. The many, many, long hours of forced solitude *inside* the belly of a great fish—smelly, slimy, pitch black, alone with his equally dark thoughts. And the fact that it took him *three days* of this before he decided to pray speaks to the depth of his dark feelings!

I could go on for as many days discussing how this story engaged my emotions and those of the various groups. Very powerful.

Figure 7.2. Jonah Awaits Nineveh's Destruction (by Sarah Drobnack)

TOM: How difficult did you find focusing on concrete characters, their conversations, actions, and so forth, rather than abstract concepts?

RAY: Not at all. As you well know, characters, with their words and actions, are who carry and create these incredible stories! We have all sat in a classroom or church where we've been blessed to hear a passage cleverly converted into creative concepts crafted to sound appealing to the ear and to our memories.

Sometimes these are to create mnemonics which may help keep the message with us beyond the end of the service. Sometimes these are to demonstrate the style or even the brilliance of the speaker. I'm guilty of attempting both of those at various times. Even in the States there were occasions after I had preached that my loving wife would look at me and quizzically ask, "What was that?"

This is even more profound yet less understood when overseas with a group of people whose value system strongly tilts honor-shame. It took me years to recognize that those in such cultures would *never* tell me that they did not understand what I was attempting to communicate. They were *always* incredibly gracious and grateful for my "excellent message." Except that many of my messages were *not* excellent.

My creative communication was built on clever concepts I crafted in my own mind, which made perfect sense to me and, apparently, at times, *only* me! In strongly honor-shame cultures, they would never think of shaming a speaker by confessing that they did not understand or that my communication failed to succeed. I spent years blindly believing I was doing a great job. That is, until some of those same people cared enough to help me understand that simple is better, that the Bible is good enough as it is, and I needed to stop trying so hard. I, and many who have endured my teachings since then, are very grateful.

Now, after a few "reeducation camps," I spend a lot more time thinking about what it would be like to walk in the sandals of each character. For example, idol-worshipping sailors sliding around the slick deck of the ship during the storm. A stubborn prophet pitifully sliding around the inside of the stomach of the profound and obedient fish! God's prophet slinking around the great city of Nineveh in stinky clothes, dried and crusty, not wanting to be there, yet begrudgingly delivering God's message. Everyday sinners repenting on the spot, pleading with a God they have only heard about, then discovering his power. A frustrated, fainting prophet fearing that God will be faithful to receive the humble prayers of the very people he despises.

And there are so many others! The more time we spend ruminating on how it might have been for each character in the story, the more we are prepared in our spirits to receive amazing insights.

One thing some interpreters should learn is that there are indelibly delicious insights embedded in each aspect of the characters and their interactions. The more we slow down to ponder and pay attention to each character, each comment, each action—*especially each commotion*, the more we will learn.

It's quite easy and very profitable once we realize that the characters are not driving us towards a point, *they are the point*! They are not fodder for a sermon; rather, they are formational for spiritual growth. Characters are us.

While serving in Belize, a new believer expressed it well when he declared how much he loved learning through Bible stories, "*I love this*! First, you get into the stories and it's good. Then, you realize that those people in the stories are *you* and you need to live like the people in the stories, so you change your life! *It's great!*"[2] A frequent response was clearly stated by one of the Floridian women, "I know the Bible well and read it often, but I have *never* encountered a study like this. This is amazing for how it makes you notice things that you had never seen before."

TOM: What is your impression of using character-centric questions?

RAY: The use of character-centric questions is a bit like using a magnifying glass or a spotlight, causing us to focus on particular characters or moments in the ongoing story. Consider these questions as tools creating a *freeze-frame* in the video. These questions create the effect of stopping all action long enough to capture a moment of the film and really investigate it in detail. And they serve as guardrails and guidelines to appropriate interpretation.

Many stories proceed forward too quickly to be fully grasped. Our minds will see, hear, and even subconsciously "*feel all the feels*" of the event, but it is not until we slow down to a pace where we can consciously consider how each moment, each scene, each event, each detail contributes to the overall appreciation of how the story is developing. We begin to acknowledge and appreciate that it is *less* about how the story is progressing and *more* about how each character is developing as they encounter and move through each situation. Their appearance, their moment-by-moment choices, words and actions, reveal the unfolding of a person in process.

---

2. Conversation with Kekchi believer in Southern Belize, ca. 2011.

Figure 7.3. God Sends a Worm (by Sarah Drobnack)

TOM: Any thoughts on "defamiliarization" in relation to the scroll of Jonah?

RAY: I think that "defamiliarization"—making the familiar unfamiliar or vice versa—has been shown to be very necessary in Jonah's journey. For example, prophets are expected to obey God, listen to his messages, repeat them to the intended audience. Nathan did this for King David. Isaiah and Jeremiah did this even when given horrific prophecies to deliver. Jonah decides against being an obedient, loyal prophet, and this counter-expectation gets our attention as it is rather shocking!

Other instances where the unexpected was plain to see, at least for the listener, yet not for Jonah, was when the pagan sailors who had been crying out to other gods turned and prayed to the living God! Not even Jonah, the one who claimed he worships God, had done this at this point in the story.

On top of that, Jonah answers one of the questions posed by the sailors with this information: "I am a Hebrew, and the God whom I worship is the eternal one, the God of heaven. He made the sea and the land, so he controls them" (Jonah 1:9 VOICE). Yet unbelievably, Jonah is foolishly trying to run away from the very same God whom he *knows* has not only *made* but *controls* the entire earth!

The immediate godly response of the ungodly people of Nineveh provides another dramatic example. They had completely defeated the Israelites and their God in the past, yet instantly believed the message from a God they did not worship. Not only that, but they also extend their concerns to the animals in their care. Such unexpected elements pull our attention aside to focus on the potential *why* behind these observations, thereby challenging automatized, routine perceptions.

We are drawn inside Jonah's story effectively enough that we, too, are *inside* the belly of the great fish before we realize that this story is about us. We are not merely passive observers offstage, but actively engaged onstage as reflections of this same story. The setting, characters, their experiences, all collectively form their world which invites us in and carries us along; they take us all the way to the point that we slow down as it dawns on us that we too, play a part in this never-ending narrative.

TOM: What did some of the pivotal people in Jonah teach us about God?

RAY (*emotional moment*): This is taking me to tears! There were so many precious insights shared as people realized and called out what they were seeing about God's pursuit of us. Even when we are stubborn, racist, resistant, recalcitrant, refusing to comply, God keeps coming! Even when we miss the point, miss the grace we personally are given, miss the blessings happening to others, miss the transformed lives around us who have been swayed by God because we are too wrapped up in our own selves and excuses, God keeps coming!

Some respondents shared deeply and wept, even as I am now. One dear woman from the Philippines expressed that she, too, is Jonah and then went on to share that God has been calling her for some time to go to a certain people group, but she had been unwilling. From time spent together processing this story, she was convicted that it is time for her to be obedient and go to the people God loves.

Another woman, this time a Floridian, said that God had laid the country and the people of Russia on her heart. She had been wondering about this. As she reflected on Jonah's journey and the incredible impact of seeing 120,000 people saved, she shared that she was feeling confirmed in her heart to seriously consider going to Russia!

Precious moments like these are a major factor which drives me to continue to admire and relish this type of dialogical discussion. I could never make such suggestions to others as I don't know their hearts or what God might be prompting them to do. Yet, when encountered by such people, processing with peers and being nudged by the Holy Spirit, we often hear the most incredible confessions. As some pastors were overheard to say at an orality training in Lenexa, Kansas, "*This is revival!*"

TOM: What surprised you most about character theology? What was the most challenging? Most comfortable?

RAY: Characters are *not* flat, nor are their stories. The participants gathered to relive and reflect on the characters are *not* flat either. The absence of flatness brings about a dynamic that is at once both terrifying to the uninitiated and terrific to the experienced facilitator.

Terrifying because one cannot fully predict where the conversation and discoveries will go. Terrific because one cannot fully predict where the conversation and discoveries will go. While that may seem at odds with each other, it really is not. It becomes a matter of adjusting our expectations, acknowledging our inability to control everything that may be shared, and our willingness to allow other people and the Holy Spirit to speak freely.

Adjusting teacher expectations could be compared to riding a horse. For uninitiated riders, the immense power of the animal beneath them is terrifying because they are not sure what might happen. They fear the uncontrolled release of that power with them becoming a helpless heap being dragged along the ground against their will.

Yet, when an experienced rider sits astride the same magnificent mount, that power is unleashed with control and understanding. Little nudges of the knees, soft kicks with the heels, whispered words, leaning slightly in a certain direction, all converge to compel the pair forward to places and at speeds that would not be possible if they were not in harmony with each other.

The potential discomfort of the unknown becomes much more comfortable once the storyteller turned facilitator embraces the power of collective discovery through character theology. It actually is quite thrilling!

TOM: Researchers have shown many storytellers do not connect individual stories to the big picture. Participants therefore leave with a fragmented Bible. How would you connect the scroll of Jonah to the grand narrative so that participants see it is as part of the bigger story rather than a stand-alone story?

RAY: Ah, yes. In other words, why is this scroll part of the really big Scroll, that is, the Bible? As I noted earlier, there can be many ways to look at the various characters and movements of events and people in the Bible. Here's something to consider.

In general, most people view the Old Testament and that entire time period as God's relationship and interactions with his chosen people, the Hebrews. For some, it is apparent that God loves the Hebrew people, and beyond a few isolated exceptions, that's it. Further, most consider that evangelism and God's concern for other people, namely, the gentiles, did not become a focus until New Testament times. This is an error.

God has expressed immense love for everyone from the very beginning. True, the Hebrew people, following along after God's choosing and then covenants with Abram, Isaac, and Jacob have held a special place—the apple of God's eye—but that did not leave others beyond God's love and compassion.

When God commanded people to be fruitful, multiply, and fill the earth, it was not so that he could later decide his favorites. God's word, first spoken and then written, did not limit access to himself or just a chosen people.

Did Jonah evidence ethnocentrism—God exists for the Hebrew people only? As a "chosen people," it is not difficult to see how this could develop. Learning that your God is also making himself, his goodness and compassion available to others, especially feared and hated enemies, could be a putrid pill to swallow.

Evangelism did not start with Jesus. Yes, John the Baptizer announced *a new way*, but *not a new plan*. In fact, John simply declared that it was time for what had been announced through the prophet Isaiah hundreds of years earlier to be brought into the spotlight.

God has always made room in his heart for those who desire a relationship with him, regardless of their ethnicity, background, or circumstances. Ask Hagar, Ishmael, Rahab, Ruth, Naaman, and now the Ninevites. We will see this continue with Canaanites, Samaritans, even a traveling Ethiopian eunuch. Nevertheless, this broad inclusiveness was not always appreciated by some Israelites/Jews. It took even Peter a while and a vision to recognize "God has made no distinction between them and us" (Acts 15:9 VOICE).

God knows people. He knows our hearts. He knows that change does not always come easily or is readily embraced. Jonah's journey, to express God's compassion on an enemy is a step towards preparing people to hear Jesus's challenge to love our enemies and pray for them.

The grand narrative will later return to the Ninevites. About one hundred years later, they returned to their rebellious ways, and God decided that enough was enough. Nahum delivered the prophecy Jonah wished to see fulfilled during his day. The city, the people, and the animals were all destroyed. It's a sobering reminder that repentance at one time is not a permanent reprieve.

248   PART 2: CHARACTER THEOLOGY DEMONSTRATED

Jesus also used the story of Nineveh's original repentance as a "call to action" for those seeking a sign from him.

> Jonah spent three days and three nights in the belly of a great fish, as the Son of Man will spend three days and three nights in the belly of the earth. One day, the people of Nineveh will rise up in judgment and will condemn your present generation—for the Ninevites turned from sin to God when they heard Jonah preach, and now One far greater than Jonah is here. (Matt 12:40–41 VOICE)

We can clearly see that Jonah's scroll is not an isolated story. Rather, it is an integral piece of a much wider, much grander story for all time.

Figure 7.4. Jonah Wishes He Was Dead (by Sarah Drobnack)

TOM: How did the groups relate to the art visuals?

RAY: The visuals were very helpful in creating awareness, especially of the vast distance Jonah was willing to travel to attempt to run away from the Lord! That was about as far as a person could go in those days, and the map made that clear in an instant. Check out fig. 6.1.

The accusing fingers of the sailors, the image in the midst of the stomach of the great fish, the abrupt deposit onto the beach, the sitting under his shelter with and without the vine all helped give pause and attention to important details in the story. So take a look at figs. 6.1–4 and 7.1–4 as well. Note also these are very helpful memory markers.

Then there was the worm too! The worm became a favorite character for quite a few. One participant pointed out that he would like to be like the worm, who was just doing what worms do. Yet this particular worm was provided by God. God arranged for that worm to be in this exact spot on this exact day. The participant said that the worm filled his belly while fulfilling God's purpose at the same time. So he wanted that same opportunity!

TOM: Any changes made from one telling to the next?

RAY: Not so much changes, as an emphasis in attempting to convey Jonah's twofold prayer. I found that both for the remembering on my part as well as the telling, it was helpful to use my left hand for the first half of his reflective prayer; then my right hand, along with a slight turn of the body, for the second half of his prayer. Then bringing both hands together above my head to symbolize the temple, which Jonah mentions twice. His prayer, with its Hebrew form, was a bit challenging.

TOM: I noticed you jumped right into the story without providing any background. Why?

RAY: Of course you noticed, you don't miss much of anything! This became a personal choice in consideration not just of North American or Western audiences who have access to so many resources, including background materials, but in deference to most of the oral learners I work with globally, who do not have such resources. They have what is shared on the day the story is told. That is their primary, and in some cases, their only resource. I wanted to see the story unfold in its simplicity as well as keeping it more reproducible.

TOM: When interpreting a book or story, interpreters tend to initially focus on what the book is *saying* rather than what the author is *asking*. We noted in the book that knowing the question or questions behind the text that the author is asking can serve as guardrails and guidelines for interpretation. What question or questions do you think the author of Jonah wants us to answer?

RAY: Obviously, you enjoy challenging questions, like this one. It makes me squirm a little bit trying to figure out what the author, whom I've never met, wanted us to wrestle with. Honestly, before processing this story together with some of our global colleagues, I would have likely given a much narrower answer. I'm reminded that Paul told a younger Timothy, "So work with fear and trembling to discover what it really means to be saved" (Phil 2:12 CEV).

Now, after learning from those in three EBCs—remember, these were my first attempts at storying a complete book of any size—I would suggest that any of the following could be the questions behind the scroll the author is *asking*:

1. Are we arbitrators of God's will?
2. Do we get to decide who is worthy of God's love?
3. Is obedience to God optional?
4. Do we have the right to disagree with God?
5. Do we care about what God cares about?
6. Is God the God of *all* creation or just the Hebrew people?

The corralled answers—what the author is *saying*—of course, have *major* implications for our walk with God.

TOM: Fascinating! I like that! Here's another question: Why would God end the book with a question?

RAY: This one struck us every time. Why indeed would God leave us hanging? Several expressed their desires to know what happened with Jonah. Did his heart soften? Did he remain stubborn and vengeful? Did he go home frustrated or angry at God for not destroying the city, all its people and animals?

The consensus each time seemed to be that God closed the story so that each of us would continue to seek the answer as to how the story should end. We realized, in rather sobering moments, that the ending reflects deeply our own hearts, some of which cannot be spoken.

TOM: You've told the Jonah story to Westerners who tend to give strong emphasis to individualism and to those from Africa and Asia who tend to give strong emphasis to collectivism. From their questions and comments, did either of these emphases stand out? If so, what?

RAY: That's another great question. Yes, there were some variations in how these groups assessed the story. In general, the Westerners were more focused on the person of Jonah, an individual on an individual quest. The more communally minded Africans and Asians reflected more on the groups, namely the sailors and the population of Nineveh, both people and animals. Their comments seem so casual at first, to a Westerner, until one realizes they are more naturally inclusive while we remain more naturally individualistic.

TOM: Any participants gain a *new* Bible?

RAY: Absolutely! Several commented that they now had new appreciation of this story, having encountered thoughts they previously had never considered. This model of exploration constantly creates new venues for examining the treasures God has embedded in every story and every pivotal character in the Bible, which reawakens a desire to go back to the stories with *a new set of eyes to see and a new set of ears to hear*.

TOM: What's going to keep you up tonight after this interview?

RAY: Not much, I greatly value my sleep! Ha! However, I always wonder: Did I do enough? Did I offer enough opportunity for people to truly walk into the story and explore all that God would want them to discover? Did I get in the way anywhere? What can I do better next time?

The beauty of critical character-centric questions is usually overwhelmed by the incredible comments shared by the group, the eye-opening *aha* moments, which I never saw coming. The heartfelt, teary-eyed confessions tenderly shared after the Spirit has nudged someone. These warm my own heart and soul and send me into grateful sleep, praise our Lord.

TOM: Anything you would like to ask me?

RAY: Yes, how can we make all this orally based character theology more accessible to the Ifugao, the idol-worshipping farmers in the Sahel, the subsistence-level laborers throughout most of the world and those who will never read this book? How can we build and encourage reproducibility such that everyone has access and capacity to learn from and to share character theology effectively?

TOM: Accessibility assumes we know the needs of the recipients and have the right personnel with the right tools to accomplish this. Let's start big picture and work our way down a short list.

We need to first *rethink* theology—our interpretation of Scripture—and how we got there—hermeneutics. This book raises numerous questions that require humble dialogue between participants representing the assemblies, academies, and agencies. And not just in the West, but the East as well, which *is* happening, and they now may be leading the parade.

Part of that discussion must center on the "big forgot," the role of *orality* pre-canon, as the canon was being constructed, and post-canon.

We need a "theology of orality." The ties to the inner workings of the Trinity will not be far. That will help the "big forgot" become the "big *re*-membered." That will make the "fatal flaw" of the lost voice heard again.

Another part of the discussion should be technology, the digital world, AI. What is the future of writing? Who can afford and handle what kind of technology? What values will drive all this? Who controls the content of AI?

Still another discussion topic must be formal and nonformal theological education. Most theological education today is too Western—too conceptual (recall the ladder of abstraction), too individualist, too focused on questions related to the Minority World, too fragmented, too pedagogically antiquated, too sterile. Fortunately, a number of dissertations have/are focusing on the role of orality in theological education, including hermeneutics and character theology.

We need collections of Bible characters, artwork, and other symbols and rituals that serve as teachers and memory hangers. Their appropriation, of course, will have to be culturally sensitive. We also need a virtual Center for All Things Oral.

Providing access for *all* will require personnel, training, and materials that address those who are strongly oral to those who respect and proficiently use both, e.g., the Ifugao, to the highly literate who have no clue about orality even though social media drives their daily lives. Such a continuum means there is *no single approach*! *If*, and that's a big *if*, *if* Western and Eastern Bible teachers and trainers can change, so can theological education, and so will the world.

All this requires seeing orality not just as another communication tool, but one that is universal, natural, relational—read people, read the room—not to mention its ties to the Trinity. Can such discussion result in application for all? It's already started, and it's multiplying, but we have lots of work to do. It will be interesting to see if the Majority World will lead the Minority World in this orally based endeavor.

TOM: Anything you would like to say to our readers?

RAY: Yes, yet first allow me to respond a bit to your keen insights that suggest potential pathways forward. You said so much in such a concise way that it will need much more space to unpack, which may require subsequent publications.

First, I agree that some of these vital conversations are happening, and on a slowly growing global scale. We need this. Turning the wheels of tradition, of academia, of long-standing theological thought is a *slow* process, and must be *carefully* crafted by concerned people who take their responsibilities seriously. Don't stop. Maintain the integrity of the disciplines while focusing on current needs.

In the area of technology blending with orality, there are advances being shaped even now as we speak by various agencies. Some focus more locally while others are massively global. In our work at Spoken Worldwide, we are field testing a variety of these approaches, including visual manuals, kinetic outlines, app assisted learning for storytelling teachers that lead to teach/reteach models empowering several generations of local language leaders.

As you mentioned, these require feedback from the field to understand effectiveness for local leaders. As we listen, we are refining approaches, techniques, and tactics, following the model set in Prov 27:17, "In the same way that iron sharpens iron, so a person sharpens the character of his friend" (VOICE).

Strongly oral communities, being more communal in nature, have many local proverbs that carry the idea *we are all in this together*. Practically speaking, we need each other—those studying orality and theology and technology right alongside those living theology, using orality, and testing technology.

Back to your question. We seek to deploy one more tool into this vital work—*character theology*. Character theology is a simple, natural, relational way to seek a story's significance. Check out fig. 7.5. This integrative approach to story analysis focuses on concrete, conflictive events, what Ryken calls "an experiment in living."[3]

This "experiment in living" is scattered across scenes. When conflict hits—"Jonah, go to Nineveh"—characters must make hard choices: Jonah heads to Tarshish. Sometimes they are rewarded—the sailors are saved, sometimes not—Jonah gets thrown into the sea, swallowed by a fish, yet still goes to Nineveh. The result is we receive a more *defined* painted portrait of God and what he desires of us. *Characters reveal the Creator*!

---

3. Ryken, *How Bible Stories Work*, 117.

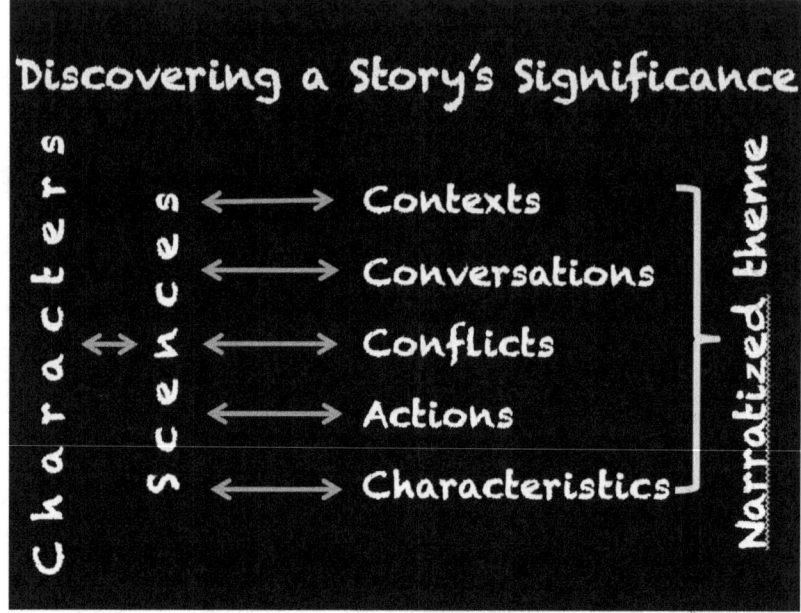

Figure 7.5. Discovering a Story's Significance

Note I didn't rush to articulate the theme or possible secondary themes. Rather, we worked through the whole story—all four chapters. This allows the answer to bubble up to the surface. Good narrative interpretation *begins* by listeners reliving, by experiencing what the characters in the story experienced, *not* by quickly identifying headliners and one-liners.

After reliving the story, I then broke the book into action scenes. This helps capture the flow of the book. While doing so I identified the geographical contexts as they changed—Joppa, Tarshish, sea, coastland, Nineveh, outside of Nineveh—over the course of the book, as well as the characters involved in each scene.

Geography is context and therefore important to the characters involved. Geography also helps identify the protagonist and antagonist as well as other pivotal players in a story.

Characters leave behind dropped breadcrumbs through their conversations and actions, especially when conflict happens. We want to collect and scour these suggestive clues as they point to possible conflict solutions as well as provide identifying characteristics of key characters, and ultimately the Creator.

Just as the characters paint a picture of God, they also paint their *own* portrait through defining characteristics. Our final goal is to determine what God's world should look like.[4] The conclusion will be more than an idea, more than a headliner, more than a one-liner. Orality requires a narratized idea!

TOM: What is your "narratized idea" of Jonah?

RAY: After processing this with others, after learning from them, I would say *God continually pursues us*. That simple statement is loaded with deep implications and "needs to ruminate for some time to be more fully appreciated." One of our African brothers said that, and it really caught my attention and continues to do so.

For oralists, it needs some meat on the bone rather than a simple propositional statement like this one which many Western exegetes appreciate. As Ryken and Longman, among others, have pointed out in the book, stories were never designed for *one-liners*. Was that part of the African's thinking when referencing the need for rumination? Was he looking for more meat on the bone?

While in Florida, the group helped me see that there is a plot and a subplot going on in Jonah's journey. The more we discussed these, the more it made me question which is the real reason for this story.

Did God send Jonah to Nineveh for Nineveh's sake? Or, did God send Jonah to Nineveh, to reveal the depths of Jonah's character? This takes us back to the questions behind the book that the author wants us to answer.

In Jonah's journey, he ran away, yet God chased him down and redirected him. He did not want to obey yet was compelled to obey through extraordinary circumstances which only God could deploy. He tried to submit to death, even wanted to die, a few times, yet God did not permit that, extending his life in the same way that God extended grace. Jonah failed to see the grace God was repeatedly granting him even while people around him were repenting. He didn't even *get it* when God provided the vine and then took it away. God was *still* pursuing Jonah's heart while also extending extraordinary grace to *all* the people and animals of Nineveh.

TOM: Thanks, Ray, for your many helpful insights. Your last statement, whether the author's propositional idea or not, definitely put some meat on the bones. Oralists will not only appreciate this, they will also *remember* it.

From the voices of the participants in chapter 6 and the storyteller in chapter 7, it seems obvious. Not only did the participants gain a richer, fuller, more impactful message through character theology, so did the storyteller! And some received a *new* Bible!

---

4. Ryken, *How Bible Stories Work*, 121.

Because of the power and persuasiveness of character theology, the same lies in store for other groups. For some EBC discussion group, somewhere, at some time, incredible theological insights await discovery. Some, like those noted in chapters 6 and 7, will also discover a *new* Bible!

It is now time to tighten the loose ends that may have arisen over the course of the book.

Tightening the Threads

> To shift the tracks of history requires leaders
> who are equipped to critically assess and engage
> the contours of contemporary culture.
>
> —MICHAEL COOPER AND ANDREW JOHNSON

> You cannot swim for new horizons until you
> have courage to lose sight of the shore.
>
> —WILLIAM FAULKNER

> Faith is not a conclusion you reach . . . it's a journey you live.
>
> —AIDEN WILSON TOZER

IN AN 1889 EDITION of *Punch* magazine, Genius entered a patent office and asked, "Isn't there a clerk who can examine patents?" A young boy replied, "Quite unnecessary, Sir. Everything that can be invented has been invented."[1]

Will Bible teachers and trainers from around the globe make the same fatal mistake this young lad did? Has everything in the hermeneutic and theology worlds already been invented? If innovation dies, what else dies?

---

1. See D. Crouch, "Tracing the Quote," para. 3.

In *The Facilitator Era*, I (Tom) raised this question: "Will character theology take the world by surprise in the Fourth Era [of missions] just as CBS (Chronological Bible Storying) has in the Third Era?"[2] Time will tell.

Something strongly required in an oral-aural-digital-AI plus world seems lacking in Minority World theology—*human experience*. The central question, therefore, this book seeks to answer intellectually, practically, impactfully, and with fidelity and faithfulness to Scripture, is: *Why is it important to know and practice character theology when interpreting and communicating Author-author truths*?

How did we get to where we are today in relation to interpreting the narrative sections of Scripture? In chapter 1, Richard Hays reminded us that during the Reformation the chief hermeneutic challenge was to relate Scripture to *tradition*. During the Enlightenment the chief hermeneutic challenge was to relate Scripture to *reason*. Have we entered another era?

Hays believes, and we agree, we have "passed into an era in which the urgent question is the relative authority of Scripture and *experience*."[3] As time passes, the primary societal question related to culturally colored hermeneutics changes, possibly through God-ordained reasons—"*that people of every culture and religion* would search for this ultimate God" (Acts 17:26 VOICE [emphasis original]).

For centuries, abstract systematic theology has reigned as queen not just in the Minority World but the Majority World as well, even if pedagogically challenging (never shame your Western teacher who may have played a role). Sadly, it continues today. J. O. Terry laments, "It is sad to see seminary students coming to the field today loaded with theological knowledge, but lacking presentation skills and understanding of how the rest of the world prefers to learn."[4]

For a certain era, systematics served as an excellent fit for a specific segment of the world's population (the science-Enlightenment–based West). But times have changed, as have pedagogical preferences.

Just as different eras required different hermeneutic focuses, the same is true of today. Has *evidence that demands a verdict* been replace by *demonstration that requires his cast of characters*? *Has a case for Christ been decided through the voices and actions of a cast of characters*? Is it time to steal past those pesky and persistent "watchful dragons" and anoint a new theology

---

2. T. Steffen, *Facilitator Era*, 149. In *Scripture and Strategy*, published in 1994, mission scholar David Hesselgrave identified CBT (now CBS) as one of the major contributions of twentieth-century missions.

3. Hays, *Moral Vision*, 211 (emphasis added).

4. Personal email to Tom, Oct. 13, 2022.

queen who *serves and supplements all* theologies? Or possibly more appropriate, another queen who *complements* the present queen.

> What will be the hermeneutics of the electronic age?

What would make such change possible? The new queen does so by wedding the ear, eye, and heart (oral layering of the sensory), thereby offering a richer, fuller, more appealing, more impactful message that surpasses stand-alone, cold, categorized propositions.

All the above can be accomplished *without* throwing the former queen overboard along with Jonah! One protects the other. The sensory keeps systematics human while systematics keeps the sensory honest.

There are, however, at least two caveats. The first assumes each side—sensory and systematics—is willing to listen to the other. The second assumes Bible communicators are not "future blind," i.e., they have the "inability to see anything beyond the present" or are not able to "anticipate the future."[5]

Contrasting Two Eras

In relation to the narrative sections of Scripture, yes, a new era has supplanted a former era—from verdict to demonstration, from literate to postliterate, from intellectual encounters to character encounters, from truth to post-truth, from statements and plans to songs and stories, from text to voice, from print to screen. These changes require a new hermeneutic focus without necessarily jettisoning everything from previous eras. Bible interpreters must constantly keep abreast with the continually changing cultural terrains of different eras. They must also be cognizant of the inherent shortcomings of each. Table 8.1 summarizes some of the main distinctives between the eras the authors noted in previous chapters.

So, Which Is It?

Many view the Bible as the written words of God. But is something vital missing that impacts interpretation, teaching, and application? Chapter 3 spotlighted the "big forgot" in hermeneutics—*orality*. It also noted the "fatal flaw" of the excluded *voice*. Blinded by a print culture, too many exegetes missed these, and sadly continue to do so. This shortcoming opens the

---

5. Cooke, "Dangers," para. 2.

door to misunderstanding and misapplying the orally voiced nature of the spoken-written words of God.

Too much foreign accent is still associated with orality by far too many. It's time for Bible interpreters to shake that foreign accent and become more natural, more native.

Modern Era	Postmodern Era
Written words of God	Spoken-written words of God
Critical thinking	Character thinking
Individualism	Collectivism
Science-based hermeneutic	Orally based hermeneutic
Cerebral culture	Character culture
Science-based theology	Character-based theology
Single truth only	Multiple truths possible
Fragment focused	Totality focused
Grand narrative lost	Grand narrative recovered
Rationalist reading	Relational "reading"
Head hermeneutic	Heart hermeneutic
Content-focused questions	Character-focused questions
Correctness	Coreness
Systematic theology	Character theology

Table 8.1 Contrasting Two Eras

Are Bible characters—who display vital aspects of orality, e.g., through voice and sound, symbols, metaphors, rituals, relationships—the new, nonconventional, strange, unexpected, unexplored frame of reference? The "defamiliarization" that makes the familiar hermeneutic seem odd, even bizarre for the narrative genre?[6] Do Bible characters make the "'normal' method of evaluation seem arbitrary and strange"[7] for some 80 percent of the world?

Do characters offer Bible interpreters a corrective that advances beyond the "habitual associations and automatic responses"[8] associated with a grammar-focused hermeneutic? Does the demonstrative role of characters shockingly surprise as they point exegetes towards an oral hermeneutic? Does oral hermeneutics guide Bible interpreters to the foothills of character theology?

6. Resseguie, "Defamiliarization in the Gospels," 25.
7. Resseguie, "Defamiliarization in the Gospels," 31.
8. Victor Erlich, as quoted in Resseguie, "Defamiliarization in the Gospels," 25.

There remains, however, another "defamiliarization" that precedes characters. Theologians and those who studied under them tend to *come to the text as theology*. Character theology argues we must come to the text first as genre. The "strange" here is that *genre precedes theology*—the text must be heard/read/viewed in light of the story. The "strange" here is that without first respecting the narrative genre, the resultant theology, including its appeal and impact, are weakened.

Yet most shocking and stretching of all the "defamiliarization" hermeneutic codes tendered is how the Trinity chose to reveal their character to the highest creation. By Trinitarian choice and construct, *characters reveal their Creator. We grasp and engage God most naturally and precisely through his interaction with biblical characters and their interaction which each other*! Characters communicate the Creator.

The Author-authors gave us much more than the written words of God; they gave us the *spoken-written* words of God. This requires something beyond today's privileged hermeneutic models that focus strongly on grammar; it requires a hermeneutic that centers on a character's conversations, conduct, contexts, conflicts, and commitments so that the nations can begin to observe the Creator's distinguishing and defining features. For example, contrast the animistic sailors in the storm and the brutal, idol-worshipping Ninevites who bowed and worshipped the Creator with God's disobedient *prophet* Jonah who fled in the opposite direction and sulked because God extended grace rather than a switch. Such contrasted conversations and conduct demonstrate "defamiliarization" which challenges group think.

Assumptions Requiring Adjustments

Substituting oral for textual hermeneutics to interpret the narratives within the spoken-written words of God will require some major paradigm shifts for many. We have identified ten. This doesn't mean the absence of scholarship surrounding the topics; rather, unawareness tends to prevail. If these paradigm shifts can occur, a sea change surrounding Christianity around the world could occur. Minimally, these include:

1. Orality has little to do with textual construction.
2. Propositions dominate Scripture.
3. Textually based hermeneutic theories are sufficient.
4. All stories have a single meaning.
5. Propositional logic is superior to all other forms of logic.

6. Theological compartmentalization is completely nailed down.
7. Systematized rational theology is superior to narrative relational theology.
8. Objective conceptual categories trump subjective concrete characters.
9. Fragments surpass holism.
10. Scripture is understood best when read privately, silently, and piecemeal.

In our search for accuracy (through science-Enlightenment-based textual hermeneutics) over attractiveness (the sensory), have scholars made Scripture more difficult to comprehend for most Christ followers? By prioritizing grammar over the human experience of characters, has the interpretation of biblical narratives become more difficult for the masses? How does oral hermeneutics offer a more *concrete culture* than the current *cerebral culture* dominating the hermeneutic guilds?

Oral hermeneutics recognizes the sensory side of the text that requires imagination and emotions has too often been lost, thanks in part to modernity. Mburu reminds us, "We read them [narratives] not just for the purpose of extracting principles, but for the joy of being a part of the story.... We automatically orient ourselves in such a way as to understand both the artistry and the words of the text, recognizing that both make up the message."[9] Because of its holistic nature, oral hermeneutics fills this gap by utilizing the role of the sensory to lead to lived biblical values.

Beyond Current Theologies

Some theologians and Bible teachers seem to believe all major theology has been identified, summarized, and categorized. Anything newly discovered is conveniently tucked under one of the preexisting categories of convenience.

While we all have the same Bible, culture colors *how* and *what* we perceive. As Justo Gonzàlez posits, "The landscape is the same for all of us. Yet each one sees it from a different perspective, and will thus describe it differently."[10] While we may have accurately extracted *a* theology, we must never assume we have extracted *the* theology. Millennia of hermeneutic church history argue otherwise.

Wise exegetes include a blank slide at the end of their PowerPoint presentation for the new insights that will emerge after reviewing the landscape,

---

9. Mburu, *African Hermeneutics*, 62–63.
10. Gonzàlez, *Santa Biblia*, 17.

often through the lens of those from different cultures. Character theology continually calls us back to the same landscape, but from different vantage points, to discover fresh insights. Can we really understand God until we see him through the eyes of all the cultures of the world?

Because all Bible stories are "hermeneutically unfinished"[11] they can advance people of "the Way" beyond current theologies to new expressions; they can also add dimension and depth to present levels of spirituality and service. How is such blossoming best accomplished? By gathering regularly with those of different cultures to *engage* Bible characters rather than to *study* them.

Beyond Concepts and Content to Character Accents

For character theology to become a strong ally in today's hermeneutical and theological guilds, exegetes must move beyond prioritizing abstract-philosophical concepts and content to concrete-relational characters. If the gospel message must be contextualized for different audiences, so must the interpretive hermeneutic model match the pedagogical moment. This requires moving *beyond* textual hermeneutics to oral hermeneutics; *beyond* systematic theology to character theology.

> Are Bible characters the new, nonconventional, strange, unexpected, unexplored frame of reference? The "defamiliarization" that makes the familiar hermeneutic seem odd, even bizarre for the narrative genre?

Oral hermeneutics is *not* the poor cousin of textual hermeneutics. Nor is character theology the poor cousin of systematic theology. Based strongly on ancient Semitic language and culture, oral hermeneutics's natural outgrowth—character theology—is a layered relational theology that speaks to the heart; it strikes the senses; it appreciates the aesthetics; it helps interpreters experience and express emotion; it connects with listeners; it respects the narrative genre, all without asking one to check reason at the door. See fig. 8.1 for some of the key accents of character theology noted previously.

Character theology makes Scripture ring true because we see ourselves mirrored in the lives of some of the Bible's colorful cast of characters. Through the contours of their conversations and conduct (e.g., courage,

---

11. Kelber, *Oral and Written Gospel*, 61.

compassion, conflict, collaboration [or the lack thereof]) we learn ways to become more Godlike personally and collectively. Like focusing binoculars, character theology makes the contrasts between God's character and our character clearer, crisper, brighter, and does so speedily.

Bible characters become contagious; we can't resist their human experience because Bible characters R us. Unlike grammar for most, the conversations and conduct of characters are easily caught, modeled, and multiplied.

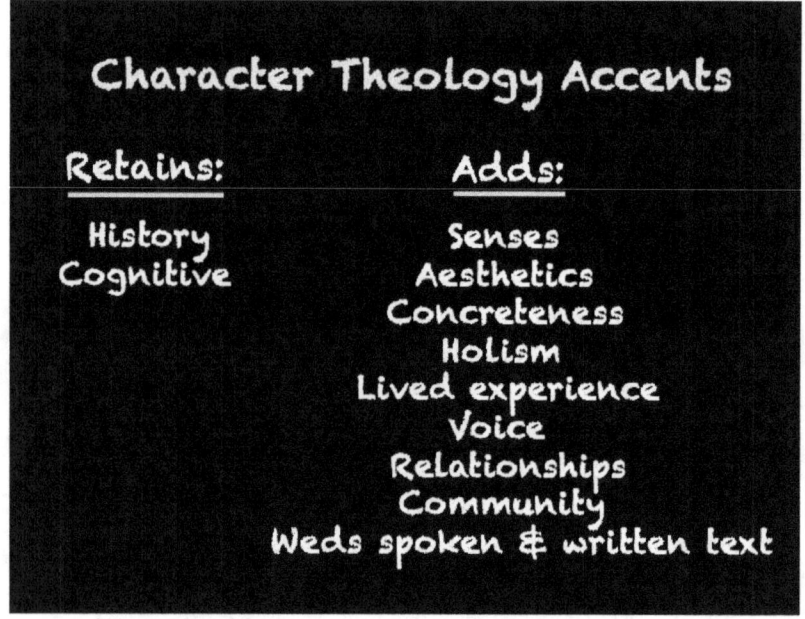

Figure 8.1. Character Theology Accents

Character theology takes interpreters on an imaginative, emotionally packed journey of twists and turns, highs and lows, as they attempt to decipher what the Holy Spirit wishes them to internalize as they forge faith and faithfulness. Character theology asks that we align our lives with selective ancients, e.g., the pioneers and veterans of faith (Heb 12:1). Why? Because we become whom we hang with. Character theology focuses strongly on concrete experiences demonstrated through human relationships.

Character theology partially accomplishes this episodic journey of triumphs and tragedies through the grand narrative. From Genesis to Revelation, key characters concretize central truths and themes of the overall story, all centered on the Chief Character.

Character theology requires truth be imaged and demonstrated as well as stated and analyzed. One-liners *cannot* do justice to a story or a character. Rather, an orally layered "narrative statement" and "inferences from events" are required—something that puts some meat on the bone requires an embodied explanation, a demonstrated idea, not just a documented one; it demands personalness and holism; it requires *human experience*. Character theology is derived from orally layered (verbal and visual) interpretation.

Character theology acknowledges that voice permeates the written text and that to grasp a fuller understanding of Scripture requires listening to the sound script. Scripture weds the spoken text to the written text, thereby integrating sound and sight. Such integration makes character theology not just a powerful pedagogical tool, but a universal one as well.

Character theology allows for, but does not insist on, multiple truths within a specific story. Character theology accepts the possibility for Author-author design to be multi-intentional in nature. Not tied to a science-based hermeneutic model that permits only a single truth, character theology recognizes and respects the ambiguous oral foundation and nature of Scripture, which may include more than one truth being espoused.

What keeps OH-CT interpretation in the ballpark? What moves interpreters beyond reader response? To move beyond interpretational interests, everyone comes with an agenda; for interpretational integrity here are a few guardians we highlighted throughout the book (review fig. 5.2). To help minimize fabrication or falsification, these components take interpreters *behind* the text, *within* in the text, and *beyond* the text:

- Prayer, humility, revision
- The grand narrative
- The author's questions behind the text
- Repetition and rhythm within the text
- Individual and corporate shame of interpreters
- Communal listening, dialoguing, debating
- Church tradition over the centuries
- The Grand Interpreter who guides into *all* truth

Character theology relies strongly on human experience to uncover biblical truths and introduce members of the Trinity. Human experience lived out through the lives of Bible characters serves as the principal interpretive key to uncover the truths of Scripture even as it incrementally paints a more detailed and defined portrait of the face of God. It also makes a masterpiece out of our messy attempts to paint our own portrait, our family's portrait, our community's portrait, and our nation's portrait.

Not requiring formal training, character theology unleashes an army of viable amateur Bible story interpreters. This opens the door for critical-contextual ethno-theology as co-constructors seek core truths and blossom in their interpretive prowess.

Character theology explores the most fundamental issues of life. Bible storytellers are character highlighters. Highlighted characters simulate life, navigating responding recipients from, to, or even beyond their present words and deeds. Character theology is practical, personal, and public.

Character theology relies on more than the cognitive in the interpretive process. That is due to the narrative-centric nature of Scripture where orality's fingerprints are found emblazoned throughout. Character theology, therefore, takes a more holistic approach, valuing not only the cognitive, but also a story's attractiveness and impactfulness. Recall Piper's desire for himself and all others was not just to *understand* the author's words but "to penetrate through language to the reality that words represent."[12] In other words, to *experience* them. Character theology seeks holistic coreness through artistic accuracy.

Bible characters should be found upstream of any theological system, e.g., systematic theology or biblical theology. In character theology, what's downstream determines what is discovered upstream.

Dirty water upstream results from dirty water downstream. It's time for a revised filtration system upstream in relation to the narrative genre. The good news is dirty water can be purified. Part of the purification process includes becoming curious cultural watchers. How does your audience hold meetings? Dialogue? Tell stories? Use logic? Interpret stories? Read characters and contexts? Ask questions? Apply new insights? Remember over time?

Some will feel answering such questions will require time away from "real ministry." Anyway, they already *know* the answers. Mark Twain's quip is apropos: "What gets us in trouble is not what we don't know. It's what we know for sure that just ain't so."[13]

---

12. Piper, *What Is Saving Faith*, 89.

13. See https://www.goodreads.com/quotes/738123-what-gets-us-into-trouble-is-not-what-we-don-t.

Character-Centric Pathways

Character theology challenges most Bible interpreters to not just *revisit* their hermeneutic model but to *revise* it. As "literary tourists," print has domesticated too many exegetes. The "big forgot" (orality) and the "fatal flaw" of the excluded voice have blinded many Bible interpreters to other legitimate hermeneutic and theological possibilities, including those practiced by the first contributors and custodians of the *spoken-written* words of God (ch. 4). God's highest creations received much more than the written words of God; they received the *spoken*-written words of God.

A significant part of the following review will include how one perceives hermeneutics. Here are some top perceptions. Rather than assembling for Bible study, we prefer a more relational gathering—engaging Bible characters. Rather than relying on professionally trained teachers, we prefer participatory discovery with the aid of a teacher-facilitator. Rather than initiating questions about what the story is saying, we prefer to attempt to answer the author's questions that fostered the story. Rather than focusing on grammar as the main means (recall menu entrées) to discover meaning, we prefer interpreters "read" characters and rooms (context). Rather than interpreters being book smart, we prefer they be street smart *and* book smart.

Oral hermeneutics, whose answers are anchored in characters navigating a crisis in search of a satisfactory solution, provides a much broader, more appealing, and reasonable pathway to truths and ethics than most interpreters have surmised; it serves up some down-home case study cuisine (engagement).

Following are some examples of thick character-centric pathways that retain the multi-accents that comprise character theology's relational (personal-collective) nature:

1. The *definition of story* centers on characters.
2. *Characters* receive self-author characterization.
3. Abstract *plot* is driven by concrete characters involved in events.
4. The *mystery* of the story revolves around "Who dunnit?" and "What happens next?"
5. One *listens* to a story with an ear for characters.
6. *Conversations* center on relationships between characters.
7. The *Trinity and Scripture* reveal character-based communication.
8. The *grand narrative of Scripture* is centered on the Chief Character.

9. *Hermeneutics* centers on interpreting characters.
10. *Logic* requires character thinking.
11. *Questions* center on the characters involved.
12. *Rationality* requires character support.
13. *Concepts* are character-based.
14. *Propositions* require layered character-based summaries.
15. Good *teaching* requires an audience-attentive relationship.
16. *Curriculum* centers on characters.
17. *Titles* and *themes* emphasize key characters.
18. *Learning* is character-centered.
19. *Ethics* focus on what characters demonstrate.
20. Downstream *theology* reflects upstream characters.
21. *Application* involves emulating the words and works of select Bible characters.
22. *Character formation* is based on real or fictional characters.
23. Through identity and intimacy, *we become* whom we hang with.
24. Aid to *accomplish all this* is a person—the Grand Interpreter.

The above list will require major paradigm shifts for many print-oriented exegetes. As card-carrying members of Facts Anonymous the authors understand this all too well. Can we learn to think in characters? Read characters? Read rooms? Has our chatter changed to conviction? How strongly do you see yourself moving towards a hermeneutic focused on human experience? Many are getting there, even if they take the long route as we did.

Why is everything of significance anchored to characters? Can we learn to move beyond appreciation of characters to appropriation of characters? Can we learn to habitually live in a speaking text? *How character-centric are all our communicative, interpretive, theological, curricular, applicational, and recall components*? Being character-centric is being concrete-centric. Wise Bible interpreters discover divine truths as they live the story through the eyes of the Spirit-selected characters involved. The sacred canon conveys character-based and character-shaped communication that conveys the Chief Character.

Only fear—the gateway to the status quo—can stop Bible communicators. Universalizing and maintaining the status quo of the Western hermeneutical and theological guilds will minimally alienate some three-fourths of today's world. We may have to change our idea of what constitutes the *best* hermeneutic model for the story genre. Can we become comfortable and confident with oral hermeneutics? With character theology? Is it time to sample some "seemingly" forbidden food (Acts 10)? If Christianity is to become and remain relevant in this present era, exegetes have two pathways—oral hermeneutics and character theology.

> What if that antique in the attic is a Picasso painting waiting to be discovered?

Have Bible communicators underappreciated what the majority of the world (not to mention the Holy Spirit) assumes as natural and normal? Is it time for some hard reflection on the cultural boundedness, and hence limitations, of our grammatic-historical hermeneutic model without jettisoning it? Recall when schoolteachers tried to teach left-handers how to write right-handed so they would be "normal," rather than appreciate the contribution of a different writing style? That experiment didn't go so well. Natural is natural.

The grammatical-historical model did *not* begin history; it was *added to* history. Bible interpreters must move beyond being *comfortable* with their hermeneutic theory to being *capable* of articulating the assumptions that drive it.

Can Bible communicators learn to rest in the reality that there is more than one legitimate hermeneutic model? Other potential theologies? Is it still necessary to continually push a string when interpreting the narrative genre or thinking about theologies?

Does there have to be a hermeneutical hierarchy that limits the possibilities of other reasonable and relevant theologies? Is the Spirit doing a "new thing"? What if that antique in the attic is a Picasso painting waiting to be rediscovered?

It's very easy to slide under the warm, familiar hermeneutic blanket designed for a specific cold climate. But should dialogue surrounding hermeneutic models ever cease (recall the lad's comment that "everything that can be invented has been invented"), especially when major communication transitions are presently taking place (oral to print to digital-virtual-AI)?

The eminent F. F. Bruce offers some sage advice: "Perhaps we may learn not to depend exclusively on past experiences; they will not be sufficient for the needs of the present. Daily grace must be obtained for daily need."[14] It's

---

14. Bruce, *Hard Sayings of Jesus*, 268.

time to welcome back some old friends—oral hermeneutics and character theology—and reinstate them as full family members.

Which do people want to hear and see? Solid exegetical sermons or stories of the lives of Bible characters? Titles such as "The Book of Numbers" or the Hebrew translation—"In the Wilderness"? Evidence that demands a verdict or Someone who is more than a carpenter?

Bible communicators can no longer remain in an imagined era that no longer exists. Nor can they continue to offer lackluster theologies to "all the nations." It's time to check the current calendar and modify the menu at the Old Faithful Fact Church and Buffet Seminary. It's time to re-narrativize, re-dramatize, re-characterize, re-symbolize, re-ritualize divine discourse—the spoken-written words of God; it's time to offer something that will resonate (relationships), reveal truth (characters), and take up residence long-term (imaged memory); it's time for a natural theology (character theology) that can go global; it's time for Bible teachers to refamiliarize themselves with what the ancients took for granted—orality; it's time for Bible communicators to scoot over to the other side of the car so that the learners can get behind the wheel and *learn to drive by driving*; it's time for character theology.

Character Theology Reveals the Chief Character

Stories require a setting, a time, a conflict (plot) played out in a sequence of scenes and events. But to make sense and pack a more powerful punch, stories require something more concrete, more significant, more sensory, more strategic, more relational. Stories require *characters*. While all the components that comprise a story are necessary (and integrated), concrete characters *drive* these elements in a story.

Stories serve as pathways for characters to express themselves. *Without characters there is no story*. Characters, such as Jonah, pagan sailors, a king, Ninevites, a fish, a worm, serve as pathways to express theology and ethics. *Without characters there is no living theoretical or practical theology*. That is why character theology is so important.

Character theology is not just for:

1. Conveying a more robust, appealing, impactful message (affective sensory enactment wrapped in rational cold evidence) found in the lived lives of concrete characters, nor just for
2. Offering a genre-sensitive tool that allows the text to set the agenda when interpreting the conversations and actions of a sovereignly

selected few of the three thousand plus characters whose stories comprise *more than half* the spoken-written words of God, nor just for

3. Opening the door for the common Christian to become a competent interpreter of Scripture's stories, nor just for

4. Unifying the many individual stories through the grand narrative; *rather*, character theology's major contribution is

5. *Revealing the relationship-seeking Chief Character* behind creation and the canon through his interfacing with biblical characters and their interfacing with each other.

Composed of a colorful cast of characters, character theology takes us *beyond* abstract, fragmented, siloed words and grammar. One does not have to be a grammarian or even print-oriented to interpret and understand Scripture's stories. A relationally based character theology serves holistically as the mother of meaning, meditation, modeling, modification, and memory. Character theology is natural, universal, relational! And one of its strong suits is it *has currency* with today's generations because it is recognizable and respectable.

Character theology has the tendency to make the unfamiliar appear as familiar or the old and familiar appear as new and unfamiliar (recall "defamiliarization" in ch 2). Character theology's strong focus on human experience (actionized beliefs and behaviors) of characters calls for imagination-based reason that makes the unexpected become the expected and the expected become the unexpected. For example, the greatest is the one who serves, not served; the first shall be last; let the dead bury the dead; deformities or ailments are the result of former sin.[15] Bible characters have an immediate and intimate way of shattering our present, stable, and secure world or stabilizing an insecure world, whichever the case.

Character theology is a relational theology that includes characters not only to reveal salvific history but also to equip all willing Creator-worshipers for service among the nations. Encouraged by the facilitative *"guide on the side"* (recall the driver's ed trainer), Christ followers become *co-performers* (*reenactors*) *on the stage* with the Chief Character as the moving and memorable sacred story expands globally. They have discovered their story is sacred because it is integrated with the Chief Character's sacred story and are therefore enabled to take the offensive and raid the darkness (John 12:36).

While difficult to grasp for many, including the authors, the Supreme One for some curious reason courageously (human perspective) chose to reveal his personage most naturally and precisely through the interactions

---

15. A common holistic belief then (Ps 107:17; John 9:2; 2 Cor 10:10).

of people along with his interactions with his highest creation—*people*. Through demonstration and display rather than mere, cold, codified lists of systematized definitions and propositions, Author-author–selected personages, such as Jonah, whisper to us characteristics of the Triune God.

> *How character-centric are all our communicative, interpretive, theological, curricular, applicational, and recall components?*

With the Bible ancients behind us and a hungry-for-heroes audience before us, the future of Christianity looks a little brighter today because it loves to wed characters, including the Chief Character, to abstract ideas and concepts.

Orality's strong emphasis on the interaction of concrete characters draws the listening audience up onto the public stage to become coactors who share in the conversations (sound) and experiences (actions) of the Author-author–chosen actors. Literacy's strong emphasis on print allows individuals reading privately in silence to remain offstage as distant objective observers and analyzers of the text that results in a system of theological propositions. Without eliminating either orality or print (two eyes provide greater depth perception), and adding the digital-virtual-AI world, which best characterizes today's world? *The road map to the recovery and expansion of Christianity in the twenty-first century will be through Bible characters.*

In review, character theology is composed of interacting Bible characters—with their Creator and with each other. Sovereignly selected by the Author to fulfill specific roles, key Bible characters purposely reveal and distinguish the Eternal's personality to the nations through visualized demonstration. Tellers and told, therefore, should not just look "at" these message-bearing beings, but "through" them, to see, hear, smell, enjoy, fear what they embody through words and deeds.

Chosen Bible characters drop breadcrumbs that reveal the Creator. *Through a perpetual parade of personalities, the Eternal One sovereignly chose to reveal himself to the nations most naturally and precisely through his interactions with people and their interaction with each other.*

Each chosen character offers the Author a brush and fresh canvas on which to paint one or more of his attributes for the whole world to see. All who in steadfast faith follow the Savior should desire as a first-order ambition the longing to be so like the Great Revealer that their presence among others radiates a glimpse of Jesus's presence. *Why should the devil have all the good characters?*

Bible characters create choices. How they navigated earthy life—through wisdom, wit, worthlessness—demonstrates the very essence of the Great Revealer, demanding ongoing deliberations. Will we become "living epistles"? "And what more shall I say? I do not have time to tell about Gideon, Barak, Samson and Jephthah, about David and Samuel and the prophets" (Heb 11:32 NIV).

The authors hope you—the diligent reader who reached the end of the book—are like the women in the parable of the lost coin. After meticulous effort (she lit a lamp, swept the whole house, searched diligently), she *rediscovered* the missing silver coin. The ten coins were unified again. We hope you, too, have rediscovered something valuable that should never have been lost—human experiences found in character theology that reveal the Chief Character.

> *Why should the devil have all the good characters?*

We know considering something unfamiliar like oral hermeneutics and character theology is not easy. As Sharon Brown surmises, "Sometimes on the way to better, things get worse for a while."[16] And we hope, like the determined, yet surprised and rejoicing women Jesus spoke about, you will invite your "friends and neighbors" and shout, "Celebrate with me! I've found the hermeneutic and theology that were lost!"

Concluding Reflections

Endings generate *new* beginnings—*new* stories, *new* characters, *new* forms of logic, *new* memories, *new* hermeneutics, *new* theologies, new applications, new participants entering the covenant community. The authors encourage the reader to remain curious and courageous in Christianity's common cause—grasping God.

In that this is new ground for many, please sharpen the authors' shortcomings. Coin new terminology that brings greater clarity. Add your voice to the growing conversation on character interpretation through future articles, volumes, podcasts, videos.

Most important, *try it; give it a chance*. Secure more than a front row seat. Step up onto the stage and become coactors. Scripture will come alive

---

16. Sharon Brown, *Sensible Shoes*, 141.

as never before for you and your audience, as it did with the participants and storyteller in the three EBCs.

You may enable some participants to receive "*a brand-new Bible*"! For sure the church will be blessed, and the Speaking One will gain many more worshipping workers from among the nations, and his "praise will echo through eternity" (Ps 111:10 VOICE).

> *Why is it important to know and practice character theology when interpreting and communicating Author-author truths?*

Bible communication can't be much more concrete than when portrayed through characters. Character theology turns verbal information into visual speaking images through concrete-relational characters. Character theology relates, sticks, and transforms people from among the nations, resulting in "singing joy-filled songs *of praise to You*" (Ps 67:4 VOICE [emphasis original]). Character theology provides motivation and meaning. Character theology provides a natural, universal, relational way for the world to engage God through *his* chosen cast of characters.

We began this book with a question: Who doesn't love a good story? As modeled in the scroll of Jonah, we conclude the book by asking the reader to pause for a moment and once again ponder the challenging question that drove this book: *Why is it important to know and practice character theology when interpreting and communicating Author-author truths?*

Appendix

Four Value Frames of the Gospel

GOSPEL FRAMES	GUILT/ INNOCENCE	SHAME/ HONOR	FEAR/ POWER	POLLUTION/ PURITY
LANGUAGE	Moral law	Moral code	Moral custom	Moral values
NAMES FOR GOD	Just One Righteous Judge	King Jealous Lover Patron	Victor Deliverer All-Powerful	Cleanser Pure One
NAMES FOR SATAN	Liar Accuser	Challenger Debater	Adversary Prowling lion	Dirty one
GOD'S ISSUE	Justice challenged	Lost face	Power usurped	Holiness polluted
PEOPLE'S ISSUE	Broke God's law	Dishonored patron	Usurped God's power	Polluted community code
SIN	Broken law	Broken relationship	Challenged power	Polluted community code
RESULTS	Separation from a holy God	Estrangement Humiliation Identity loss	Controlled Possessed	Contamination
COSTS	Punishment	Abandonment	Domination	Separation
ARENA	Private-Public	Public-Private	Public-Private	Public-Private
PLAYERS	Self-Society	Society-Self	Society-Self	Society-Self
FOCUS	Internal behavior	Public action	Internal emotion	Internal action
EMOTION	Regret	Unworthy	Powerless	Dirty
OUTCOME	Restitution	Relationship	Control	Acceptance
ACTION	Confess Correct Fix Apologize	Beat self Hide Retaliate Suicide	Appease Manipulate Placate	Appease Manipulate Placate
INTERVENER	Substitute	Mediator	Victor	Purifier

FOUR VALUE FRAMES OF THE GOSPEL

GOSPEL FRAMES	GUILT/ INNOCENCE	SHAME/ HONOR	FEAR/ POWER	POLLUTION/ PURITY
RESULT	Forgiveness Pardon Obedience	Loyalty Inclusion Reaffirmation	Freedom Peace	Purified Spotless

Source: T. Steffen, *Worldview-Based Storying*, 245–46.

Bibliography

Abernethy, Alexis D. "Exploring the Role of Embodiment in Worship." *Fuller* 13 (2019) 68–71. https://fullerstudio.fuller.edu/wp-content/uploads/2019/01/Issue-13.pdf.
Adams, Edward. "Paul's Story of God and Creation." In *Narrative Dynamics in Paul: A Critical Assessment*, edited by Bruce W. Longenecker, 19–43. Louisville: Westminster John Knox, 2002.
Adams, Marilee. *Change Your Questions, Change Your Life: 10 Powerful Tools for Your Life and Work*. San Francisco: Berrett-Koehler, 2009.
Adeney, Miriam. "Feeding Giraffes, Counting Cows, and Missing True Learners." In *Communicating Christ through Story and Song: Orality in Buddhist Contexts*, edited by Paul H. DeNeui, 77–107. Pasadena, CA: William Carey, 2008.
Adewuya, J. Ayodeji. *An African Commentary on the Letter of James*. Global Readings. Eugene, OR: Cascade, 2023.
Adeyemo, Tokunboh, ed. *Africa Bible Commentary: A One-Volume Commentary Written by 70 African Scholars*. Grand Rapids: Zondervan Academic, 2006.
Alter, Robert. *The Art of Biblical Narrative*. New York: Basic, 1981.
———. *The World of Biblical Literature*. New York: Basic, 1992.
Alves, Rubem A. *The Poet, the Warrior, the Prophet*. Edward Cadbury Lectures. Philadelphia: Trinity, 1990.
Arrington, Aminta. *Songs of the Lisu Hills: Practicing Christianity in Southwest China*. University Park: Penn State University Press, 2021.
Assmann, Jan. "Form as a Mnemonic Device: Cultural Texts and Cultural Memory." In *Performing the Gospel: Orality, Memory, and Mark*, edited by Richard A. Horsley et al., 67–82. Augsburg: Fortress, 2011.
Auerbach, Erich. *Mimesis: The Representation of Reality in Western Literature*. Translated by Willard R. Trask. Princeton Classics. Princeton, NJ: Princeton University Press, 2003.
Autero, Esa J. "Seeing the New Testament through Asian Eyes." *Evangelical Review of Theology* 46 (2022) 180–84.
Bailey, Kenneth E. *The Cross and the Prodigal: Luke 15 through the Eyes of Middle Eastern Peasants*. Downers Grove, IL: InterVarsity, 2005.
———. "Informal Controlled Oral Tradition and the Synoptic Gospels." *Them* 20 (1995) 4–11.
———. *Jacob and the Prodigal: How Jesus Retold Israel's Story*. Downers Grove, IL: InterVarsity, 2003.

Bal, Mieke. *Narratology: Introduction to the Theory of Narrative*. 2nd ed. Ontario: University of Toronto Press, 1997.
Barr, James. *The Bible in the Modern World*. London: SCM, 1963.
Barrick, William D. "Living a New Life: Old Testament Teaching about Conversion." *TMSJ* 11 (2000) 9–38.
Bartholomew, Craig G. "Three Horizons: Hermeneutics from the Other End—An Evaluation of Anthony Thiselton's Hermeneutic Proposals." *EuroJTh* 5 (1996) 121–36.
Bates, Colin W. "5 Listening Insights from the Chinese Character for Listening." Colinwbates, n.d. https://www.colinwbates.com/chinese-character-for-listening/.
Bauckham, Richard. *Jesus and the Eyewitnesses: The Gospels as Eyewitness Testimony*. 2nd ed. Grand Rapids: Eerdmans, 2017.
Berger, Daniel R. *Oral Interpretation of the Bible*. Eugene, OR: Wipf and Stock, 2003.
Bishop, Ryan. "There's Nothing Natural about Natural Conversations: A Look at Dialogue in Fiction and Drama." *Oral Tradition* 6 (1991) 58–78.
Blomberg, Craig L. *Interpreting the Parables*. 2nd ed. Downers Grove, IL: InterVarsity, 2012.
Bock, Darrell L. "Opening Questions: Definition and Philosophy of Exegesis." In *Interpreting the New Testament Text: Introduction to the Art and Science of Exegesis*, edited by Darrell L. Bock and Buist M. Fanning, 23–32. Wheaton, IL: Crossway, 2006.
Bohannan, Paul. *How Culture Works*. New York: Free, 1995.
Boomershine, Thomas E. *First-Century Gospel Storytellers and Audiences: The Gospels as Performance Literature*. Biblical Performance Criticism 17. Eugene, OR: Cascade, 2022.
Botha, Pieter J. J. *Orality and Literacy in Early Christianity*. Biblical Performance Criticism 5. Eugene, OR: Cascade, 2012.
Bradt, Kevin M., SJ. *Story as a Way of Knowing*. Kansas City, MO: Sheed & Ward, 1997.
Bream, Shannon. *The Mothers and Daughters of the Bible Speak: Lessons on Faith from Nine Biblical Families*. Northhampton, MA: Broadside, 2022.
Brockmeier, Jens, and Hanna Meretoja. "Understanding Narrative Hermeneutics." *StoryWorlds: A Journal of Narrative Studies* 6 (2014) 1–27.
Brooks, Will. *Interpreting Scripture across Cultures: An Introduction to Cross-Cultural Hermeneutics*. Eugene, OR: Wipf & Stock, 2022.
Brown, Michael Joseph. "Hearing the Master's Voice." In *Engaging Biblical Authority: Perspectives on the Bible as Scripture*, edited by William P. Brown, 10–17. Louisville: Westminster, 2007.
Brown, Sharon Garlough. *Sensible Shoes: A Story about the Spiritual Journey*. Sensible Shoes. Downers Grove, IL: InterVarsity, 2013.
Brown, Stuart. "Empiricism." Encyclopedia, Oct. 18, 2023. From *Europe, 1450 to 1789: Encyclopedia of the Early Modern World*. https://www.encyclopedia.com/history/encyclopedias-almanacs-transcripts-and-maps/empiricism.
Bruce, F. F. *The Canon of Scripture*. Downers Grove, IL: IVP Academic, 1988.
———. *Hard Sayings of Jesus*. Hard Sayings Series. Downers Grove, IL: IVP Academic, 1983.
Brueggemann, Walter. *Abiding Astonishment: Psalms, Modernity, and the Making of History*. Louisville: Westminster/John Knox, 1991.

———. *The Land: Place as Gift, Promise, and Challenge in Biblical Faith.* London: SPCK, 1978.
———. *Texts under Negotiation: The Bible and Postmodern Imagination.* Minneapolis: Fortress, 1993.
Bruner, Jerome. *Acts of Meaning: Four Lectures on Mind and Culture.* Cambridge, MA: Harvard University Press, 1990.
———. *The Culture of Education.* Cambridge, MA: Harvard University Press, 1996.
Bruno, Chris, et al. *Biblical Theology According to the Apostles: How the Earliest Christians Told the Story of Israel.* New Studies in Biblical Theology. Downers Grove, IL: IVP Academic, 2020.
Buchanan, Andrew. "Biblical Theology for Oral-Preference Communities." *Missiology: An International Review* 49 (2021) 250–62.
Burke, Kenneth. *A Rhetoric of Motives.* Berkeley: University of California Press, 1969.
Caldwell, Larry W. *Doing Bible Interpretation! Making the Bible Come Alive for Yourself and Your People.* Sioux Falls, SD: Lazy Oaks, 2016.
———. "Towards the New Discipline of Ethnohermeneutics: Questioning the Relevancy of Western Hermeneutical Methods in the Asian Context." *JAM* 1 (1999) 21–43.
Carr, David M. *Writing on the Tablet of the Heart: Origins of Scripture and Literature.* Oxford: Oxford University Press, 2005.
Chafer, Lewis Sperry. *Prolegomena, Bibliology, Theology Proper.* Vol. 1 of *Systematic Theology.* Grand Rapids: Kregel, 1976.
Chan, Sam. *Evangelism in a Skeptical World: How to Make the Unbelievable News about Jesus More Believable.* Grand Rapids: Zondervan Academic, 2018.
Chan, Simon. *Grassroots Asian Theology: Thinking the Faith from the Ground Up.* Downers Grove, IL: IVP Academic, 2014.
Chiang, Samuel E. and William Coppedge. "Connecting Orality, Language, and Culture." *Orality Journal* 6 (2017) 7–12.
Chiang, Samuel E., and Grant Lovejoy, eds. *Beyond Literate Western Models: Contextualizing Theological Education in Oral Contexts.* Hong Kong: International Orality Network, 2013.
Chou, Abner. *Hermeneutics of the Biblical Writers: Learning to Interpret Scripture from the Prophets and Apostles.* Grand Rapids: Kregel Academic, 2018.
Clanchy, M. T. *From Memory to Written Record: England 1066–1307.* 2nd ed. Malden, MA: Blackwell, 1993.
Clark-Sole, Jaime. *Women in the Bible.* Interpretation: Resources for the Use of Scripture in the Church. Louisville, KY: Westminster John Knox, 2020.
Colijn, Brenda B. *Images of Salvation in the New Testament.* Downers Grove, IL: IVP Academic, 2010.
Conquergood, Dwight. "Performance Studies: Interventions and Radical Research." *Drama Review* 46 (2002) 145–56.
Cooke, Phil. "The Dangers of Being 'Future Blind.'" Phil Cooke, Dec. 13, 2022. https://www.philcooke.com/the-dangers-of-being-future-blind/.
Cooley, Charles Horton. *Human Nature and the Social Order: The Interplay of Man's Behaviors, Character and Personal Traits with His Society.* Edmonton: Adansonia, 2018.
Cooper, Michael T., and Andrew Johnson. "A New Theological Education Initiative." YouTube, Feb. 28, 2023. From *Ephesiology: Podcast and Master Classes.* https://youtu.be/thOy3ZIfifM.

Coppedge, Billy. "Towards a Theology of Orality: Reevaluating the Significance of Orality for L4 and 2050." Lausanne, Dec. 15, 2022. https://lausanne.org/about/blog/towards-a-theology-of-orality.

Coppedge, William A. *African Literacies and Western Oralities? Communication Complexities, the Orality Movement, and the Materialities of Christianity in Uganda.* American Society of Missiology Monograph Series. Eugene, OR: Pickwick, 2021.

Cordeiro, Wayne. *The Divine Mentor: Growing Your Faith as You Sit at the Feet of the Savior.* Minneapolis: Bethany, 2007.

Corduan, Winfried. "Humility and Commitment: An Approach to Modern Hermeneutics." *Them* 11 (1986) 83–88.

Cross Bridge Church. "Engaging Jonah." YouTube, June 9, 2023. https://www.youtube.com/watch?v=1weH8zLAklk.

Crouch, Andy. "The Return of Shame." *Christianity Today* 59 (2015) 32–41.

Crouch, Dennis. "Tracing the Quote: Everything that can be Invented has been Invented." *Patentlyo*, Jan. 6, 2011. https://patentlyo.com/patent/2011/01/tracing-the-quote-everything-that-can-be-invented-has-been-invented.html.

Daly, James. "Life on the Screen: Visual Literacy in Education." Edutopia, Sept. 14, 2004. https://www.edutopia.org/life-screen.

Danesi, Marcel. *Poetic Logic: The Role of Metaphor in Thought, Language, and Culture.* Madison, WI: Atwood, 2004.

David, Susan. "The Gift and Power of Emotional Courage." TED, Nov. 2017. https://www.ted.com/talks/susan_david_the_gift_and_power_of_emotional_courage?language=en.

Dean, Edith. *All of the Women of the Bible.* San Francisco: HarperOne, 1988.

Deere, Jack. *Surprised by the Voice of God: How God Speaks Today through Prophecies, Dreams, and Visions.* Grand Rapids: Zondervan Academic, 1996.

DeMarco, Donald. "Did Jesus Ever Laugh?" Catholic Exchange, May 2, 2023. https://catholicexchange.com/did-jesus-ever-laugh/.

DeMuth, Mary E. *The Most Misunderstood Women of the Bible: What Their Stories Teach Us about Thriving.* Washington DC: Salem, 2022.

Dewey, Joanna, ed. *Orality and Textuality in Early Christian Literature.* Semeia Studies. Atlanta: Scholars, 1995.

Dewey, John. *Democracy and Education.* New York: Macmillan, 1966.

Dickie, June Frances. "Zulu Song, Oral Art Performing the Psalms to Stir the Heart." PhD diss., University of KwaZulu-Natal, 2017.

Dorsey, David A. *The Literary Structure of the Old Testament: A Commentary on Genesis-Malachi.* Grand Rapids: Baker Academic, 2004.

Dunn, James D. G. *New Testament Theology: An Introduction.* Library of Biblical Theology. Nashville: Abingdon, 2009.

———. *The Oral Gospel Tradition.* Grand Rapids: Zondervan, 2013.

Duvall, J. Scott, and J. Daniel Hays. *Grasping God's Word: A Hands-On Approach to Reading, Interpreting, and Applying the Bible.* 3rd ed. Grand Rapids: Zondervan Academic, 2012.

Edwards, Viv, and Thomas J. Sienkewiez. *Oral Cultures Past and Present: Rappin' and Homer.* Language Library. Oxford: Basil Blackwell, 1990.

Eisenhower, William D. "Why Should the Devil Have All the Good Stories?" Paper presented at Evangelical Theological Society conference, Philadelphia, Nov. 16–18, 1995.

Elliot, Matthew A. *Faithful Feelings: Rethinking Emotion in the New Testament.* Grand Rapids: Kregel Academic, 2006.

Enns, Peter. *Inspiration and Incarnation: Evangelicals and the Problem of the Old Testament.* Grand Rapids: Baker Academic, 2005.

Erickson, Diane M. "A Developmental Re-Forming of the Phases of Meaning in Transformational Learning." *Adult Education Quarterly* 58 (2007) 61–69.

Erickson, Millard J. *Evangelical Interpretation: Perspectives on Hermeneutical Issues.* Grand Rapids: Baker, 1993.

Estes, Douglas. *Questions and Rhetoric in the Greek New Testament: An Essential Reference Resource for Exegesis.* Grand Rapids: Zondervan Academic, 2017.

Evans, A. Steven. "Matters of the Heart; Orality, Story, and Cultural Transformation: The Critical Role off Storytelling in Affecting Worldview." *Missiology: An International Review* 38 (2010) 185–99.

Eve, Eric. *Behind the Gospels: Understanding the Oral Tradition.* Minneapolis: Fortress, 2013.

Fee, Gordon D., and Douglas Stuart. *How to Read the Bible for All Its Worth: A Guide to Understanding the Bible.* Grand Rapids: Zondervan, 1982.

Finnegan, Ruth. *Literacy and Orality: Studies in the Technology of Communication.* Updated ed. N.p.: Lulu, 2014.

———. *Oral Literature in Africa.* World Oral Literature Series 1. Cambridge: Open Book, 2012.

———. "What Is Orality—If Anything?" *Byzantine and Modern Greek Studies* 14 (1990) 130–49.

Fisher, Walter R. *Human Communication as Narration: Toward a Philosophy of Reason, Values, and Action.* Columbia: University of South Carolina Press, 1987.

———. "Narration as a Human Communication Paradigm: The Case of Public Moral Argument." *Communication Monographs* 51 (1984) 1–22.

Flanders, Christopher, and Werner Mischke, eds. *Honor, Shame and the Gospel: Reframing Our Message and Ministry.* Littleton, CO: William Carey, 2020.

Flemming, Dean. *Contextualization in the New Testament: Patterns for Theology and Mission.* Downers Grove, IL: IVP Academic, 2005.

Fokkelman, J. P. *Reading Biblical Narrative: An Introductory Guide.* Louisville: Westminster John Knox, 1999.

Fox, Everett. *The Five Books of the Bible: Genesis, Exodus, Leviticus, Numbers, Deuteronomy.* New York: Schocken, 1995.

Frei, Hans W. *The Eclipse of Biblical Narrative: A Study in Eighteenth and Nineteenth Century Hermeneutics.* New Haven, CT: Yale University Press, 1974.

Freire, Paulo, and Antonio Faundez. *Learning to Question: A Pedagogy of Liberation.* London: Continuum, 1989.

Gadamer, Hans-Georg. *Truth and Method.* Bloomsbury Revelations. Reprint, New York: Bloomsbury Academic, 2013.

Gamble, Harry Y. *Books and Readers in the Early Church: A History of Early Christian Texts.* New Haven, CT: Yale University Press, 1995.

Gardner, Paul D., ed. *New International Encyclopedia of Bible Characters.* Zondervan's Understand the Bible Reference Series. Grand Rapids: Zondervan, 2001.

Gaventa, Beverly Roberts. "Toward a Theology of Acts: Reading and Rereading." *Interpretation* 42 (1988) 146–57.

Gener, Timotea D., and Stephen T. Pardue. *Asian Christian Theology: Evangelical Perspectives.* Cumbria, UK: Langham Global, 2019.

Georges, Jayson, and Mark D. Baker. *Ministering in Honor-Shame Cultures: Biblical Foundations and Practical Essentials*. Downers Grove, IL: IVP Academic, 2016.

Gerhardsson, Birger. *Memory and Manuscript: Oral Tradition and Written Transmission in Rabbinic Judaism and Early Christianity*; with *Tradition and Transmission in Early Christianity*. Biblical Resource Series. Grand Rapids: Eerdmans, 1998.

Goldberg, Michael. *Theology and Narrative: A Critical Introduction*. Nashville: Abingdon, 1982.

Goldingay, John. "Biblical Story and the Way It Shapes Our Story." *Journal of the European Pentecostal Theological Association* 17 (1997) 5–15.

———. "How Far Do Readers Make Sense? Interpreting Biblical Narrative." *Them* 18 (1993) 5–10.

Goleman, Daniel. *Emotional Intelligence*. 10th anniv. trade pbk. ed. New York, Bantam, 2005.

Gonzàlez, Justo L. *Santa Biblia: The Bible through Hispanic Eyes*. Nashville: Abingdon, 1996.

Goody, Jack. *The Domestication of the Savage Mind*. Themes in the Social Sciences. Cambridge: Cambridge University Press, 1977.

Gottschall, Jonathan. *The Storytelling Animal: How Stories Make Us Human*. Boston: Houghton Mifflin Harcourt, 2012.

Gregersen, Hal. *Questions Are the Answer: A Breakthrough Approach to Your Most Vexing Problems at Work and in Life*. New York: Harper Business, 2018.

Grima, Benedicte. *The Performance of Emotion among Paxtun Women: "The Misfortunes Which Have Befallen Me."* New York: Oxford University Press, 2005.

Grudem, Wayne. *Systematic Theology: An Introduction to Biblical Doctrine*. Grand Rapids: Zondervan Academic, 1994.

Gunn, David M., and Danna Nolan Fewell. *Narrative in the Hebrew Bible*. Oxford Bible Series. New York: Oxford University Press, 1993.

Haight, Roger. *Spirituality Seeking Theology*. Modern Spiritual Masters. Maryknoll, NY: Orbis, 2014.

Harris, William V. *Ancient Literacy*. Cambridge, MA: Harvard University Press, 1989.

Harvey, John D. *Listening to the Text: Oral Patterning in Paul's Letters*. ETS Studies 1. Grand Rapids: Baker, 1998.

Havelock, Eric A. *The Muse Learns to Write: Reflections on Orality and Literacy from Antiquity to the Present*. New Haven, CT: Yale University Press, 1988.

Haven, Kendall. *Story Proof: The Science behind the Startling Power of Story*. Westport, MA: Libraries Unlimited, 2007.

———. *Story Smart: Using the Science of Story to Persuade, Influence, Inspire, and Teach*. Santa Barbara, CA: Libraries Unlimited, 2007.

Hayakawa, Samuel I. *Language in Action: A Guide to Accurate Thinking, Reading and Writing*. New York: Harcourt, Brace and Company, 1939.

Hays, Richard B. *The Moral Vision of the New Testament: A Contemporary Introduction to New Testament Ethics*. New York: HarperCollins, 1996.

———. *Reading with the Grain of Scripture*. Grand Rapids: Eerdmans, 2020.

———. "Scripture-Shaped Community: The Problem with Method in New Testament Ethics." *Imagination: A Journal of Bible and Theology* 44 (1990) 42–50.

Hearon, Holly E. "The Implications of 'Orality' for Studies of the Biblical Text." *Oral Tradition* 9 (2004) 96–107.

---. "The Interplay between Written and Spoken Word in the Second Testament as Background to the Emergence of Written Gospels." *Oral Tradition Journal* 25 (2010) 57–74.
Henry, Carl F. H. *God Who Speaks and Shows: Fifteen Theses, Part Two.* Vol. 3 of *God, Revelation and Authority.* Wheaton, IL: Crossway, 1999.
Herring, Josh. "Re-Enchanting the World." *An Unexpected Journal: Imagination* 2 (2019) 135–61.
Hibbert, Evelyn, and Richard Hibbert. *Training Missionaries: Principles and Possibilities.* Pasadena, CA: William Carey, 2016. Kindle.
Hiebert, Paul G. *Anthropological Insights for Missionaries.* Grand Rapids: Baker Academic, 1985.
---. *Anthropological Reflections on Missiological Issues.* Grand Rapids: Baker Academic, 1994.
---. "Conversion and Worldview Transformation." *International Frontier Missions* 114 (1997) 83–86.
---. "Critical Contextualization." *International Bulletin of Missionary Research* 11 (1987) 104–12.
---. *Transforming Worldviews: An Anthropological Understanding of How People Change.* Grand Rapids: Baker Academic, 2008.
Hodge, Charles. *Systematic Theology.* Vol. 1. New York: Scribner, Armstrong, and Co., 1873.
Hood, Jason B., and Matthew Y. Emerson. "Summaries of Israel's Story." *CurBR* 11 (2013) 328–48.
Hooper, Walter. *C. S. Lewis: A Companion & Guide.* New York: Harper-Collins, 1996.
Horsley, Richard A. "Oral and Written Aspects of the Emergence of the Gospel of Mark as Scripture." *Oral Tradition* 25 (2010) 93–114.
---. *Whoever Hears You Hears Me: Prophets, Performance, and Tradition in Q.* Harrisburg, PA: Trinity, 1999.
Inge, John. *A Christian Theology of Place.* Explorations in Practical, Pastoral and Empirical Theology. New York: Routledge, 2003.
Innis, Harold A. *The Bias of Communication.* Buffalo, NY: University of Toronto Press, 2008.
Institute in Basic Youth Conflicts. *Character Sketches from the Pages of Scripture, Illustrated in the World of Nature.* 3 vols. Hinsdale, IL: Institute, 1976.
Jaengmuk, Manot. "Walk through the Bible Study Program and the Local Thai." BTh thesis, Bangkok Bible College, 1992.
Jagerson, Jennifer. "Hermeneutics and the Methods of Oral Bible Storytelling for the Evangelization and Discipleship of Oral Learners." *Great Commission Research Journal* 4 (2013) 251–61.
---. "The Quintessential Characters, Stories, and Texts of the Old Testament." In *The Return of Oral Hermeneutics: As Good Today as It Was for the Hebrew Bible and First-Century Christianity*, by Tom Steffen and William Bjoraker, 325–34. Eugene, OR: Wipf & Stock, 2020.
---. "Transformation through Narrative: Exploring the Power of Sacred Stories among Oral Learners in Ethiopia." PhD diss., Talbot School of Theology, 2016.
Jakobson, Roman, et al. *Verbal Art, Verbal Sign, Verbal Time.* Minneapolis: University of Minnesota Press, 1985.
Jordan, James B. *Through New Eyes: Developing a Biblical View of the World.* Eugene, OR: Wipf and Stock, 1999.

Jousse, Marcel. *The Oral Style*. RLE Folklore. Abingdon, UK: Routledge, 2016.

Jusu, John, ed. *NLT Africa Study Bible: God's Word through African Eyes*. Chicago: Oasis International, 2016.

Kaiser, Walter C. "The Meaning of Meaning." In *Introduction to Biblical Hermeneutics: The Search for Meaning*, by Walter C. Kaiser and Moisés Silva, 29–46. Rev. ed. Grand Rapids: Zondervan Academic, 2007.

———. "Must We Go beyond the Bible? The Theological Use of the Bible." In *Introduction to Biblical Hermeneutics: The Search for Meaning*, by Walter C. Kaiser and Moisés Silva, 83–94. Rev. ed. Grand Rapids: Zondervan Academic, 2007.

Kaplan, Robert B. "Foreword." In *Contrastive Rhetoric Revisited and Redefined*, edited by Clayann Gilliam Panetta, vii–xx. New York: Routledge, 2008.

Karpf, Anne. *The Human Voice: How This Extraordinary Instrument Reveals Essential Clues about Who We Are*. New York: Bloomsbury, 2006.

Keener, Craig S. *Spirit Hermeneutics: Reading Scripture in Light of Pentecost*. Grand Rapids: Eerdmans, 2016.

Kelber, Werner H. *Jesus and Tradition: Words in Time, Words in Space*. Newcastle upon Tyne, UK: Scholars, 1994.

———. *The Oral and the Written Gospel: The Hermeneutics of Speaking and Writing in the Synoptic Tradition, Mark, Paul, and Q*. Minneapolis: Fortress, 1983.

Keller, Timothy J. *The Prodigal Prophet: Jonah and the Mystery of God's Mercy*. New York: Viking, 2018.

Kelly, Kevin. *The Inevitable: Understanding the 12 Technological Forces That Will Shape Our Future*. New York: Penguin, 2016.

Kinlaw, Dennis F. *Let's Start with Jesus: A New Way of Doing Theology*. Grand Rapids: Zondervan Academic, 2005.

Knowles, Malcolm S., et al. *The Adult Learner: The Definitive Classic in Adult Education and Human Resource Development*. 8th ed. New York: Routledge, 2012.

Koehler, Paul F. *Telling God's Stories with Power: Biblical Storytelling in Oral Cultures*. Pasadena, CA: William Carey, 2010.

Koeshall, Anita. "Navigating Power." In *Devoted to Christ: Missiological Reflections in Honor of Sherwood G. Lingenfelter*, edited by Christopher L. Flanders, 65–78. Eugene, OR: Pickwick, 2019.

Koller, Charles W. *How to Preach without Notes*. Grand Rapids: Baker, 2007.

Koyama, Kosuke. "We Had Rice with Jesus." In *Theology in Action: Papers and Extracts on Doing Theology in Today's World*, edited by Jae Shik Oh and John C. England, 19–32. Manila: East Asian Christian Conference, 1972.

Kranz, Jeffery. "Word Counts for Every Book of the Bible (Free Download")." Overview Bible, May 14, 2014. https://overviewbible.com/word-counts-books-of-bible/.

Le Paul, Andrew T. *Write Better: A Lifelong Editor on Craft, Art, and Spirituality*. Downers Grove, IL: IVP, 2019.

Lee, Charlotte I. *Oral Interpretation*. Cambridge, MA: Riverside, 1952.

Lee, Margaret Ellen, and Bernard Brandon Scott. *Sound Mapping the New Testament*. Salem, OR: Polebridge, 2009.

Lewis, C. S. *On Stories: And Other Essays on Literature*. New York: Harcourt, 1982.

Lin, Tom. *Losing Face and Finding Grace: 12 Bible Studies for Asian-Americans*. Downers Grove, IL: IVP, 1996.

Lingenfelter, Judith E., and Sherwood G. Lingenfelter. *Teaching Cross-Culturally: An Incarnational Model for Leaning and Teaching*. Grand Rapids: Baker Academic, 2003.

Lingenfelter, Sherwood. *Transforming Culture: A Challenge for Christian Mission.* Grand Rapids: Baker, 1992.

Lingenfelter, Sherwood G., and Marvin K. Mayers. *Ministering Cross-Culturally: An Incarnational Model for Personal Relationships.* Grand Rapids: Baker Academic, 2016.

Lockyer, Herbert. *All the Men of the Bible.* Grand Rapids: Zondervan, 1988.

———. *All the Women of the Bible.* Grand Rapids: Zondervan, 1988.

Loewen, Jacob A. "Bible Stories: Message and Matrix." *Practical Anthropology* 11 (1964) 49–54, 60.

Longenecker, Bruce W., ed. *Narrative Dynamics in Paul: A Critical Assessment.* Louisville: Westminster John Knox, 2002.

Lord, Albert B. *The Singer of Tales.* Edited by David F. Elmer. 3rd ed. Hellenic Studies Series 77. Milman Parry Collection of Oral Literature 4. Washington, DC: Center for Hellenic Studies, 2019.

Losch, Richard R. *All the People in the Bible: An A–Z Guide to the Saints, Scoundrels, and Other Characters in Scripture.* Grand Rapids: Eerdmans, 2008.

Loubser, J. A. *Oral and Manuscript Culture in the Bible: Studies on the Media Texture of the New Testament–Explorative Hermeneutics.* Biblical Performance Criticism 7. Eugene, OR: Cascade, 2013.

———. "Orality and Literacy in the Pauline Epistles. Some New Hermeneutical Implications." *Neotestamentica* 29 (1995) 61–74.

MacDonald, George. *A Dish of Orts, Chiefly Papers on the Imagination, and on Shakespeare.* New York: Forgotten, 2012.

Madinger, Charles. "Coming to Terms with Orality: A Holistic Model." *Missiology: An International Review* 38 (2010) 201–13.

———. "Orality and 21st Century Asian Mission." *Asian Missions Advance* 29 (2023) 25–33. https://www.asiamissions.net/wp-content/uploads/2022/12/AMA78_CharlesMadinger.pdf.

Matthews, Michael. *A Novel Approach: The Significance of Story in Interpreting Reality.* Victoria: TellWell, 2017.

Matthews, Victor H. *More than Meets the Ear: Discovering the Hidden Contexts of Old Testament Conversations.* Grand Rapids: Eerdmans, 2008.

Maxey, James. *From Orality to Orality: A New Paradigm for Contextual Translation of the Bible.* Biblical Performance Criticism 2. Eugene, OR: Cascade, 2009.

———. "New Testament and African Orality: Implications for Exegesis and Orality." Paper presented at the OTSSA Conference on Bible Translation, University of KwaZulu-Natal, Pietermaritzburg, S. Afr., 2005.

Mburu, Elizabeth. *African Hermeneutics.* Plateau State, Nigeria: Hippo, 2019.

McCall, Thomas H. "Relational Trinity: Creedal Perspective." In *Two Views on the Doctrine of the Trinity*, edited by Stephen R. Holmes et al., 113–37. Counterpoints: Bible and Theology. Grand Rapids: Zondervan Academic, 2014.

McCarthy, Michael C. "We Are Your Books: Augustine, the Bible, and the Practice of Authority." *JAAR* 75 (2007) 324–52.

McGrath, Alister E. "Engaging the Great Tradition: Evangelical Theology and the Role of Tradition." In *Evangelical Futures: A Conversation on Theological Method*, edited by John G. Stackhouse Jr., 139–58. Grand Rapids: Baker, 2000.

———. *Narrative Apologetics: Sharing the Relevance, Joy, and Wonder of the Christian Faith.* Grand Rapids: Baker, 2019.

McKee, Robert. *Story: Substance, Structure, Style, and the Principles of Screenwriting.* New York: Harper-Collins, 1997.

McLean, Max. "Mark's Gospel: On Stage with Max McLean." YouTube, Nov. 16, 2020. From Vision Video. https://youtu.be/rVFQfPTJPq8.

McMahan, Eva M. *Elite Oral History Discourse: A Study of Cooperation and Coherence.* Tuscaloosa: University of Alabama Press, 1989.

Mezirow, Jack, and Associates. *Learning as Transformation: Critical Perspectives on a Theory in Progress.* San Francisco: Jossey-Bass, 2000.

Miller, Mark. *Smart Leadership: Four Simple Choices to Scale Your Impact.* Dallas: Holt, 2022.

Mitchell, Jolyon P., and Sophia Marriage, eds. *Mediating Religion: Conversations in Media, Religion and Culture.* New York: T&T Clark, 2003.

Mugambi, J. N. K. *African Heritage and Contemporary Christianity.* Nairobi: Longman Kenya, 1989.

Munson, Robert H. *Theo-Storying: Reflections on God, Narrative, and Culture.* Baguio City, Phil.: MM-Musings, 2012.

Myers, Scott. "Writers on Characters." Go into the Story, Jan. 2, 2021. https://gointothestory.blcklst.com/writers-on-characters-ccbfad3ad463.

Newbigin, Lesslie. "The Gospel and Our Culture: A Response to Elaine Graham and Heather Walton." *Modern Churchman* 34 (1992) 6.

———. *The Gospel in a Pluralistic Society.* Grand Rapids: Eerdmans, 1989.

Nida, Eugene. *Customs and Cultures: Anthropology for Christian Missions.* Pasadena, CA: William Carey, 1975.

Niditch, Susan. *Oral World and Written Word: Ancient Israelite Literature.* Library of Ancient Israel. Louisville: Westminster John Knox, 1996.

Niles, John D. "Introduction to the Special Issue: Living Epics of China and Inner Asia." *Journal of American Folklore* 129 (2016) 253–69.

Nussbaum, Martha. "Narrative Emotions: Beckett's Genealogy." *Ethics* 98 (1988) 225–54.

O'Connor, Flannery. *Mystery and Manners: Occasional Prose.* New York: Farrar, Straus, & Giroux, 1969.

O'Donnell, Douglas Sean, and Leland Ryken. *The Beauty and Power of Biblical Exposition: Preaching the Literary Artistry and Genres of the Bible.* Wheaton, IL: Crossway, 2022.

Ong, Walter. *Interfaces of the Word: Studies in the Evolution of Consciousness and Culture.* Ithaca, NY: Cornell University Press, 1977.

———. *Orality and Literacy: The Technologizing of the Word.* New York: Methuen & Co., 1982.

Ordway, Holly. *Apologetics and the Christian Imagination: An Integrated Approach to Defending the Faith.* Steubenville, OH: Emmaus Road, 2017.

Osborne, Grant R. *The Hermeneutical Spiral: A Comprehensive Introduction to Biblical Interpretation.* Downers Grove, IL: InterVarsity, 1991.

Paauw, Glenn R. *Saving the Bible from Ourselves: Learning to Read & Live the Bible Well.* Downers Grove, IL: IVP Academic, 2016.

Packer, James I. "In Quest of Canonical Interpretation." In *The Use of the Bible in Theology: Evangelical Options*, edited by Robert K. Johnson, 35–55. Eugene, OR: Wipf and Stock, 1997.

Palmer, Parker J. *The Courage to Teach: Exploring the Inner Landscape of a Teacher's Life.* San Francisco: Wiley and Sons, 2017.

Paris, Ben. "Failing to Improve Critical Thinking." *Inside Higher Ed*, Nov. 29, 2016. https://www.insidehighered.com/views/2016/11/29/roadblocks-better-critical-thinking-skills-are-embedded-college-experience-essay.
Payette, Francis A. "The Role of the Holy Spirit in Transformational Learning." Didache, n.d. https://didache.nazarene.org/index.php/volume-3-1/678-v3n1-transformational/file.
Peterson, Eugene H. *As Kingfishers Catch Fire: A Conversation on the Ways of God Formed by the Words of God*. Colorado Springs, CO: Waterbrook, 2017.
———. *Leap over a Wall: Earthy Spirituality for Everyday Christians*. New York: HarperCollins, 1997.
Peterson, Jordan. "Why We Remember Stories." YouTube, n.d. https://www.youtube.com/watch?v=c6bj94DdRmU. Link discontinued.
Pink, Daniel H. *A Whole New Mind: Why Right Brainers Will Rule the Future*. New York: Riverhead, 2006.
Piper, John. *What Is Saving Faith? Reflections on Receiving Christ as a Treasure*. Wheaton, IL: Crossway, 2022.
Platt, Richard L. *He Gave Us Stories: The Bible Student's Guide to Interpreting Old Testament Narratives*. Brentwood, TN: Wolgemuth & Hyatt, 1990.
Postman, Neil. *Amusing Ourselves to Death: Public Discourse in the Age of Show Business*. New York: Penguin, 2006.
Postman, Neil, and Charles Weingartner. *Teaching as a Subversive Activity: A No-Holds-Barred Assault on Outdated Teaching Methods—with Dramatic and Practical Proposals on How Education Can Be Made Relevant to Today's World*. New York: Delta, 1971.
Praeger, Michele. "Edouard Glissant: Toward a Literature of Orality." *Callaloo* 15 (1992) 41–48.
Price, Tom. "What Does Michael O'Sheal Mean When He Say Art Can . . ." YouTube, Feb. 23, 2023. From Forum of Christian Leaders. https://www.youtube.com/watch?v=QqBSN8nhv_E.
Ramm, Bernard. *The Christian View of Science and Scripture*. Grand Rapids: Eerdmans, 1954.
Resseguie, James L. "Defamiliarization in the Gospels." *Mosaic: An Interdisciplinary Critical Journey* 21 (1988) 25–35. https://www.academia.edu/44663872/Defamiliarization_in_the_Gospels.
———. *Narrative Criticism of the New Testament: An Introduction*. Grand Rapids: Baker Academic, 2005.
Rhoads, David M. "From Narrative in Print to Narrative in Performance." *Oral History Journal of South Africa* 5 (2017) 1–24.
———. "Performance Criticism: An Emerging Methodology in Second Testament Studies—Part I." *BTB* 36 (2006) 118–33.
———. "Performance Criticism: An Emerging Methodology in Second Testament Studies—Part II." *BTB* 36 (2006) 164–84.
———. "Performing the Letter to Philemon." Docplayer, 2008. First published in *Journal of Biblical Storytelling* 17. https://docplayer.net/201346685-Performing-the-letter-to-philemon-by-david-m-rhoads-first-published-in-the-journal-of-biblical-storytelling-17-11-2008-used-by-permission.html.
Rice, Wayne. *Reinventing Youth Ministry (Again): From Bells and Whistles to Flesh and Blood*. Downers Grove, IL: InterVarsity, 2010. Kindle.

Richards, E. Randolph, and Brandon J. O'Brian. *Misreading Scripture with Western Eyes: Removing Cultural Blinders to Better Understand the Bible.* Downers Grove, IL: IVP, 2012.

Richter, Sandra L. *The Epic of Eden: A Christian Entry into the Old Testament.* Downers Grove, IL: IVP Academic, 2008.

Ricoeur, Paul. *History and Truth.* Translated by Charles A. Kelbley. Evanston, IL: Northwestern University Press, 1965.

———. *Interpretation Theory: Discourse and the Surplus of Meaning.* Fort Worth: Texas Christian University Press, 1976.

Ridderbos, Herman N. *Paul: An Outline of His Theology.* Grand Rapids: Eerdmans, 1975.

Rodrigues, Rafael. *Oral Tradition and the New Testament: A Guide for the Perplexed.* Guides for the Perplexed. London: T&T Clark, 2014.

Ryken, Leland. "The Bible: God's Story-Book." *Christianity Today* 23 (1979) 34–38.

———, ed. *The Christian Imagination: The Practice of Faith in Literature and Writing.* Rev. ed. Colorado Springs, CO: Shaw, 2002.

———. *How Bible Stories Work: A Guided Study of Biblical Narrative.* Reading the Bible as Literature. Bellingham, WA: Lexham, 2018.

———. *How to Read the Bible as Literature . . . and Get More Out of It.* Grand Rapids: Zondervan, 1984.

———. *Words of Delight: A Literary Introduction to the Bible.* Grand Rapids: Baker, 1993.

Ryken, Leland, and Tremper Longman III, eds. *A Complete Literary Guide to the Bible.* Grand Rapids: Zondervan Academic, 1993.

Sachs, Jonah. *Winning the Story Wars: Why Those Who Tell (and Live) the Best Stories Will Rule the Future.* Boston: Harvard Business, 2012.

Salway, Larry. "General Conferences 2012—5th Legislative Session (A) (Jun 5, 8:30 AM)." YouTube, June 5, 2012. From the Wesleyan Church. http://www.youtube.com/watch?v=fMXxwnvm7nQ&feature=plcp.

Sanders, James A. *From Sacred Story to Sacred Text: Canon as Paradigm.* Eugene, OR: Wipf and Stock, 1987.

Sandy, D. Brent. *Hear Ye the Word of the Lord: What We Miss if We Only Read the Bible.* Downers Grove, IL: IVP Academic, 2024.

Sarna, Nahum M. *Genesis.* JPS Torah Commentary. New York: Jewish Publication Society, 2001.

Schank, Roger. *Tell Me a Story: Narrative and Intelligence.* Rethinking Theory. Evanston, IL: Northwestern University Press, 1995.

Schillebeeckx, Edward. *Church: The Human Story of God.* New York: Crossroad, 1993.

Schultze, Dell, and Rachel Sue Schultze. *God and Man.* Manila: Self-published, 1984.

Scott, Susan. *Fierce Conversations: Achieving Success at Work & in Life One Conversation at a Time.* New York: New American, 2017.

Shaw, Perry. "Moving from Critical Thinking to Constructive Thinking." *Evangelical Review of Theology* 45 (2021) 128–40.

———. *Transforming Theological Education: A Practical Handbook for Integrative Learning.* Cumbria, UK: Langham Global, 2014.

Shaw, Perry, et al., eds. *Teaching across Cultures: A Global Christian Perspective.* Cumbria, UK: Langham Global, 2021.

Shaw, Susan M. *Storytelling in Religious Education.* Birmingham: Religious Education, 1999.

Shearer, Darren. *Marketing Like Jesus: 25 Strategies to Change the World*. Houston: High Bridge, 2014.
Sheed, William G. T. *Dogmatic Theology*. Edited by Alan W. Gomes. 3rd ed. North Charleston, SC: P&R, 2003.
Shoemaker, Stephen H. *Godstories: New Narrative from Sacred Texts*. King of Prussia, PA: Judson, 1988.
Short, Sharon W. "Formed by Story: The Metanarrative of the Bible as Doctrine." Supplement, *Christian Education Journal* 9 (2012) 110–23.
Simmons, Annette. *The Story Factor: Inspiration, Influence, and Persuasion through Storytelling*. New York: Basic, 2006.
Singhal, Arvind, et al., eds. *Entertainment-Education and Social Change: History, Research, and Practice*. Routledge Communication. Abingdon, UK: Routledge, 2003.
Slade, Darren M. "Christian Hermeneutics: The Problem of Using Solely Historical-Grammatical Methods for Christian Exegesis." Academia, Nov. 13, 2016. https://www.academia.edu/30803427/Christian_Hermeneutics_The_Problem_of_Using_Solely_Historical_Grammatical_Methods_for_Christian_Exegesis.
Snodgrass, Klyne R. *Stories with Intent: A Comprehensive Guide to the Parables of Jesus*. Grand Rapids: Eerdmans, 2008.
Song, C. S. *In the Beginning Were Stories, Not Texts: Story Theology*. Cambridge, UK: Clarke, 2011.
Stafford, Tim. "Mere Mission." *Christianity Today* 1 (2007) 39–41.
Stallter, Thomas M. *The Gap between God and Christianity: The Turbulence of Western Culture*. Eugene, OR: Resource, 2022.
Steffen, Tom. "A Clothesline Theology for the World: How A Value-Driven Grand Narrative Can Frame the Gospel." In *Honor, Shame, and the Gospel: Reframing Our Message and Ministry*, edited by Christopher Flanders and Werner Mischke, 37–56. Pasadena, CA: William Carey, 2020.
———. *The Facilitator Era: Beyond Pioneer Church Multiplication*. Eugene, OR: Wipf & Stock, 2011.
———. "Pedagogical Conversions: From Propositions to Story and Symbol." *Missiology: An International Review* 38 (2010) 141–59.
———. "The Role of Grand Narrative." Presentation in Narrative as an Educational Philosophy course, Biola University, Sept. 23, 2008.
———. "Saving the Locals from Our Theologies: Part One." *JAM* 19 (2018) 3–33.
———. *Worldview-Based Storying: The Integration of Symbol, Story, and Ritual in the Orality Movement*. Richmond: Orality Resources International, 2018.
Steffen, Tom, and William Bjoraker. *The Return of Oral Hermeneutics: As Good Today as It Was for the Hebrew Bible and First-Century Christianity*. Eugene, OR: Wipf & Stock, 2020.
Steffen, Tom A. *Passing the Baton: Church Planting That Empowers*. La Habra, CA: Center for Organizational & Ministry Development, 1997.
———. *Reconnecting God's Story to Ministry: Crosscultural Storytelling at Home and Abroad*. Downers Grove, IL: IVP, 2006.
Stephanous, Andrea Zaki. *Arabic Christian Theology: A Contemporary Global Evangelical Perspective*. Grand Rapids: Zondervan Academic, 2019.
Sternberg, Meir. *The Poetics of Biblical Narrative: Ideological Literature and the Drama of Reading*. Biblical Literature. Bloomington, IN: Indiana University Press, 1987.

Stetzer, Ed. "How 450 Sermons Revealed Four Preaching Truths." Sermon Central, Sept. 1, 2021. https://www.sermoncentral.com/pastors-preaching-articles/ed-stetzer-how-450-sermons-revealed-four-preaching-truths-1726.

Stock, Augustine. "Chiastic Awareness and Education in Antiquity." *BTB* 14 (1984) 23–27.

Stout, Harry S. "Theological Commitment and American Religious History." *Theological Education* 25 (1989) 44–59.

Strate, Lance. "Time-Binding in Oral Cultures." *Et Cetera* 43 (1986) 234–46.

Stringer, Trisha, and Stephen Stringer. "New Hope: A Theo-Dramatic Approach to Trauma Healing." In *New and Old Horizons in the Orality Movement: Expanding the Firm Foundation*, edited by Tom Steffen and Cameron D. Armstrong, 232–50. Eugene, OR: Pickwick, 2022.

Taylor, Daniel. *The Healing Power of Stories: Creating Yourself through the Stories of Your Life*. New York: Doubleday, 1996.

Team Ifugao. *Ifugao Evangelism*. Manila: Self-published, 1981.

Tennent, Timothy C. *Theology in the Context of World Christianity: How the Global Church Is Influencing the Way We Think About and Discuss Theology*. Grand Rapids: Zondervan Academic, 2007.

Thigpen, L. Lynn. *Connected Learning: How Adults with Limited Formal Education Learn*. Eugene, OR: Pickwick, 2020.

———. "The Dark Side of Orality." In *Honor, Shame, and the Gospel: Reframing Our Message and Ministry*, edited by Christopher Flanders and Werner Mischke, 117–26. Pasadena, CA: William Carey, 2020.

Thiselton, Anthony C. *Two Horizons: New Testament Hermeneutics and Philosophical Description with Special Reference to Heidegger, Bultmann, Gadamer, and Wittgenstein*. Grand Rapids: Eerdmans, 1980.

Thomaskutty, Johnson, ed. *An Asian Introduction to the New Testament*. Philadelphia: Fortress, 2022.

Tickle, Phyllis. *The Great Emergence: How Christianity Is Changing and Why*. Grand Rapids: Baker, 2008.

Tiede, Bob, ed. "339 Questions Jesus Asked." Leading with Questions, n.d. https://339questionsjesusasked.com/wp-content/downloads/eng-P8VoLUagOIjvyerRXfmATLRLDqIZ6qMG.pdf.

———, ed. "Great Leaders Ask Questions: A Fortune 100 List." Leading with Questions, n.d. ttps://leadingwithquestions.com/wp-content/downloads/Q9foLUagOIjvyerRXfmATLRLDqIZ6qMG.pdf.

Tiede, Bob, and Reed Davidson, eds. "262 Questions Paul the Apostle of Christ Asked." Leading with Questions, 2002. Available by request from leadingwithquestions.com.

Tucker, Ruth A. *The Biographical Bible: Exploring the Biblical Narrative from Adam and Eve to John of Patmos*. Grand Rapids: Baker, 2013.

Turner, Mark. *The Literary Mind: The Origins of Thought and Language*. New York: Oxford University Press, 1996.

Tverberg, Lois, and Bruce Okkema. *Listening to the Language of the Bible: Hearing It through Jesus' Ears*. Holland, MI: En-Gedi Resource, 2004.

Van der Toorn, Karel. *Scribal Culture and the Making of the Hebrew Bible*. Cambridge MA: Harvard University Press, 2007.

Vanhoozer, Kevin J. *The Drama of Doctrine: A Canonical Linguistic Approach to Christian Theology*. Louisville: Westminster John Knox, 2005.

———. "A Drama-of-Redemption Model." In *Moving beyond the Bible to Theology*, edited by Gary T. Meadors, 151–99. Grand Rapids: Zondervan, 2009.

———. *Is There a Meaning in This Text? The Bible, the Reader, and the Morality of Literary Knowledge*. Grand Rapids: Zondervan, 1998.

Vella, Jane. *Learning to Listen, Learning to Teach: The Power of Dialogue in Educating Adults*. San Francisco: Wiley & Sons, 2002.

Wadholm, Robert R. *On Hermeneutics*. Ellendale, ND: Invariable, 2017.

Walton, John H., and D. Brent Sandy. *The Lost World of Scripture: Ancient Literary Culture and Biblical Authority*. Downers Grove, IL: InterVarsity, 2013.

Ward, Richard F. "Pauline Voice and Presence as Strategic Communication." In *Orality and Textuality in Early Christian Literature*, edited by Joanna Dewey, 95–107. Semeia 65. Atlanta, GA: Scholars, 1995.

We Are Social. "Digital 2022: Another Year of Bumper Growth." We Are Social, Jan. 26, 2022. https://wearesocial.com/uk/blog/2022/01/digital-2022-another-year-of-bumper-growth-2/.

Webber, Robert E. *The Younger Evangelicals: Facing the Challenges of the New World*. Grand Rapids: Baker, 2002.

Wendland, Ernest R. *Finding and Translating the Oral-Aural Elements in Written Language: The Case of the New Testament Epistles*. New York: Mellen, 2008.

———. "Interpreting the Bible: An Overview of Hermeneutics." Academia, 2017. https://www.academia.edu/34661504/INTERPRETING_THE_BIBLE_An_Overview_of_Hermeneutics.

———. "'My Tongue Is the Stylus of a Skilled Scribe' (Ps 45:2c): If So in the Scriptures, Then Why Not Also in Translation?" *Verbum et Ecclesia* 32 (2013) 1–8.

———. *Orality and Its Implications for the Analysis, Translation, and Transmission of Scripture*. Dallas: SIL International, 2013.

———. "Studying, Translating, and Transmitting the 'Orality' (Oral-Aural Dimension) of Scripture with Two Case Studies: Solomon's Song and John's Apocalypse." Academia, 2010. https://www.academia.edu/40049048/Studying_Translating_and_Transmitting_the_Orality_of_Scripture?email_work_card=title.

———. *Translating the Literature of Scripture: A Literary-Rhetorical Approach to Bible Translation*. Dallas: SIL International, 2003.

Williams, Peter J. *Can We Trust the Gospels?* Wheaton, IL: Crossway, 2018.

Winger, Thomas M. "Orality as the Key to Understanding Apostolic Proclamation in the Epistles." DTh diss., Concordia Seminary, St. Louis, MO, 1997.

———. "The Spoken Word: What's Up with Orality?" *Concordia Journal* 29 (2003) 133–51. https://www.academia.edu/29401898/The_Spoken_Word_Whats_Up_with_Orality.

Wintle, Brian, ed. *South Asia Bible Commentary on the Whole Bible*. Grand Rapids: Zondervan Academic, 2015.

Wiseman, Liz, with Greg Mckeown. *Multipliers: How the Best Leaders Make Everyone Smarter*. New York: HarperCollins, 2010.

Wisher, William Jr., and Warren Lewis. *The 13th Warrior*. Based on *Eaters of the Dead*, by Michael Crichton. Burbank, CA: Buena Vista, 1999.

Witherington, Ben III. *Paul's Narrative Thought World: The Tapestry of Tragedy and Triumph*. Louisville: Westminster/John Knox, 1994.

———. "Why Ignoring the Rhetorical Shape of Oral Texts Including NT Letters Won't Do." Bible & Culture, Dec. 2, 2020. https://www.patheos.com/blogs/bibleandculture/2020/12/02/why-ignoring-the-rhetorical-shape-of-oral-texts-including-letters-wont-do/.

Worthington, Jonathan D. "Orality's Breadth and Depth." *Journal of Global Christianity* 8 (2023) 8–27.
Wright, G. Ernest. *God Who Acts: Biblical Theology as Recital*. Studies in Biblical Theology 8. London: SCM, 1962.
Wright, N. T. *The New Testament and the People of God*. Minneapolis: Fortress, 1992.
———. *Scripture and the Authority of God: How to Read the Bible Today*. New York: HarperOne, 2011.
Wu, Jackson. "Biblical Theology for Oral Cultures in World Mission." In *World Mission: Theology, Strategy, and Current Issues*, edited by Scott N. Callaham and Will Brooks, 269–89. Bellingham, WA: Lexham, 2019.
———. "The Doctrine of Scripture and Biblical Contextualization: Inspiration, Authority, Inerrancy and the Canon." *Them* 44 (2019) 312–26.
———. *Saving God's Face: A Chinese Contextualization of Salvation through Honor and Shame*. Pasadena, CA: WCIU, 2012.
Wuellner, Wilhelm. "Where Is Rhetorical Criticism Taking Us?" *CBQ* 49 (1987) 448–63.
Yancey, Philip. *The Bible Jesus Read*. Grand Rapids: Zondervan, 1999.
Yeh, Allen, and Tite Tiénou, eds. *Majority World Theologies: Theologizing from Africa, Latin America, and the Ends of the Earth*. Evangelical Missiological Society 26. Littleton, CO: William Carey, 2018.
Yenawine, Philip. "Thoughts on Visual Literacy." Visual Thinking Strategies, Aug. 12, 2016. From *Handbook of Research on Teaching Literacy through the Communicative and Visual Arts*. http://vtshome.org/wp-content/uploads/2016/08/12Thoughts-On-Visual-Literacy.pdf.
Yong, Amos. *Theology and Down Syndrome: Reimaging Disability in Late Modernity*. Studies in Religion, Theology, and Disability. Waco, TX: Baylor University Press, 2007.
Yong, Amos, with Jonathan A. Anderson. *Renewing Christian Theology: Systematics for a Global Christianity*. Waco, TX: Baylor University Press, 2014.
Yutang, Lin. *From Pagan to Christian: The Personal account of a Distinguished Philosopher's Spiritual Pilgrimage Back to Christianity*. New York: World, 1959.
Zoba, Wendy Murray. "Bright Unto the End." *Christianity Today*, Oct. 1, 2001. https://www.christianitytoday.com/ct/2001/october1/6.56.html.
Zondervan. *The Books of the Bible, New International Version*. 4 vols. Grand Rapids: Zondervan, 2017.

www.ingramcontent.com/pod-product-compliance
Lightning Source LLC
Chambersburg PA
CBHW061430300426
44114CB00014B/1613